The Catholic Biblical Quarterly
Monograph Series
35

The Most Magic Word

Essays on Babylonian and Biblical Literature

BY
William L. Moran

EDITED BY
Ronald S. Hendel

The Catholic Biblical Quarterly
Monograph Series
35

Produced in the United States of America

Library of Congress Cataloging-in-Publication Data

Moran, William L.
The most magic word : essays on Babylonian and biblical literature / by William L. Moran; edited by Ronald S. Hendel.
p. cm. — (The Catholic Biblical quarterly. Monograph series ; 35)
Includes bibliographical references and index.
ISBN 0-915170-34-5
1. Assyro-Babylonian literature—History and criticism.
2. Assyro-Babylonian literature—Relation to the Old Testament.
3. Gilgamesh. 4. Atrahasis (Old Babylonian epic) I. Hendel, Ronald S.
II. Title. III. Series.
PJ3611 .M67 2002

2002010486

In memory of William L. Moran

Hoc erat in votis: modus agri non ita magnus,
hortus ubi et tecto vicinus iugis aquea fons
et paulum silvae super his foret. auctius atque
di melius fecere. bene est. nil amplius oro . . .

This is what I prayed for: a piece of land not so very large,
where there would be a garden, and near the house a spring
  of ever-flowing water,
and up above these a bit of woodland. More and better
have the gods done for me. I am content. Nothing more do I ask.
Horace, *Satires,* 2.6 (trans. after H. Rushton, LCL)

das zaubernde Wort zu irgendeiner Zeit
the most magic word of any time
Rainer Maria Rilke

Contents

Foreword

William L. Moran was for many years the Andrew Mellon Professor of the Humanities at Harvard University, where he was a benevolent sage and strict pedagogue of Akkadian. He was held in awe by all of his students, and beloved by those fortunate enough to know him well. He was a man who combined the best of the everyday and academic worlds, who read Ovid and Horace on Boston's Red Line and crowed about Larry Bird's game in the Harvard Semitic Museum. I never met someone who so conformed to Montaigne's definition of the life well-lived: "Il n'est rien si beau et légitime que de faire bien l'homme et dûment, Ni science si ardue que de bien et naturellement savoir vivre cette vie." ("There is nothing so beautiful and legitimate as to play the man well and properly, no knowledge so hard to acquire as the knowledge of how to live this life well and naturally" [trans. D. Frame].)

Like Gilgamesh, he acquired this knowledge through his wanderings—born in Chicago, he taught classics, studied with W. F. Albright, Benno Landsberger, and Thorkild Jacobsen, taught Bible at the Pontifical Biblical Institute in Rome, and finally Assyriology at Harvard, where Jacobsen introduced him to his future wife, Suzie. Bill and Suzie retired in 1990 to their Maine woods. In early winter 2000, Bill passed away, a few months after giving his blessing to the idea and plan of this volume. We all miss him.

Moran's oeuvre, published and unpublished, is a marvelous concatenation of insight, erudition, and wisdom. This volume is a selection of his gem-like essays, drawing on his lasting passion for savoring the words and conceptualities of Babylonian and biblical literature.

Constructing this volume has been a rare delight. I wish to acknowledge the encouragement, advice, and aid of John Huehnergard, Suzanne Drinker Moran, Tzvi Abusch, Mark Smith, Paul Kobelski, and Scott Nikaido.

R.S.H.
Berkeley, California

CHAPTER I

Rilke and the Gilgamesh Epic

Most of us accord to poets writing about poetry special attention and respect, for they have stood, we feel, not only in the outer chambers of reading, theory, and criticism, but within the sacred precincts of poetry itself. They are the seers who have seen. We know that their criticism need not be the best criticism, and we are aware that they may be as dogmatic, one-sided, and perverse as any other critic.[1] Nevertheless, they remain critics apart whose mere impressions of a work command our serious consideration and reflection. To most Assyriologists, therefore, it will be of interest to learn that Rainer Maria Rilke read the Gilgamesh Epic and left us a record of his impressions.[2]

In 1916 Georg Burckhardt's very free version of the Gilgamesh Epic was published by the Insel Verlag, which in 1905 had become Rilke's

[1] A case in point: John Berryman on Rilke (a jerk) and his poetry (those goddammed angels for chrissake).

[2] I learned of this in Idris Parry's review, *Times Literary Supplement* (1977) 828, of the Rilke–von Nostitz correspondence (see n. 6). He remarked that Rilke's "interesting enthusiasm" for the Gilgamesh Epic was already known from the Katharina Kippenberg correspondence. This latter reference I followed up and I have cited the appropriate passage in a review of Röllig et al., *Altorientalische Literaturen*, *JAOS* 100 (1980) 189-90. The von Nostitz correspondence, however, continued to elude me until Dr. Francesca Rochberg-Halton tracked it down and very kindly sent me the text. As she remarked in an accompanying letter, the von Nostitz statement gives an even clearer impression of the poet's response to the epic. Hence this note—and my thanks to her.

main publisher, and whose owner, Anton Kippenberg, and his wife, Katharina, had become his close friends. This version seems to have introduced the poet to the epic and to have led him, too, to the earlier, literal translation by Ungnad in 1911. Of his decided preference for the latter and of his response to the epic we learn in three letters written in December, 1916.

The first was written on December 11, to Katharina Kippenberg, who was also engaged in editorial work. In the course of the letter Rilke bursts out:

> Gilgamesch ist ungeheuer! ich kenns aus der Ausgabe des Urtextes und rechne es zum Grössesten, das einem widerfahren kann. Von Zeit zu Zeit erzähl ichs dem und jenem, den ganzen Verlauf, und habe jedesmal die erstaunendsten Zuhörer. Die Zusammenfassung Burckhardts ist nicht durchaus glücklich, bleibt hinter der Grösse und Bedeutung zurück—, ich fühle: ich erzähls besser. Und mich gehts an.[3]

She replied a few days later, telling Rilke how pleased she was to read what he had to say about the epic, but also defending the publication of Burckhardt's version. She writes that the manuscript had been shown to Zimmer (sic), who is identified as "assyriologische Autorität," and who, she says, was not only enthusiastic about it, but even suspected that the translator was himself an Assyriologist desirous of concealing his identity. She adds: "Dennoch fühlt man ganz genau, dass es hätte besser gemacht werden können, und die nächste Auflage wird nachgedichtet von Rainer Maria Rilke."[4]

Unfortunately, Rainer Maria Rilke was not to be so easily charmed and ensnared as that. The reason he gives for his refusal is rather curious: "Oh nein, den Gilgamesch werd ich nie anders als mündlich erzählen, da find ich von einem zum anderen Mal mehr Ausdruck."[5]

[3] Rainer Maria Rilke, Katharina Kippenberg, *Briefwechsel* (Wiebaden, 1954) 191-92: "Gilgamesh is overwhelming! I know it from the edition of the original text, and I consider it the greatest thing one can experience. From time to time I tell its story to this one and that one, the whole story, and every time I have the most astonished listeners. The synthesis of Burckhardt is not altogether happy; it doesn't achieve the greatness and significance [of the epic]—I feel I tell the story better. It involves me." [trans. W.L.M.—Ed.]

[4] *Briefwechsel*, 194-95.

[5] *Briefwechsel*, 198.

The matter rested there, and in the correspondence with Katharina Kippenberg we hear no more about Gilgamesh.

However, not many days later, "am Sylvester-Tage," in a letter to Helene von Nostitz, Rilke described at even greater length his appreciation of the epic.

> . . . haben Sie in der Inselbücherei den Band gesehen, der etwas wie ein *resumé* eines altassyrischen Gedichts enthält: den Gilgameš? Ich habe mich mit der genauen gelehrten Übersetzung (von Ungnad) eingelassen und an diesen wahrhaft gigantischen Büchstücken Maasse und Gestalten gelebt, die zum Grössesten gehören, was das zaubernde Wort zu irgendeiner Zeit gegeben hat. Am Liebsten würd ichs Ihnen erzälhlen—, das Insel-Bändchen, so geschmackvoll es zusammengestellt sein mag, unterschlägt doch die eigentliche Gewalt des fünftausend Jahre alten Gedichts. In den (wie ich annehmen muss, ausgezeichnet übersetzten) Fragmenten ist ein wirklich riesiges Geschehen und Dastehen und Fürchten, und selbst die weiten Text-Lücken wirken irgendwie konstruktiv, indem sie die herrlich-massiven Bruchflächen auseinanderhalten. Hier ist das Epos der Todesfurcht, entstanden im Unvordenklichen unter Menschen, bei denen zuerst die Trennung von Tod und Leben definitiv und verhängnisvoll geworden war. Ich bin sicher, auch Ihr Mann wird die lebhafteste Freude haben, die Seiten durchzusehen. Ich lebe selt Wochen fast ganz in diesem Eindruck.[6]

One would like to see this "interesting enthusiasm" commented upon by a competent scholar and examined in the light of the poet's personality, his life at the time, during the trying and barren years of the Great War, and, perhaps most important of all, his conception of art and poetry.[7] Striking is the poet's sense in the epic of massiveness, the gigantic, the marvelous, which he must also have conveyed in his

[6] Rainer Maria Rilke, Helene von Nostitz, *Briefwechsel* (Frankfurt-am-Main, 1976) 99.

[7] To judge from the little I have read in the Rilke literature, I would not be surprised if such a scholar began by warning us of Rilke's rather limited literary culture—it seems questionable whether he read more than parts, if anything at all, of the Divine Comedy, Hamlet, and (is this really possible?) Faust—and of his penchant for discovering unsuspected riches in unknown works or in apparently insignificant figures; see J. F. Angelloz, *Rainer Maria Rilke: Leben und Werk* (Zürich, 1955) 256. In Rilke's enthusiasm for the Gilgamesh Epic one should perhaps also allow for a certain posturing and one-upmanship.

own telling of the tale.[8] One can easily imagine the astonished listeners and the spell of *das zaubernde Wort*, and then one also begins to sense the measure of our loss in his refusal to give us his own translation. This, we may be confident, would have matched even Pasternak's standard for translations, works standing on the same level as the originals and themselves unrepeatable. It would have been, as Chapman hoped his Homer would be, "Poesie to open Poesie."

[8] Even to the amateur it seems evident that Rilke was not least impressed by what he thought the extreme antiquity of the epic. One senses a certain romanticism that makes of the epic a kind of literary Stonehenge, raised in the mists of the dawn of history, now destroyed or surviving only in fragments, with the power and pathos that attach to remnants of the ancient past.

CHAPTER 2

The Epic of Gilgamesh: A Document of Ancient Humanism*

Philology has been described as the "art of slow reading," and nowhere else is this art more appropriate, indeed at times even essential, than in reading an epic. For distinctive of the epic and lending it its peculiar power and dignity is the leisure with which the epic poet moves through his tale. His pace is slow; he may even digress. He lingers over scenes and events. And, as we read his work, we should linger too, and not only linger, but, as Schiller once wrote to Goethe, linger with love—*sich mit Liebe verweilen.*

It is as a philologist, a lover of words, a slow reader, with Schiller as my guide, that I speak. I can hardly hope, I know, to introduce you to the Gilgamesh epic. Most of you are familiar with it, I am sure, and some of you will recall Thorkild Jacobsen's lecture on the epic before this Society not many years ago. You may also be acquainted with Bernarda Bryson's splendid adaptation of the epic for your children and grandchildren, and as these children have grown to high school and college age and have been introduced to the genre of the epic in various languages and cultures, you may have heard them discussing Gilgamesh and comparing it with, say, the *Odyssey* or *Beowulf.*

In fact, in the last decade it has become almost impossible to ignore our epic. Two more scholarly translations have appeared, one by Stephanie Dalley, another by Maureen Kovacs. Robert Silverberg, the

*Lecture delivered to the Canadian Society for Mesopotamian Studies, November 14, 1990.

distinguished science-fiction writer, turned the epic into a first-rate novel, *Gilgamesh the King*. Another novelist, the late John Gardner, shortly before his tragic death completed his re-englishing of the text, and it was published in 1984. In this decade, too, our epic returned to the world of music. On October 18, 1988, at the Theatre der freien Volksbühne in Berlin, a seven-act opera, *The Forest*, by Robert Wilson and David Byrne, was performed for the first time, and not long after that at the Brooklyn Academy of Music. It was conceived, we are told, as a modern response to the ancient message of the Gilgamesh epic.

In a word, the Gilgamesh epic is becoming part of world literature. Its appeal is universal. Its images and tale arrest the fancy of a child. The profundity of these images, their immense, almost endless, significance, and the understanding of man in a tale told with a simple but compelling art, command the esteem and admiration of even the most sensitive and the most critical. One of the most renowned poets of the 20th century, Rainer Maria Rilke, could declare the Gilgamesh epic the greatest thing one could experience.

If therefore I cannot introduce you to the Gilgamesh epic, I must ask you to allow me to linger over the text, here and there, in various ways, but always with love, and to introduce you to *my* Gilgamesh epic.

This request is not as egotistical as it may sound. It has been said that everyone should write his own Faust. In a very real sense, everyone must write his own Gilgamesh. We have two versions of the epic, one from the Old Babylonian period, written in the early second millennium, which is extremely fragmentary. This version a poet-editor, in the late second millennium, in still undetermined proportions of revision, expansion, deletion, and oral variation, reworked into the standard version that will be our concern. But this version too is fragmentary, in places extremely so. This situation, together with our still very imperfect knowledge of the Mesopotamian literary tradition in general, renders any interpretation tentative and subjective. The best I can do, then, is present to you *my* Gilgamesh.

I begin at the beginning. Among relatively recent discoveries bearing on the reconstruction of the epic, the most important concern the prologue. One fragment has restored a few precious signs at the end of the opening lines; another has filled in a 25-line break that had so tormented interpreters of the past. We now have almost intact the entire introduction. Moreover, we now know that the first 26 lines are the creation of the later poet-editor of whom I just spoke. Obviously, these lines merit the closest attention, for here, if anywhere, we may expect to hear the authorial-editorial voice speaking most clearly. Here, if anywhere, we may hope to determine his point of view, how he read, and would have us read, the ancient tale that follows.

He immediately presents Gilgamesh, introducing him as "one who saw everything,"

> Possessed of wisdom, knowing all,
> He saw what was secret, revealed what was hidden,
> Brought back knowledge of days before the Flood,
> From a long journey returned, weary but at peace.
> On stone he chiselled each wearying toil.

There is a paradox here that my translation obscures. When the two words for "weary" and "at peace," or their congeners, are elsewhere used together as here, they are antonyms: one means "weary, exhausted," and it is related to the word for "wearying toil" in the next line; the other word means just the opposite, "rested, refreshed." Gilgamesh is both. The paradox is brief but important. It focuses our attention on the contrast of the externally exhausted body and what can only be, internally, a spirit refreshed and at peace, a peace which the context implies came to Gilgamesh with wisdom and knowledge. What this wisdom and knowledge were the epic will reveal.

The poet-editor continues. He refers briefly to two other achievements of Gilgamesh, the building of the famous walls of his native city Uruk and of its famous sanctuary, the temple of the goddess Ishtar. Then suddenly he addresses us, you and me, individually, a fact that is almost always lost in translation. As Leo Oppenheim so rightly stressed, the poet is no bard, real or fictive, Homer-like, singing his tale in some banquet hall. He speaks to a "thou":

> Look at its wall, . . . gaze on its bastions,
> Go up on the walls of Uruk and walk about,
> Examine the terrace and study the brickwork,
> If its brickwork not be all of baked bricks,
> Its foundation not laid by the Seven Sages.
> One *sar* city, one *sar* orchards, one *sar* pasture and pond—
> and fallow fields of Ishtar's house—
> Three *sar* and fallow fields . . .

The poet addresses us as readers, and we are alone, with tablet in hand. No other epic begins this way, and we are becoming increasingly aware, first from the theme of wisdom, now from this unparalleled form, that if what we are reading is epic it is perhaps epic of a special kind.

On reading the next five lines, which conclude the poet-editor's expansion of his earlier source, the impression of novelty yields to conviction, and the author's purpose, I believe, becomes clear. I shall read them but continue on into the hymn to Gilgamesh of the earlier source, and this will bring us to the end of the old 25-line gap and to the beginning of the narrative. (The tablet is slightly broken on the left edge and therefore some readings, none of which seriously affects the sense, are dubious.)

Find the copper chest,
Remove the locks of bronze,
Open the cover to the treasure there,
Take up and read diligently the tablet of lapis lazuli,
How he, Gilgamesh, every hardship bore.

(Now begins the old hymn, and note the change style.)

He was a giant among kings, in stature most renowned,
Brave, in Uruk born, a butting ox,
Marching in the vanguard, the leader,
In the rearguard marching too, the one his brothers trust,
A mighty net, protector of his band,
A raging flood, destroying even walls of stone,
Son of Lugalbanda, Gilgamesh, perfect in strength,
Child of the noble cow, Lady Wild-Cow Ninsun,
Gilgamesh, proud, perfect, awesome.
Opening passes in the hills,
Digging wells on mountain slopes,
Crossing Sea, Wide-Deep, to the rising sun,
The universe surveying, life ever seeking,
In his power reaching Utnapishtim, the Faraway One,
Restoring shrines by the Flood destroyed.

Who among the multitudes of men
Can rival him in kingship,
Like Gilgamesh can say, "I am king."
Like Gilgamesh was chosen the day that he was born,
Two parts being god, one part man?

Before turning to the lines about the chest and the lapis lazuli tablet, let us consider briefly the prologue a whole, this long (46 lines), unparalleled combination of quasi-hymn, address to a reader, and concluding hymn. You will perhaps have noted that it is only in the very last line of the expansion, as the poet-editor is about to join his older source, that he mentions his hero's name. For 25 lines, directly or indirectly, we have been reading about him without being told just who he is, so that when we finally do come to the name Gilgamesh, it emerges from the previous silence with a certain emphasis or foregrounding. And this leads to the lines that follow, in which the name reappears in line 33, again in line 35, and in a kind of crescendo, at the very end:

Who among the multitudes of men
Can rival him in kingship,
Like Gilgamesh can say, "I am king,"
Like Gilgamesh was chosen the day he was born?

A more literal translation in the last line, instead of "was chosen," would be "his name was called." Another reading that has been proposed is "his name was famous." In any reading, the nameless hero of lines 1–25 is nameless no more. The prologue looks like a baroque elaboration of the old simple poetic device of speaking of an action and identifying the subject in only a general way, and then in a parallel line saying the very same thing, only this time identifying the subject by name.

Since we know the hymn only here and from a reference elsewhere to the opening line, "He was a giant among kings, in stature most renowned," we cannot be sure in what follows of what belongs to the older source, and what, if anything, to our poet editor. It is true that no king is called a "wild ox" or a "net" after the Old Babylonian period, and in the references to physical strength, birthplace, royalty, and legitimation, we recognize themes of the ancient royal hymnology. But that does not take us very far. We can say only that, if anything was added, it was nothing discordant. The hymn is of a piece to the unique dignity, kingship, and power of Gilgamesh.

This Gilgamesh, I hardly need point out, is not the Gilgamesh of the opening lines. This Gilgamesh is a powerful giant, the strongest of men, performing one feat of strength after another, moving across the world and the cosmic sea, reaching Utnapishtim, and finally stopping there, we feel, only because there is no more distant place to go. Of course when we get to these lines now, we have read what has gone before and we are conditioned by it. We know that there is another Gilgamesh. But think how different it would be if we didn't.

Far different is the figure of the Gilgamesh to whom we are first introduced. This Gilgamesh is a man who has suffered and is spent. Every one of the feats that the hymn celebrates is here simply "wearying toil." And lest we forget this, just as we are about to begin the hymn, we are reminded that "Gilgamesh every hardship bore." Opening passes in the hills, digging wells on mountain slopes, and so on—all hardships, pain, exhaustion. There is something almost unheroic in the tenor of all this, in insistence on pain and exhaustion, usually dominant considerations only for non-heroes. Here Gilgamesh seems as much the sage who has suffered as the hero who has triumphed.

To the difference of the two figures there is, as we noted in passing, a corresponding difference of styles: for the traditional hero, the traditional hymn and the conventional celebratory tone; for the exhausted man of suffering, language that is flatter, more matter of fact, a style that, fittingly, reports more than celebrates.

And now to the copper chest and the lapis lazuli tablet lying within. Certainly we must identify the inscription mentioned earlier, "on stone he chiseled each wearying toil," with the lapis lazuli tablet we are now instructed to read so diligently. Not only does it seem, in context, unlikely that the two are distinct, but, as we shall see, good and proper kings were supposed to leave inscriptions in chests. Note, too, how strongly "each wearying toil," *kalû mānaḫti*, is echoed in sound and paralleled in sense by what we are now told to read about on the tablet, how Gilgamesh bore *kalû marṣāti*, "every hardship."

Open to discussion is the proper rendering of the term *narû*, the object on which Gilgamesh chiselled the account of his labors, usually a "stele" and hitherto so translated here. But if the lapis lazuli tablet and the *narû* are the same thing, we should no longer think of a stele like the Code of Hammurabi, a large inscribed standing stone on public display. Our *narû* lies in a chest.

And where is the chest? A text that I shall cite shortly suggests that we should think of it as lying in a room of some temple, perhaps the temple of Ishtar, the only temple that has been mentioned. That the chest was part of a foundation deposit, as has been proposed, to me does not seem likely. Perhaps, however, since we are dealing with literary fiction, the question should not be pressed.

These are minor issues. The main one is the implications of these lines for interpretation. It has been argued that by implying that his source for the narrative that follows—and certainly this is implied—was the *narû* inscribed by Gilgamesh himself, and by inviting the reader to a comparison with the original, our poet-editor wishes to authenticate his tale. And this is true, I believe, but I also believe that such an analysis does not go far enough, for it ignores the implications within the literary tradition of the particular type of authentification.

The best parallel for this particular type is found in the composition known as the *Legend of Narām-Sîn*. Now this composition is the clearest example of what Professor Grayson calls "pseudo-autobiography." The formal characteristics of the genre, due to the accidents of preservation, are still not firmly established, but the genre certainly imitates, with modifications, the old *narû*-stele form. It has a famous king of the past speak in the first person and tell of some events in his life, often fabulous and legendary. Then, where the old *narû*-stele form concluded with blessings and curses depending on how the stele was treated, 'pseudo-autobiography' has the king address the reader and instruct him on the conduct of his life, basing the instruction on his own experiences as just recounted. On the evidence at hand, this didacticism is an essential feature of the genre.

In the *Legend of Narām-Sîn*, which in its later rather than its Old Babylonian form is instructive for our purposes, we find Naram-Sin, the famous king of Akkad, in the broken first line already addressing the reader: "Read diligently the *narû*. . . ." It is, moreover, now virtually certain that we should restore the beginning of the line to read "Open the chest." The text that follows is at first badly broken. Narām-Sîn tells of an earlier king's failure to leave a *narû*, as he should have done, thereby depriving Narām-Sîn of his guidance. A fabulous tale about bird-men follows, and the narrative section concludes with Narām-Sîn's reporting an oracle he says he received from the goddess Ishtar. The king then addresses the reader:

> Whosoever thou art, whether governor or prince or anyone else,
> Whom the gods shall call to rule over a kingdom,
> I have made for thee a chest and inscribed a *narû* for thee,
> And in the city of Cuthah, in the temple Emeslam,
> In the chamber of the god Nergal, deposited it for thee.
> Find this *narû* and listen to what this *narû* says, and then . . .

And there follows a long exhortation reflecting the oracle of Ishtar as just reported.

I need not belabor the obvious parallels to our Gilgamesh passage: the address to the reader, the chest, the *narû* within, the command to read it diligently. Were these parallels from a form of didactic literature isolated, and were there no other indications of didacticism, latent or expressed, in the rest of the epic, then naturally one would hesitate to draw from these parallels any firm conclusions. But, of course, as we have just seen, this is not true. Gilgamesh is presented as a wise man from the very opening lines, and this has not been overlooked by modern interpreters. Jean Nougayrol, Erica Reiner, Thorkild Jacobsen, Giorgio Buccellati—to name only some of the more recent ones—have in various ways analyzed the epic as a kind of *Bildungsroman*, the story of Gilgamesh's education and progress to maturity, and the implications we would see in these lines only confirm how essentially correct they have been. I propose, therefore, that in this imitation of "pseudo-autobiography" our poet-editor gives us final and formal guidance on how we are to read what follows: as *narû*-epic, epic, but epic in a new key, epic in "the key of wisdom" (Buccellati).

The hymn is over, the narrative begins. At this point I feel like Aeneas when asked by Dido to tell of the fall of Troy and all that had befallen him. Not, of course, that for me to tell my tale would be an "unspeakable sorrow" (*infandum dolorem*). On the contrary. But I share with Aeneas the obvious problem of time.

> The dewy night is falling from the sky,
> And sinking stars summon us to sleep.
> (*Aeneid* II 8–9)

I cannot tell the whole tale, let alone linger over it, but let me remind you of all that follows: Gilgamesh oppressing Uruk; Enkidu, given by the gods to be a match for Gilgamesh, born in the steppe, seduced by the harlot, drawn from his animal state into the civilized life of Uruk; the struggle and then friendship of Gilgamesh and Enkidu; their expedition against the monster Huwawa; their triumphant return to Uruk; the confrontation with the goddess Ishtar and the vision of *eros* as also *thanatos*; the death of Enkidu; the unassuageable grief of Gilgamesh and his new, obsessive fear of death; his journey across the world to the one immortal, the survivor of the Flood, Utnapishtim, only to learn the terrible truth of the inevitability of death, even for him, even for the greatest of kings and the strongest of men, a man indeed even partly divine.

Let us now step back, if only briefly, look at the narrative as whole, and linger long enough to see at least the structure of this truly epic tale.

The principal structure, I submit, is articulated by repetition, repetition of periods of time associated with a repeated symbolism. The periods of time are three periods of "six days and seven nights" ("seven days and seven nights" in the Old Babylonian version); the symbolism, that of bathing and clothing 'rites of passage,' symbols of an inner transformation.

The first period is the "six days and seven nights" during which Enkidu and the harlot make uninterrupted love. As you will recall, this epic performance over, Enkidu tries to run again with his animal companions, and he fails. He is no longer an animal; he has been transformed within. As the poet says, "He now has wisdom, broad understanding." He has begun his transformation into a human being.

Then on the way to Uruk with the harlot, he meets shepherds who place before him bread and beer, the food and drink of men. Here the text breaks off and for the sequel we must go to the Old Babylonian version. There we find Enkidu adjusting very quickly and in truly heroic fashion; of the beer he drinks seven kegs. Then, relaxed and singing away, his face aglow,

> With water he washed
> His hairy body,
> Anointed himself with oil,
> Became a man,
> Put on a garment,
> Was human.

The humanization of Enkidu, it is generally and perhaps correctly held, is complete at this point, but I would like to propose one last step, and it is the moment—described so far, I admit, only in the Old Babylonian, but certainly present in the later version—when Enkidu bows down and acknowledges the kingship of Gilgamesh:

> It is as one unique your mother bore you,
> Wild-Cow of the pen, Ninsuna.

Placed high, high over men, are you.
The kingship of the people Ellil has decreed for you.

This event must be seen, I believe, against the background of the Mesopotamian view of kingship. In this view, kingship is the final and perfect ordering principle of human existence, and in its absence humanity is incomplete, even savage. This is implied, for example, by the Sumerian King List, where we find kingship bringing order to human affairs. It is in the myth of Etana; without kingship man lacks counsel. And it has a new and striking illustration in a recently published myth where we find the Birth-goddess told, "It was you who created primal-man (*lullû-amēlu*), so fashion too a king, counselor-man."

Enkidu was born primal-man (*lullû-amēlu*), and I propose that until he comes into the city and begins life under a king he is still not entirely removed from his original condition. Only in Gilgamesh does he find counsel, and in counsel his full humanity.

The narrative then moves on until another period of six days and seven nights intervenes, a period associated this time, however, with the negative symbolism of a refusal to bathe and to dress in the clothes of men. I refer to the mourning of Gilgamesh over the death of his friend Enkidu.

The fragmentary state of the seventh and eighth tablets leaves the actual course of events at Enkidu's death somewhat obscure. According to the Old Babylonian version, however, paralleled by a fragment of the standard version, Gilgamesh later on tells the alewife that when Enkidu died,

All day and night I wept over him
And would not have him buried,
As if my friend might rise at my cries,
For seven days and seven nights,
Until a maggot dropped from his nose.

And I think we may safely assume that somewhere in the breaks of the seventh or eighth tablet the description of the grief of Gilgamesh included this information.

In the course of his protracted and unremitting grief, as Gilgamesh rocks back and forth over his friend's corpse, he pulls out his hair, tears off his finery as though something taboo and untouchable, and in his last words to his beloved friend he says:

I will leave my body covered with grime,
Wrap it in a lion-skin and roam in the steppe.

The transformation of Gilgamesh in this week of mourning is profound. We witness not only the physical death of Enkidu, but the ethical death of Gilgamesh as well. The hero who had once voiced so eloquently the heroic ideal, declaring his contempt for death, chiding Enkidu for fearing it even for a moment as long as there be prospect of fame, is about to reject that ideal utterly and all the values associated with it. Consumed with a fear of death, Gilgamesh the hero dies and Gilgamesh the anti-hero is born.

And the transformation goes even deeper. In setting out, as he is about to do, to find immortality, Gilgamesh rejects not only conventional heroism but his very humanity.

Therefore, the grime, the unbathed body, the animal skin, the absence of human garb, speak of more than an identification with the dead Enkidu and a return to the world of the steppe from which his friend had once come. They are also emblematic of the anti-hero and the would-be god, the anti-man.

There remains a last week and a last transformation. Utnapishtim tells Gilgamesh the story of the Flood. Then to convince him that he does not have the stuff of immortality, Utnapishtim challenges Gilgamesh:

Lie not down to sleep
For six days and seven nights.

And immediately sleep, an image of death as an old man, death's twin for the Greeks, pours over Gilgamesh and he sleeps and sleeps until Utnapishtim touches and wakes him. It is the seventh day.

And now, finally, Gilgamesh yields. Now, finally, he accepts his mortality and therefore his humanity. Now, finally, the would-be god, the anti-man, is no more. In evidence of this he allows himself to be bathed, his skins cast off and carried away by the sea, and a new cloak to cover him. Thus he is ready for the journey back, back from the rim of the world, where the immortals dwell, back from the steppe, the haunt of animals and death, Uruk, where he as a man belongs.

The consistency and comprehensiveness of this overall analysis convinces me of its essential correctness. It was first proposed, though only partially and tentatively, by Hope Wolff, a student of comparative literature, who buried it in a footnote.[1] She recognized the repetitions of the time periods and their association with changes of character, though the changes she proposed were somewhat different from mine. She did not see the repeated association with bathing and clothing, which recognized, her position becomes, I believe, immeasurably stronger, for the symbolism not only bears on changes of character but cuts to the very heart of the epic and its central concern, on being human.

Of the many merits of Emily Vermeule's 1975 Sather Lectures, *Aspects of Death in Early Greek Art and Poetry*, not the least was the inclusion among her illustrations of the old Charlie Brown strip showing Snoopy lying at the entrance to his doghouse, under a huge icicle, and fearing imminent death, saying to himself with ever increasing emphasis, "I don't want to die. I'm too **young** to die. I'm too **nice** to die. I'm too **ME** to die."

Of what Snoopy speaks we all surely know, and how often have we not said to ourselves essentially the same thing. And for the same reason we sympathize with the terrified Gilgamesh who felt very much "too me to die," and in him we recognize the very prototype of the ego's massive resistance to the prospect of death and extinction. And in his subduing that resistance, in his finally accepting, if reluctantly and fearfully, his destiny, we also recognize the essential and enviable wisdom that brought him peace.

But is this all there is to the wisdom of Gilgamesh, much though it be? I think not, but here I must warn you that my Gilgamesh epic now becomes indeed very much my own.

It is generally conceded that the Flood story was not part of the original epic. There are several arguments. The long account of 188 lines seems to be told for itself. It seriously interrupts the flow of dialogue between Utnapishtim and Gilgamesh, and if one removes the Flood story one makes the very smooth and natural transition from Utnapishtim's telling Gilgamesh about the assembly of the gods after the Flood to Utnapishtim's rhetorical question, "Now who is going to

[1] "Gilgamesh, Enkidu, and the Heroic Life," *JAOS* 89 (1969) 392 n. 2.

assemble the gods for you?" Finally, the story as told here is not an independent account; it draws on an identifiable source.

It is also generally conceded, though perhaps a little less commonly, that the one who added the story was the poet-editor of the prologue. He has a manifest interest in, and esteem for, "the knowledge of days before the Flood" that Gilgamesh brought back. He speaks too, in the prologue, of the secret things revealed by Gilgamesh, and of secret things the epic makes only two formal identifications, one of them the Flood story. If our poet-editor was not the one who added the story, he certainly directs us to it and implies its importance.

And what is that? Undoubtedly, Gilgamesh is presented in the prologue as a kind of culture-hero through whose sufferings we share to some extent in his experience and knowledge, knowledge especially of such arcane matters as what exactly happened at the Flood. After all, it might well be asked: if there was only one survivor of the Flood and he lives at the end of the world, how do we know the story at all? Who contacted this survivor? The epic supplies the answer.

But I think that in an epic to be read as a wisdom tale there is more to the importance of the Flood story than that. It is important, I submit, because it makes no sense.

There were two versions of the Flood story, a long and a short. In the long one, the Flood comes as the culmination of a long series of events reaching back into mythic time when man did not exist at all. It is a story that begins with some gods forced to labor for the others until they go on strike and refuse to work any longer. The solution to the crisis, proposed by the crafty god Ea, is the creation of man to form a new labor force. But this only leads to another crisis: man's ever increasing numbers eventually produce such a din that the god in charge of the earth, Ellil, can get no sleep. And so he sends the plague god to diminish man's numbers, but the crafty Ea, who is also the personal god of Utnapishtim, tells his client to have the people give the plague god all food and presents they ordinarily give their personal gods and goddesses, thereby embarrassing the plague god at afflicting those so generous to him and thus forcing him to desist. And, of course, the plan works.

Then again, the same crisis with essentially the same solution. And then again, the same cycle once more. At which point the frustrated and furious Ellil decides to annihilate man by a flood, and he puts all the gods under oath not to tell any man lest there be somehow a survivor. And once more the crafty Ea finds a way out: he keeps his oath and still informs Utnapishtim of the impending disaster and how to escape, speaking not to Utnapishtim but to a reed wall behind which Utnapishtim lies.

In this amusing, naive tale the frustrated Ellil may be a somewhat pathetic figure, bringing very much to mind that neurotic noise-hater, Ben Jonson's character Morose in *The Silent Woman*. His anger may be excessive and his decision to destroy mankind reprehensible and even short-sighted. After all, the gods need man. But his decision is also understandable, and it does make some sense.

The short version is quite different. We have two examples of it, one the account in the Gilgamesh epic, the other on a tablet from the 13th century discovered at Ras Shamra in Syria, ancient Ugarit. The latter is extremely fragmentary, but enough is preserved—the very beginning and the very end to show its basic similarity to the Gilgamesh version. It begins:

> When the gods took counsel about the lands
> They sent a flood upon the world.

Then Utnapishtim introduces himself and begins to tell of Ea's speech to the reed wall. At the very end, Utnapishtim and his wife are being given immortality.

In the Gilgamesh version, the story of the Flood begins like this:

> Shurippak—a city you yourself know,
> lying on the Euphrates' bank—
> This city was old, the gods too within it,
> And their heart moved the gods to send a flood.

It continues, as does the Ugarit tablet, with Ea's speech to the reed wall, and ends with Ellil's touching the foreheads of Utnapishtim and his wife, as they kneel at his feet, and declaring that they would no longer be like men, but like gods, immortal.

What distinguishes the short version, as you will certainly have noted, is the absence of any clear motivation for sending the Flood. In this version, the decision to destroy mankind has no prior history, no background; it simply happens. If it is not an act of sheer caprice, the motives remain a mystery. In this version, the waters wash over man for reasons we shall never know.

Unfortunately, the part of the long version in which Utnapishtim may have been given immortality is lost, and so we cannot extend the comparison of the two versions. It should be noted, however, that in the short version, or, more cautiously, the short version as preserved in the epic, the gift of immortality must strike one as no less capricious or mysterious than the sending of the Flood. The god Ellil, who had been mainly responsible for the destruction of man, and who only moments before, on arriving and finding a few survivors, had become quite enraged, now not only spares these survivors but makes them immortal. Why this extraordinary largesse? The conclusion of the story makes no more sense than its beginning. We start with an apparently arbitrary destruction of life, we end with an apparently equally arbitrary extension of life into eternity.

Recognition of the inscrutability of the gods was ancient and common in Mesopotamian religious literature, and it became an essential part of the wisdom of the sage. Indeed, in approximately the same period as the composition of the standard version of the Gilgamesh epic, we find the reflective concluding from their experience of life that not only were the gods inscrutable, but they held man to norms of behavior which they would not reveal and he could not discover. It even seemed that good was evil and evil good. It is within this tragic view of man that I would place the short version of the Flood, the primeval paradigm of the human situation.

Equally paradigmatic is the episode of the Plant of Life. The latter is the second secret identified as such and the story about it we also owe, I believe, to our poet-editor. Through the kindness of Utnapishtim and his wife, who wish to give him a farewell present and some reward for his labors, Gilgamesh secures the Plant of Life, which will give him youth if not immortality. On the way back to Uruk, however, he lays it down and plunges into the cool waters of a pool, only to watch helplessly as a serpent (or some other creature) makes off with it, sloughing its skin as it goes.

What betrays Gilgamesh here is simply his humanity, its frailty and its limitations, and he draws a conclusion that echoes the words of the alewife he had heard earlier. To his proposal to cross the sea to Utnapishtim she had said, "If it may/can be done [the word in question is ambiguous], cross over; if not, turn back." Weeping, Gilgamesh now says, "I should have turned back." With this experience of human frailty and the recognition of the radical impropriety of the whole enterprise—one should attempt neither to escape death nor even to cheat it—Gilgamesh has achieved the final wisdom.

The tale, however, does not end there. We must still hear the very end and, in my opinion, very important words of the epic. As they reach Uruk Gilgamesh says to Urshanabi, Utnapishtim's boatman who had accompanied him:

> Go up on the walls and walk about,
> Examine the terrace and study the brickwork,
> If its brickwork be not all of baked bricks,
> Its foundation not laid by the Seven Sages.
> One *sar* city, one *sar* orchards, one *sar* pasture and pond—
> and fallow fields of Ishtar's house—
> Three *sar* and fallow fields . . .

We have come full circle. Hearing the prologue, the very words earlier addressed to us as readers, we have a sense of finality and completeness. We begin in Uruk, we end there, but now, in the new context, after all that has gone before, the verifiable materiality of it all—walls and measurements and topography—tells us, and tells us forcibly, that Gilgamesh is back from a world of jeweled trees and monsters and regions not meant for man, into a definable, measurable, human world, a world indeed made by man.

And in this man-made world of Uruk, this human achievement, one senses, too, a real, if muted, pride. There seems to be an intuitive if inarticulate perception that this is the work proper to man and his destiny: to build, to create a world of his own, as well as to die. It is this consciousness of the dignity as well as of the tragedy of man that we may, with the great art historian Erwin Panofsky, describe as humanism: insistence on human values, acceptance of human limitations. For me, then, the Gilgamesh epic, *my* Gilgamesh epic, is a document of ancient humanism.

CHAPTER 3

The Tears of Things*

[My friend, whom I still love so very much,]
Who journeyed through all hardships with me,
Enkidu, whom I still love so very much,
Who journeyed through all hardships with me,
Did journey to the fate of all mankind.

For days and nights did I weep over him,
And would not let them bury him,
As if my friend might rise at my cries
—for seven days and seven nights—
Until a maggot dropped from his nose.

And since he's gone, I have not found life,
Though roaming, trapper-like, about the steppe.
And now, dear Alewife, I behold your face.
The death I ever dread may I not behold!

The Alewife addresses Gilgamesh:
"Where can you reach in your wanderings?
The life you seek you shall never find.

* From the Gilgamesh Epic, Old Babylonian Version, "Meissner Fragment," cols. ii–iii; cf. Standard Babylonian Gilgamesh X 60–75, 134–46, 233–48 (ed. S. Parpola).

For when the gods created human kind,
Death did they establish for human kind,
Life did they keep just for themselves.

You, Gilgamesh, with belly full,
For days and nights do celebrate,
And of each day a feasting make,
For days and nights do dance and play.

And let your garments be clean and fresh,
Your head be washed, your body bathed,
Your eyes upon the child that holds your hand.
Your wife should rejoice, rejoice in your embrace.
Such work is meant [for human kind]."

CHAPTER 4

Ovid's *Blanda Voluptas* and the Humanization of Enkidu*

Thorkild Jacobsen, optimo magistro et fideli amico, octogesimum septimum annum suae aetatis prospere degenti, gratulor gratoque animo opusculum offero

The Enkidu whom we first meet in the Gilgamesh Epic is a Mesopotamian Perceval, a "fole in the filde" who "in the wilde wodde went, With the bestes to play."[1] He is a strange figure, and much has been written about him and his subsequent humanization.[2] It now appears that he was modeled on other and earlier traditions about the life of primitive man.[3] Thus, at least in broad outline, the Enkidu story is the human story.

* I wish to thank Charles Rowan Beye of City University of New York and Wendell Clausen of Harvard University for generously giving of their time to read the first draft of this essay and of their knowledge to make it less the work of an amateur. They indicated omissions in the bibliography and offered criticisms that were instructive and encouraging, a gratifying *nihil obstat*. Of course, the shortcomings of the essay and any errors that may have crept into the revised version are my responsibility. Thanks, too, to I. Tzvi Abusch, who made some helpful comments from the Babylonian camp.

[1] Cited from J. Speirs, *Medieval English Poetry: The Non-Chaucerian Tradition* (London, 1971) 123.

[2] For a recent survey, see J. H. Tigay, *The Evolution of the Gilgamesh Epic* (Philadelphia, 1982) 198–213.

[3] Ibid., 202–3; G. Komoróczy, "Berosos and the Mesopotamian Literature," *Acta Antiqua* 21 (1973) 140–42; J. Bauer, "Leben in der Urzeit Mesopotamiens," *AfO* Beiheft

Parallels for the various features of this child of nature have been sought not only in Mesopotamian and other Near Eastern sources, but also in the vast materials of folklore and anthropology. Yet, broad as the sweep of the search for parallels has been, one source, and a rich one, the classical tradition, seems to have been largely overlooked. There, in fact, one discovers a picture of man's earliest days that is remarkably similar to the life of Enkidu and his probable Mesopotamian prototypes. It seems worthwhile, then, especially in view of the ever-increasing evidence for the influence of the Near East on the classical world,[4] to call attention, however briefly, to the writings of classical authors.

These writers present us with two radically opposed views of man's earliest days. Lovejoy and Boas called them primitivism and anti-primitivism,[5] which coexisted in tension and a dialectic of mutual influ-

---

19 (1982) 377–83. The Mesopotamian traditions on primitive man Berossos sums up very briefly: "they lived without laws just as wild animals" (S. M. Burstein, *The* Babyloniaca *of Berossos* (SANE 1/5 [Malibu, 1978] 155, translating *zēn d'autous ataktōs hōsper ta thēria*; see also n. 8 below).

[4] See, for example, W. Burkert, *Die orientalisierende Epoche in der griechischen Religion und Literatur* (Sitzungsberichte der Heidelberger Akademie der Wissenschaften, phil.-hist. Kl. Heidelberg, 1984) 1; M. L. West, "Near Eastern Material in Hellenistic and Roman Literature," *Harvard Studies in Classical Philology* 73 (1969) 113–34, and his commentaries in *Hesiod, Theogony* (Oxford, 1966) 28–30 (the Succession Myth) and *Works and Days* (Oxford, 1978), especially 174–77 (the metallic ages). T. Jacobsen, "The Eridu Genesis," *JBL* 100 (1981) 521, points in Sumerian literature to a most striking parallel to the life of Hesiod's Silver Age Man. See, too, idem, *The Harab Myth* (SANE 2/3; Malibu, 1984) and his discussion of the western parallels. Also much debated is Near Eastern influence on Homer, especially by the Gilgamesh tradition: T. B. L. Webster, *From Mycenae to Homer* (London, 1964); M. N. Nagler, *Spontaneity and Tradition: A Study in the Oral Art of Homer* (Berkeley, 1974); G. K. Gresseth, "The Gilgamesh Epic and Homer," *Classical Journal* 70(1974–75) 1–18; J. R. Wilson, "The Gilgamesh Epic and the Iliad," *Echos du monde classique/Classical Views* 30 n.s. 5 (1986) 25–41; G. Crane, *Calypso: Background and Conventions of the Odyssey* (Frankfurt am Main, 1988). For the diffusion and curious distortion of the legend of Gilgamesh, note his presence at Qumran as a giant called *glgmys* or [*g*]*lgmyš* (J. T. Milik, with the collaboration of Matthew Black, *The Book of Enoch: Aramaic Fragments of Qumran Cave 4* [Oxford, 1976] 313). Humbaba probably lies behind another giant called *ḥwbbš*, which corresponds to Middle Persian *hwbʾbyš* (ibid, 311).

[5] A. O. Lovejoy and B. Boas, *Primitivism and Related Ideas in Antiquity* (Baltimore, 1935). The distinction between "hard" and "soft" is also theirs. (It might be noted that Erwin Panofsky, in his famous essay, "Et in Arcadia ego: Poussin and the Elegiac Tradi-

ence.[6] According to primitivism, in both its "hard" and "soft" versions, the beginning was the best of times. In those days, it is said, man's life was either one of complete ease and constant enjoyment, or, if hard, pristinely simple, uncomplicated, free of the clutter of culture—*beatus ille qui procul negotiis.*[7] According to anti-primitivism, in the beginning life was not only hard, it was ugly and savage, a prehuman, animal existence—*thēriōdēs bios (diaita), ferus victus (fera vita).*[8] Man lived in the open, in caves or on mountains, scattered and lacking all social bonds. He ate earth, progressing to grass, plants, roots, and nuts. He went naked or clad only in animal skins. He was without law, a murderer, a cannibal. Only with the discovery or revelation of agriculture and viticulture, fire and metal and tools, navigation and speech (with eloquence), did the truly human life gradually emerge.

Among these various forms of primitivism it is of course the last variety, anti-primitivism, that is so strikingly reminiscent of the early Enkidu and Mesopotamian primitive man. Indeed, in view of other Near Eastern influences, it is hard to believe that the anti-primitivism of classical sources does not derive, ultimately, through a long and complicated process of transmission, its general inspiration and even some of its specific lore from Near Eastern sources. The classical tradi-

---

tion," in *Meaning in the Visual Arts* [Garden City, 1955] 297, does not reflect accurately their distinctions. He calls "hard" primitivism what they call anti-primitivism.) T. Cole, *Democritus and the Sources of Greek Anthropology* (Philological Monographs, American Philological Association, no. 25; Cleveland, 1967) 1, whose work Beye and Clausen called to my attention, sees the basic distinction as between "the myth of the Golden Age and the myth of human progress—Hesiodic fantasy and Ionian science." In Homer and the epic tradition, according to Cole, glorification of a vanished age of heroic power and splendor belongs to the former. After the Ionians, if in a cyclical view of history earlier civilizations were considered more elaborate and splendid, they are "always separated from the present world by some sort of cataclysm; men are thereby reduced to the level of bare subsistence and must proceed by gradual stages to the modicum of civilization they now enjoy" (ibid., 2).

[6] In addition to Cole, see B. Gatz, *Weltalter, goldene Zeit und sinnverwandte Vorstellungen.* (Spudasmata 16; Hildesheim, 1967). The *conspectus locorum* (228ff.) is invaluable; note especially the references under *ferus priscorum temporum status.*

[7] Lovejoy and Boas also call this "cultural primitivism," which is inspired by nostalgia for the simplicity of the good old days.

[8] Cf. the language of Berossos (n. 3 above), whose use of *ataktōs* anticipated Diodorus (*ataktōi kai thēriōdei biōi*, cited by Cole, *Democritus*, 28, n. 4) and Sextus (*hot ataktos ēn anthrōpōn bios*, ibid., 189, n. 31).

tion also suggests how rich the Near Eastern traditions, written and oral, must once have been.

Within this tradition I should like to call attention to one passage in particular. It is the description by Ovid, in the *Ars amatoria* 2.467–80, of primitive man and his humanization. To show the power of love, Ovid recounts the story of cosmic and human origins:

prima fuit rerum confusa sine ordine moles
unaque erat facies sidera, terra, fretum;
mox caelum impositum terris, humus aequore cincta est,
inque suas partes cessit inane chaos;
silva feras, volucres aer accepit habendas;
in liquida, pisces, delituistis aqua;
tum genus humanum solis erravit in agris
idque merae vires et rude corpus erat;
silva domus fuerat, cibus herba, cubilia frondes,
iamque diu nulli cognitus alter erat.
blanda truces animos fertur mollisse voluptas:
constiterant uno femina virque loco.
quid facerent, ipsi nullo didicere magistro;
arte Venus nulla dulce peregit opus.

At first there was a mass, unordered, undefined,
A single sight the stars and land and sea.
Soon sky was over earth, the ground by ocean girded,
And to its place did empty void recede.
The woods received wild beasts to keep, the air the birds,
And you, O fish, did hide in flowing waters.
Then did the human race wander in lonely fields,
Was but sheer strength and body without grace.
The woods had been their home, the grass their food, and leaves their beds,
And long was each to each unknown.
Gentle love (they say) softened savage hearts:
A man and a woman, in one place, had paused.
What to do they learned by themselves. There was no teacher.
Venus performed her sweet task. There was no art.[9]

[9] The text is that of E. J. Kenney, *P. Ovidi Nasonis Amores, Medicamina faciei feminaea, Ars amatoria, Remedia Amoris* (Oxford Classical Texts; Oxford, 1961).

What is most striking in this bit of light-hearted anti-primitivism is the role Ovid assigns to sexual love. While but brute strength and graceless bodies,[10] a man and a woman meet, and their union changes their spirits. In context, the long pause between *blanda* and *voluptas* makes the latter seem like a proclamation.[11] Persuasive, soft, and gentle—*blanda* is all of these—love transforms. To quote Hermann Fraenkel: "This amounts to proposing that it was love that gave man a feeling soul in addition to his body, and that it was sexual love which taught him to know and understand and like his fellow-beings, so that he would build up society."[12]

To the reader of the Gilgamesh Epic, however, what makes Ovid's thought truly extraordinary is the parallel it provides—the closest by far that I know of—for the transformation of Enkidu by his union with the harlot. Fraenkel's statement differs little from what Morris Jastrow wrote about Enkidu many years ago, "through intercourse with a woman he awakens to the sense of human dignity.[13]

But the striking likeness granted, what are we to make of it? Though Ovid claims, in typically neoterist fashion,[14] to be citing a tradition

[10] In context, *rude* (*corpus*) must refer to crudeness, lack of refinement; cf. *artis adhuc expers et rude volgus erat* (*Fasti* 2.292). Elsewhere (*Epistulae* 4.23; *Metamorphoses* 9.270; *Tristia* 3.3) Ovid speaks of the *rude pectus* in connection with love, and there *rude* means "unerfahren, unteilhaftig" (Franz Bömer, *P. Ovidius Naso, Metamorphoses, Books 8–9* [Heidelberg, 1977] 493, on 9.720). A diligent reader of Ovid might sense a certain ambiguity about *rude corpus*.

[11] Ovid found it in *De rerum natura* 4.1085: *blandaque refrenat morsus admixta voluptas*.

[12] *Ovid: A Poet between Two Worlds* (Sather Lectures; Berkeley, 1943) 67. Fraenkel also points to *Fasti* 4.107–14 where Ovid makes love the prime mover of civilization. Clausen notes the effective juxtaposition of the virtual antonyms *blanda* and *truces*.

[13] M. Jastrow and A. T. Clay, *An Old Babylonian Version of the Gilgamesh Epic, on the Basis of Recently Discovered Texts* (Yale Oriental Series Researches 4/3; New Haven, 1920) 20. See also S. N. Kramer, "The Gilgamesh Epic and Its Sumerian Sources: A Study in Literary Evolution," *JAOS* 64 (1944) 9, n. 5.

[14] According to E. Norden, *P. Vergilius Maro Aeneis Buch VI* (3rd ed; Leipzig, 1934) 123, commenting on *ut fama est* in 4.14, this and similar expressions were used in four ways: (1) to cite as true but without criticism; (2) to emphasize, by repeated use, that one's tale is traditional; (3) occasionally to indicate that the tradition is not certain, or must be rejected or reinterpreted in rational terms; (4) to indicate one's own doubts about the tradition. Ovid reflects the second use. (I owe this reference to Clausen.) C. J. Fordyce, *Catullus* (Oxford, 1961) 276, cites as illustrative of the scholar-poet Calli-

(*fertur*), it does not follow that he merely reflects the thought of his source. Certainly in no other classical author do we find sexual intercourse intervening so decisively in the humanization of man, and nothing could be more Ovidian than the claims here made for love.[15] There are then no grounds for postulating a lost Alexandrian Enkidu known to Ovid and his model for the power of love.

However, Ovid does depend on a tradition, and the nature of the tradition and Ovid's dependence on it suggests, I think, a line of speculation on the development of the Enkidu story. One expression of the tradition that Ovid certainly knew was *De rerum natura* 5.1011–27.[16] There, as Lucretius traces the long history of early man, he tells how, after man acquired huts and hides and fire, woman was joined to man in marriage.[17] Next were children, and "then did mankind begin to grow soft. For fire made their shivering bodies less able to endure the cold under the open sky, and Venus sapped their strength, and children by their caresses easily broke the fierce spirit of their parents. And then neighbors began eagerly to unite in friendly agreement with one another neither to do nor to suffer violence."[18]

machus: "I sing of nothing unattested" (*amartyron ouden aeidō*); "the story is not mine but others" (*mythos d'ouk emos all'heterōn*).

[15] Of course Ovid was not alone in exalting love. "The elegiac poets in the time of Augustus are alien to the 'res publica,' indifferent to marriage, the family, procreation. They declare the primacy of love and the individual" (R. Syme, *History in Ovid* [Oxford, 1978] 200). Ovid was, however, unique, to his lasting woe and tribulation, in so arousing the wrath of Augustus that, ailing and at the age of fifty, he was sent into remote exile, never to return, and his *Ars* banished with him. Augustus may have been a prude, but the problem he faced was real. Marriage and procreation were the ancient world's only answer to extremely high mortality rates; see P. Brown, *The Body and Society: Men, Women and Sexual Renunciation in Early Christianity* (New York, 1988) 2.

[16] See Fraenkel, *Ovid*, 203, n. 30. This is the common opinion and it is shared by Beye and Clausen. Note especially *blanda voluptas* (see n. 11 above), and cf. *De rerum natura* 5.1014, *tum genus humanum primum mollescere coepit*, and *Ars amatoria* 2.473, *tum genus humanum* (*solis erravit in agris*), 477 (*blanda truces animos fertur*) *mollisse* (*voluptas*). M. Weber, *Die mythologische Erzählung in Ovids Liebeskunst: Verankerung, Struktur und Funktion* (Studien zur klassischen Philologie 6; Frankfurt am Main, 1983) 200, n. 30, calls our passage a "Parodie auf die epikureische voluptas-Lehre." P. Green, *Ovid: The Erotic Poems* (London, 1982) 376, questions the relevance of Lucretius only to admit that Ovid may allude to him with "his tongue, as so often, in his cheek."

[17] This latter detail seems certain even though the text may be corrupt.

[18] The translation is that of Lovejoy and Boas, *Primitivism*, 228–29.

Obviously this is a much more complex and more serious view of human development. Sexuality is present, but it is only part of the story, though an important one, and it is seen only in the context of marriage. There it diminishes man's powers—again compare Enkidu and his diminished speed—and produces children, who charm their parents into gentleness. Families are then neighbors, and this leads to the very human institution of pacts for peaceful relations. And so the story goes on. All these Lucretian solemnities, with mock didacticism, Ovid transforms—frivolously, says Cole[19]—into a light and amusing (*nullo magistro, nulla arte*) simplicity.

Lucretius had his predecessors. For them sexual love is universal, shared by gods, men, and animals.[20] It is all-powerful, taming, and subjecting, and none can escape it.[21] It bears, therefore, *in nuce*, all of society and the origins of social transformation. The sexual act is, as Cole remarks,[22] a purely natural and universal form of *koinōnia*. Cicero sums it up quite well:

> *itaque primos congressus copulationesque . . . fieri propter voluptatem; cum autem usus progrediens familiaritatem effecerit, tum amorem efflorescere tantum ut, etiamsi nulla sit utilitas ex amicitia, tamen ipsi amici propter se ipsos amentur.*

> therefore the first comings together and copulations . . . are inspired by sexual love; when, however, constant dealings with one another have created a sense of intimacy, then love blossoms to the point that, even

[19] Cole, *Democritus*, 7.

[20] See the Homeric "Hymn to Aphrodite," lines 1ff.: In their commentary, T. W. Allen, W. R. Halliday, E. E. Sikes, *The Homeric Hymns* (Oxford, 1936) 352 (reference from Beye), compare Theognis 1526–29, Sophocles fr. 941, Euripides *Hippolytus* 447, 1269; Lucretius 1.1. See also Hesiod, *Theogony* 121; *Antigone* 788–89; *Iliad* 14.199. Explaining the very early position that Love occupies in Hesiod's outline of origins, J. Griffin, *The Oxford History of the Classical World* (ed. J. Boardman et al.; Oxford and New York, 1986) 89, writes that "Love has no children of his own, but he is the principle of procreation which is to create the world."

[21] For Sophocles, Eros is "unconquerable" (*anikate machan*, Antigone 785) and, for both gods and men, "inescapable" (*phyximos oudeis*, ibid., 788); Aphrodite is "invincible" (*amachos*, ibid., 800). In the epic tradition a verb used of Aphrodite or Love (*philotēs*) is *damazō* and congeners (*Iliad* 14.199, 316, 353; *Hymn to Aphrodite* 3; also Theognis 1388), which are also used of taming animals.

[22] Cole, *Democritus*, 144, where Cole comments on the role of sex in the ethnology of Herodotus and the more general theory of Polybius.

> though nothing useful can come from friendship, still the friends themselves are loved for themselves.[23]

Now, Ovid must have known all this, but his silence about marriage and children and friendship rejects it and in effect mocks it. For the others, the story only begins with *voluptas*; for Ovid, it ends there. Nothing else matters.

All this urges us to think about the Enkidu story again and to speculate a bit. It is certainly possible and, in fact, in the light of the classical tradition, it seems even likely that in some Mesopotamian myth or myths on the development of primitive man, under the guidance of the gods, sexuality and marriage played a part not unlike what we have seen in Ovid's predecessors. Now, if Enkidu were modeled on some such tradition, obviously some adaptations would be necessary. A married Enkidu would not do. Marriage would distract from the narrative line, raise ungermane questions, and detract from the future bond with Gilgamesh. And so—we speculate—Enkidu's story was given a new twist, one worthy indeed of Ovid himself: not a wife for Enkidu, but a harlot. This is a transformation that we may suspect would have been as recognizable and as humorous to a cultivated Babylonian audience as Ovid's was to his sophisticated Roman readers. It would, too, be quite in the spirit of the description that follows of Enkidu's gawking at the bread, his mighty thirst, his beery gladness.

It is this spirit, however, that suggests another line of speculation. Perhaps the adaptations we postulate were made, not for the figure of Enkidu in the epic, but earlier, before their application to him, in the

[23] *De finibus* 1, 869, cited by Cole, *Democritus*, 84, n. 12. Cf. also *De officiis* 1, par. 54:

> *nam cum sit hoc natura commune animantium. ut habeant libidinem procreandi, prima societas in ipso coniugio est, proxima in liberis, deinde una domus, communia omnia. Id autem est principium urbis et quasi seminarium rei publicae.*

> Again, since it is by nature common to animals that they have an urge to procreate, the first society is in marriage, the next in children, then one house, all things in common. And in fact this is the beginning of the city and the nursery as it were of the state.

For the translation of *nam*, see A. W. Dyck, "On the Composition and Sources of Cicero *De officiis* 1.50–58," *California Studies in Classical Antiquity* 12 (1979) 82, n. 6. Dyck discusses the apparent inconsistencies of Cicero's thought and their possible source.

tradition on primitive man. If we look for a setting for such a tale, the *aštammu*, pub and gathering place of harlots and the bibulous, seems the most likely. There we can imagine the telling of tales, among them that of primitive man and his humanization, and we also can readily imagine that it would not go unchanged but would be adapted to the audience and reflect their interests and mood. In such a telling, to the ribald amusement and satisfaction of all, harlotry and insobriety would be recognized as quite civilizing and their contribution to man's evolution duly acknowledged. And—final step in our speculation—it was this *aštammu*-version that the epic bard, inspired by the *musa iocosa* and anticipating the principle *ludicra seriis miscere*, borrowed, bowdlerized, and attached to Enkidu.[24]

All speculation aside, certainly a reference to *Ars amatoria* 2.467–80 belongs in everyone's marginalia to *Gilgamesh* Tablet I.

The humanization of Enkidu begins with a week of love-making. It ends, it is generally held, when he has been introduced to bread, beer, clothing, and toilet. I would suggest one more step. It occurs when he reaches Uruk and, at the end of their first and decisive encounter, he addresses Gilgamesh (P vi 27–33):

kīma ištēn-ma ummaka ulidka
rīmtum ša supūri Ninsuna
ullu eli mutī rēška
šarrūtam ša nišī išīmkum Ellil

It was as one unique your mother bore you
—Wild-cow of the Pen, Ninsuna.
Placed high, high over men, are you.
The kingship of the people Ellil decreed for you.

The importance of kingship in the Mesopotamian scheme of things needs no discussion here. In brief, kingship is the final and perfect ordering principle of human existence, and in its absence the human

[24] I am aware of course that the identification of the comic and humorous across cultural boundaries is a very parlous enterprise, but the erotic, nudity, and food—all central elements of the Enkidu story—are common comic motifs, which tend to be universal; see E. R. Curtius, "Comic Elements in the Epic" and "Kitchen Humor and Other *Ridicula*," *European Literature and the Latin Middle Ages* (trans. W. R. Trask; New York, 1953) 429–31 and 431–35.

story is incomplete. This is implied by the Sumerian King List,[25] is clear from the introduction to the myth of Etana, and now has a new and striking illustration in VS 24 92:32'–33'.[26] Ea addressed Belet-ili and says: *at-ti-ma tab-ni-ma* LÚ.U_{18}.LU-*a a-me-lu* / *pi-it-qi-ma* LUGAL *ma-li-ku a-me-lu*, "It was you who created primal-man, so fashion too a king, counselor-man." As in Etana, what kingship means is counsel, guidance in both war and peace. It is the institution without which there is no human fulfillment.[27]

It would seem, therefore, that Enkidu's acknowledgment and acceptance of the kingship of Gilgamesh is not irrelevant to his humanization, especially in a narrative that has been so deeply concerned with this process. I submit, then, that until Enkidu comes into the city and begins life under a king, he is still not wholly removed from his original condition of *lullû-amēlu*. Only in Gilgamesh does he find counsel and, in counsel, full humanity.

[25] Among the pre-Etana, pre-kingship rulers, the name of the second, Kullassina-bel, "All of them (the people) are lord"(?), and the animal names of others, are perhaps meant to suggest a period of anarchy and savagery—*ho ataktos bios*. What Etana brings is order and organization (mu-un-gi-na, Jacobsen, *The Sumerian King List* [AS 11; Chicago, 1939] 80:18; gi-na = *kunnu*).

[26] For an edition of the text, see W. R. Mayer, "Ein Mythos von der Erschaffung des Menschen und des Königs," *Or* 56 (1987) 55–68.

[27] The conception of the ideal king or hero as one uniting in himself prudence and power, brains and brawn, has a long history in the West. Awareness of the polarity in Mesopotamia makes one question that in the West the phenomenon must be seen as a survival of prehistoric Indo-European religion as reconstructed by Georges Dumezil; so Curtius, *European Literature*, 171–72. In any case, the ideal is in the epic tradition down to Virgil, declining to the status of topos in Late Antiquity and the Middle Ages and surviving into the Renaissance in the formulas "arms and studies," "pen and sword" (ibid., 177–79; see also T. Greene, *The Descent from Heaven: A Study in Epic Continuity* [New Haven, 1963] 364). Note, too, in Hellenistic historiography the pairs used to describe the best rulers: "prudence and manliness" (*phronēsis, andreia*: Moses); "strength and intelligence" (*ischys, synesis*: first kings); "beauty and might" (*kallos, rōmē*: Dionysus in India); "manliness and intelligence" (*andreia, synesis*: Zeus in Crete, thereby gaining the kingship); add "manliness and judgment" (*virtus, consilium*; first kings); for the loci, see Cole, *Democritus*, 94, n. 23, who adds a number of references to authors who associate early kingship with the reign of law.

CHAPTER 5

Atrahasis: The Babylonian Story of the Flood*

Although almost a century has passed since George Smith announced his sensational discovery of "the Chaldean account" of the Deluge, until very recently our understanding of the story was seriously hampered—more seriously, it turns out, than we realized—by our meager knowledge of the broader context in which the cataclysm was conceived. In the intervening years, it is true, it had become clear that what Smith had discovered, the eleventh tablet of the Gilgamesh Epic, was derivative. However, of the Old Babylonian source, which we had learned from a scribal note consisted of three tablets totaling 1245 lines, only about 200 had been recovered, and these were pretty much *disjecta membra*.[1] There was also a Middle Babylonian fragment of little importance, and Assurbanipal's library had yielded a few fragments of later Assyrian recensions, the largest of which, by confusion of the obverse and reverse of the tablet, was being read in the wrong order;

* A review article of W. G. Lambert and A. R. Millard, *Atrahasīs: The Babylonian Story of the Flood*, with M. Civil, *The Sumerian Flood Story* (Oxford: Clarendon, 1969). 70 shillings. This review incorporates the interpretation of the epic which the writer proposed in a lecture (Feb., 1968) at Brandeis University on "The Place of the Deluge in Mesopotamian Religious Thought."

[1] All the material available before the most recent discoveries may now be conveniently found in *ANET*, 99–100 (now known to be an integral part of the Atrahasis Epic), 104–106 (E. A. Speiser), 512–514 (A. K. Grayson).

this error, until corrected by Laessøe in 1956,[2] not surprisingly resulted in some serious misunderstanding. Finally, a Sumerian version was known, but only one-third (about 100 lines) was preserved and the breaks were at crucial points.[3]

In the last five years the situation just described has been radically changed, thanks mainly to the work of Lambert and Millard.[4] What is most important is that now, instead of 200, we have well over 700 lines of the Old Babylonian version. Happily, too, they throw light just where out ignorance had previously been particularly distressing; we now have a clear picture of the events leading to the creation of man and some idea of the measures taken by the gods after the Deluge. In fact, using with due caution the later recensions together with the eleventh tablet of the Gilgamesh Epic, we can now draw a fairly detailed outline of the Old Babylonian story. The main sequence of events is clear and the roles of the principal protagonists are in much sharper focus. We are, therefore, on much firmer ground than we had been when we approach the problem of what the Atrahasis Epic as a whole is all about. It is to this central question that we shall confine our remarks here.

First, a short outline of the story. The epic begins at a period when, prior to the creation of man, some of the gods were forced to provide the labor necessary for the sustenance of their fellow deities. This they

[2] See J. Laessøe, "The Atrahasis Epic: A Babylonian History of Mankind," *BO* 13 (1956) 90–102.

[3] We do not wish to imply that we consider the Sumerian version a source of the Atrahasis Epic, though a common Sumerian background and tradition may be assumed; cf. B. Landsberger, "Einleitung in das Gilgameš-Epos," in *Gilgamesh et sa légende* (ed. P. Garelli; Paris, 1960) 34. The fact that in the Old Babylonian version the god of fresh waters is, with the single exception of *CT* 44:20, consistently called by his Sumerian (Enki) rather than his Semitic (Ea) name, may point to dependence on a Sumerian source; however, it should be noted that Sumerian provenience would not adequately explain the anomaly.

[4] In *CT* 46 Lambert and Millard published fifteen Old Babylonian and Late Assyrian copies (some of them-had been published previously). In the present volume, Lambert adds an Old Babylonian fragment (pls. 1–6), more Late Assyrian and Neo-Late Babylonian material (pls. 4, 5, 9–10; pp. xi–xii), a new copy of the Old Babylonian text published by Boissier in *RA* 28, and a list of collations (pl. 11). Through the courtesy of J. Nougayrol, *Ugaritica V*, No.167 (pp. 300–304) could also be included. Most recently, in "New Evidence for the First Line of Atra-ḫasīs," *Or* 38 (1969) 533–538, Lambert has published another small but important fragment of an Assyrian recension.

do on earth, Enlil's domain, while Anu resides in the heavens above and Enki in the fresh waters below. However, after a period of forty years or perhaps longer,[5] they find the work intolerable, they revolt, and eventually they prove adamant in their refusal to continue as the labor-force for the other gods. It is Enki who solves the dilemma by proposing the creation of man. His proposal is accepted by the gods and then carried out with his help by the mother-goddess. But even this solution proves not altogether satisfactory. Before 1200 years have elapsed, man is acting in such a way that Enlil is deprived of his sleep. He tries to solve the problem by sending a series (three) of plagues, but each is rendered ineffective by Enki, who as the personal god of Atrahasis advises his servant how man can avert the plagues or at least survive them.[6] This leads Enlil to the desperate measure of the Deluge.

Again, as in the Gilgamesh Epic, Enki thwarts Enlil of his purpose, and Atrahasis and his family survive. On the basis of the Gilgamesh Epic and the Sumerian version, we may assume that they are given immortality, but the text that is preserved is largely concerned, it seems, with carrying out Enlil's commission to Enki and the mother-goddess to put their heads together and to plan a post-diluvian order that allows for man, but on terms acceptable to Enlil.

With this brief and purposely vague outline we may now turn to the problem of understanding. Since the appearance of the new material two interpretations have been proposed.[7] According to G. Pettinato

[5] See W. von Soden, "'Als die Götter (auch noch) Mensch waren': Einige Grundgedanken des altbabylonischen Atramḫasīs-Mythus," *Or* 38 (1969) 422, n. 1.

[6] To be exact, these last remarks apply only to the first and second plagues. In the third plague Enki apparently intervenes in a somewhat different manner; see Lambert-Millard, 78ff.

[7] Of course there is a considerable literature on this subject prior to the recent discoveries. In Lambert-Millard there is a detailed outline of the contents with a number of exegetical remarks, but there is no synthesis or comprehensive interpretation. In fact, admirable as this work is in many ways, it is frequently disappointing where interpretation is concerned; many lines that cry for some word of explanation are completely ignored in the commentary. According to R. Caplice, *Or* 38 (1969) 482–483, Elena Cassin in *La splendeur divine* (Paris, 1968), at present still inaccessible to the writer, sees in "the noise which disturbed the gods . . . a sign of the teeming vitality of life, with the suggestion that the conflict of generations is a motive force in both epics [*Enūma elîš* and *Atrahasis*]." This is close to our own view, but we would emphasize the chaotic nature of the noise in the antediluvian stage (see below).

the words *ḫubūru* and *rigmu*, which are used to explain Enlil's sleeplessness, do not mean simply "din" and "cry," but connote evil conduct — in context, man's rebellious protest against his lot of having to toil for the gods. Hence in this view man is clearly a sinner and Enlil is more than justified in sending the plagues and, eventually, the Deluge.[8] For W. von Soden, the epic does not express itself unambiguously on man's guilt, and he finds its general import, *in nuce*, in the very first line, *inūma ilū awīlum*, which he renders "Als die Götter (auch noch) Mensch waren."[9] This he understands to mean that, in the poet's conception, there was a stage in the evolution from chaos in which the gods, though of course never simply men, were much more like men than they became and remained after the Deluge. He finds this view implied and elaborated in many anthropomorphisms, the first being that gods worked, suffered and rebelled. Despite considerable lacunae at the end, he believes we may assume that, in the new and present order of things, the poet had the gods put away their many too, too human traits.

Though both scholars have in our opinion rightly stressed important features of the epic, we accept neither interpretation. Pettinato's we reject as based largely on a misunderstanding of Enki's advice during the first and second plagues:

Order the heralds to cry,
Let them silence the roar in the land.
Do not reverence your gods.
Do not pray to your goddess(es).
Namtar (Adad, respectively), seek his gate,
Bring a baked-loaf before it,
Let the meal-offering please him,
So that, embarrassed at the gifts, He will raise his hand.[10]

[8] "Die Bestrafung des Menschengeschlechts durch die Sintflut," *Or* 37 (1968) 165–200, and see especially 188–159. Pettinato is of course not the first to interpret man's conduct as sinful. See, e.g., Speiser in *ANET*, 103 ("a large epic cycle dealing with man's sins and his consequent punishment through plague and the deluge"); Heidel, *The Gilgamesh Epic and Old Testament Parallels* (2d ed.; Chicago 1949) 225, 268; L. Matouš, "Zur neueren epischen Literatur im alten Mesopotamien," *ArOr* 35 (1967) 8.

[9] von Soden, "Als die Götter," 415–432, and see especially 419–427.

[10] Tabl. I 376–383 (Lambert-Millard, 68–69), Tabl. II 15'–15 (Lambert-Millard, 74–75): *qibâmāmi lissû nāgirū / rigma lišebbû ina mātim / ê taplaḫā ilīkun / ê tusalliā ištarkun / Namtara* (*Adad*, respectively) *šiâ bābšu / bilā epīta ana qudmīšu / lilliksu masḫatum*

These lines, we submit, do not urge a bold *non serviam* against the gods in general ("praktisch eine Kampfsansage an die Götter"),[11] or a "Strafmassnahme" that man in an earlier order of things may dare to take against his still not absolute masters.[12]

The unlikelihood that the people are to be told to cut off all cult to the gods with the exception of Namtar or Adad, should at least be suspected in view of the one who gives the advice. It is the clever, wily, devious Enki. This is the god who evades his oath and warns Atrahasis of the final impending disaster by speaking, not to him, but to a wall. He is the one who, in the face of a revolt, does not think of arms but conceives the new thing, man. It is he, too, who finds the compromise that establishes the post-diluvian order. This is not a god of bold confrontations. He is the sly diplomat, and it would be completely out of character if he were to urge man to a kind of showdown of power, and a necessarily futile one to boot.

Furthermore, why bother bribing Namtar and Adad, and why insist that the latter act so stealthily,[13] if there is to be an open rebellion which will force Enlil to relent! Not only is there not the slightest indication that Enlil ever felt compelled to reconsider his decisions, but when the gods suffer hunger cramps in the days of the Deluge, this seems a completely new experience for them, an unforeseen consequence of their following Enlil in his determination to annihilate man. This is hard to reconcile with alleged earlier periods of deprivation.

All of these problems disappear with the observation that the text speaks of "*your* gods" and "*your* goddess(es)", not simply of gods and goddesses. As almost countless examples show, this is the usual way of referring to personal gods.[14] If the poet had wished to include all the

niqû / lîbāšma ina katrê / lîšaqqil qāssu. The expression *rigma šubbû* (*šuppû*) could also mean "to raise a loud cry", and is so understood by Lambert-Millard and Pettinato. However, in view of the problem the *rigmu* of the people had already created, it seems much more likely that the heralds are not to be told to add to the noise but rather to go about putting it down.

11 So Pettinato, "Bestrafung," 189.

12 So von Soden, "Als die Götter," 427. How these lines can be taken, as Matouš, "Neueren epischen Literatur," 8, does, as an attempt to persuade the people to worship, escapes us.

13 See Tabl. II ii 16–19 (Lambert-Millard, 74–75).

14 See *CAD* I/J, 95ff.; cf. too *il amēli* and *il abi*, p. 95. In Tabl. III i 42 (Lambert-Millard, 90–91) Enlil is called "your god", not that he is the personal god of all the people,

gods, he would almost certainly not have used the pronominal suffix; hence, apart from all the difficulties that a reference to the entire pantheon causes here, it is not in itself a very probable reading of the text. Obviously, too, in our view Enki's counsels are duly clever and devious, really worthy of him: first of all, quiet down, then neglect for a time your individual gods and goddesses, concentrate the cult you would ordinarily give to them on the god afflicting you, making him a kind of universal personal god, until he is so embarrassed by your attentions that he either desists or adopts some way of nullifying the effects of the plague.[15]

There is, therefore, no hint of rebellion in the *rigmu* of this passage, and so such a connotation may not be read into the word, as Pettinato does, when it is found in the introduction to Enlil's complaint before the first and second plagues:[16]

> The land grew extensive,
> The people numerous,
> The land was bellowing like a bull.
> At their din the god was distressed.
> Enlil heard their cry.
> He addressed the great gods,
> "The cry of mankind has become burdensome to me,
> Because of their din I am deprived of sleep."[17]

---

but because of the contrast between Enlil and Enki, the personal god of Atrahasis (*ilī*, "my god").

[15] Note the interesting parallel to our passage in an Old Babylonian letter (R. Frankena, *Altbabylonische Briefe*, Heft II, No. 118, pp. 82–83 = *VAB* VI, No. 97, pp. 86–87) which reports on which god is causing the deaths in the city and orders a herald to proclaim assemblies (?) of all the people in honor of the god and prayers to him until he is appeased.

[16] See Pettinato, "Bestrafung," 184.

[17] *mātum irtapiš nišū imtīdā / mātum kīma lî išabbu (išappu) / ina ḫubūrišina ilu itta'dar / Enlil išteme rigimšin / issaqqar ana ilī rabûtim / iktabta rigim awīlūti / ina ḫubūrišina uzamma šitta*, Tabl. I 353–359 (Lambert-Millard, 66–67), Tabl. II i 2–8 (Lambert-Millard, 72–73); cf. also Lambert-Millard, 106–107, lines 2–8 (Assyrian recension, and note Addenda, 172). Pettinato would have Enlil uneasy with the gods. However, through *na'duru* (*itta'dar*) at times certainly denotes the specific distress of fear, Enlil's speech is not that of someone afraid. The cry of mankind is a burden, not a source of any alarm, and Enlil appears in complete control of the situation when he goes on to state the specific measures to be taken to rid himself of this burden.

The obvious meaning is that an ever-increasing population had resulted in such a din and racket that sleep became impossible, and this meaning, we maintain, is the correct one.[18] For, first of all, why mention in each case the size of the population unless it is somehow connected with the "din" and "cry"?[19] Furthermore, in the introduction to the second plague in an Assyrian recension, Enlil first notes "The people have not diminished, their numbers are more excessive than before,"[20] then goes on to complain of his distress and sleeplessness due to the "cry" and "din." The numbers of the people and the noise could hardly be associated more closely.[21] And, finally, that the problem of man, at least in part, lies precisely in his numbers is to be seen from the fact that in the post-diluvian order provision will be made for the existence of sterile as well as fertile women, of a demon that will snatch children from their mothers and thus insure a high infant mortality rate, and of institutions of religious women who may not marry—all obvious measures of population-control.[22]

These criticisms do not imply that Pettinato is wrong in stressing the importance of the din and cry of the people, or even in considering them an evil. His mistake is trying to make them a moral evil, sin.[23] In this he runs against all the evidence. The Atrahasis Epic ignores almost completely the ideas of sin and punishment, and it is not in any sense a theodicy, a justification of Enlil's ways with man. If man's sinfulness

[18] The interpretation we defend is, of course, not new.

[19] Pettinato ("Bestrafung," 183) speaks vaguely of the syntax of the passage as militating against any close connection between the size of the population and the reason for Enlil's anger.

[20] *[niš]ū lā imṭâ ana ša pāna ittatrā,* Lambert-Millard, 108, line 39.

[21] Pettinato ("Bestrafung," 183) dismisses this passage as irrelevant on the grounds that the situation is different in the two cases and adds "s. unten." We can discover nothing (pp. 191–192?) that would support any relevant distinction between the situations described in the two passages.

[22] Lambert-Millard, 102–103, lines 1–9. Note also in the Assyrian recension the last purpose (and effect) of the second plague: closed wombs giving birth to no children (Lambert-Millard, 108–111, lines 51, 61).

[23] See the perceptive remarks of Paul Ricoeur, *The Symbolism of Evil* (trans. E. Buchanan; Religious Perspective Series 18; Boston, 1969) 184–187. He also notes: "That the intention of the myth [Atrahasis] is not to illustrate the wickedness of men is confirmed further by its insertion in the famous *Epic of Gilgamesh*. The quest of Gilgamesh has nothing to do with sin, but only with death, completely stripped of all ethical significance, and with the desire for immortality" (187).

were the issue, then he should be charged with sin, but nowhere is man's responsibility expressed in terms of moral culpability. There is not a single mention of sin, a subject for which Akkadian has a rich lexical stock, until after the Deluge, when Enki defends himself before the divine assembly and bitterly reproaches Enlil for a wanton destruction that ignored all distinction between innocent and guilty.[24] If this brief reference suggests that the poet was not altogether unaware of deeper problems the Deluge might pose, it also shows that in the actions of Enlil and the people, which throughout involve only indiscriminate global masses, he has not faced them. He is definitely no Job.[25]

But man was involved in disorder, though one that ultimately was not of his own making. What man produced, *rigmu*, is not in itself an evil,[26] in fact, it is characteristically human, evidence of man's pres-

[24] Tabl. III vi 16ff., especially 25–26 (Lambert-Millard, 100–101). Though unfortunately the text is badly broken at this point, enough can be made out to establish that Enki's defense, in part at least, is substantially the one he makes in *Gilg*. XI 180ff. It is difficult to see how Heidel (*Gilgamesh Epic*, 225, 268) can find in the latter passage proof that the Deluge is a punishment for sin. Enki's reproach is precisely that Enlil ignored ethical considerations, and this is borne out by everything we know of the Deluge, which from its conception was intended to destroy man utterly, something it could not have done had sin been taken account of. It is to be admitted that the reference to sin in Enki's speech comes somewhat unexpectedly, which explains why von Soden (*ZDMG* 89 [1935] 153, n. 4) once felt that Enki's speech in *Gilg*. XI is a later addition. However, if there is an underlying polemic against Enlil throughout the epic (see below), Enki's speech may be seen as its culmination, a revelation of Enlil's character as brutal force.

[25] Nor should it be inferred from the piety of Atrahasis towards his personal god that the poet represents more conventional views. Atrahasis may be duly rewarded by Enki, but nothing suggests that the rest of the people are rightly treated as a *massa damnata*.

[26] The word runs like a theme throughout the epic. It first occurs when the rebelling gods are shouting outside Enlil's house (Tabl. I 77, Lambert-Millard, 46), then in reference to their forced labor (Tabl. I 179, Lambert-Millard, 52). It reappears at man's creation, in an unfortunately still obscure line (Tabl. I 242, Lambert-Millard, 60; cf. also Tabl. II vii 32, Lambert-Millard, 84). As we have seen, it denotes the main issue of the plagues. When the Deluge comes, *rigmu* is the thunder of the storm (Tabl. III ii 50, Lambert-Millard, 92; iii 20 [?], 23, Lambert-Millard, 94, and cf. 124, line 20), the noise of the land (Tabl. III iii 10, Lambert-Millard, 92), the cries of the people (Tabl. III in 43, Lambert-Millard, 94), the lament of the mother-goddess (Tabl. III iii 47, Lambert-Millard,

ence, and its absence suggests devastation.[27] However, in antediluvian days its volume was monstrous and chaotic. That the poet thought of it in these terms is seen in the identical descriptions of the land before the Deluge and of the Deluge-storm itself, when chaos breaks upon the world; "it was bellowing like a bull."[28]

But the form of chaos, with its chronic disorder and crises, that man's existence entailed was inevitable as long as man's procreative powers—behind which we should see his creators, Enki and the mother goddess—went unchecked. The teeming masses that necessarily resulted could not fail to produce a din that was intolerable to Enlil, who, it should be noted, is never censured for taking some limited measures against it. What is lacking prior to the Deluge is a balance of powers, the balance that obtains in the present order of things.

The origin of this balance is, in our opinion, the central question of the Atrahasis Epic, which accordingly we consider as fundamentally a cosmogonic myth. The answer defines man's established place in the universe. And unlike its Sumerian counterpart, which is also concerned with the origins of cities and kingship, the Atrahasis Epic is not interested in man's political or social institutions; at least in the text as preserved they are ignored, or if they are mentioned at all, they are mentioned only in passing, as vestiges of an earlier tradition. Rather, Atrahasis looks solely to what we may call the most essential man: his very being, his origin, his function, and his experience, at the deepest

---

94).—A similar range of meaning is attested in the omen literature (sec J. Nougayrol, *RA* 44 [1950] 26). In *En. el.* the *rigmu* of the younger gods is one source of the confusion that so disturbs old Apsu; it is perhaps to be taken here as evidence of the excessive exuberance and vitality of youth. In no case is it a war-cry (Pettinato, "Bestrafung," 196), and what is emphasized is how painful and distressing the conduct of the young gods was; nothing is said that in any way suggests an ethical judgment on it (*lā ṭābat* in line 28 is not " nicht gut" [Pettinato], but "not pleasant"; note the parallelism with *imtarṣamina* "had become painful", in the previous line, and see Y. Muffs' remarks in *Studies in the Legal Papyri from Elephantine* [Studia et documenta ad iura orientis antiqui pertinentia 8; Leiden 1969] 136 f.).

[27] Cf. *rigim amēlūti kibis alpī u ṣēni šisīt alāla ṭābi uzammâ ūgārīšu*, "I deprived his commons of the noise of men, the stamping of cattle and flocks, the cry of the pleasant work-song" (*VAB* VII, p. 56, vi 101ff.; for variants see *CAD* A/1, 328b). The few occurrences of *ḫubūru* suggest that it too was the noise typical of heavily populated areas.

[28] Tabl. III iii 15 (Lambert-Millard, 94–95). Note, too, the use of *rigmu* for the thunder of the storm and the noise of the land that the storm puts an end to (see n. 26).

level of his existence, of forces in a tension that allow him to be, but not without measure. Hence the long account of his creation, with unparalleled detail and precision on the composition of man and on the nature and function of the divine element within him.[29] Hence, too, the interest in childbirth and in customs associated with it.[30] But all is not conducive to man's being and growth. Some women are sterile, from others a demon snatches their infants, and there are even women who in the service of the gods forego marriage. There are, too, disease and famine.[31] Whence all this? The answer is the order of things established by the gods after the Deluge, an order which represents a compromise agreeable to both parties of the struggle that had gone on at the highest level of the pantheon and had led to the Deluge, Enlil supported by Anu on one side, Enki and the mother-goddess on the other.

The Deluge is, therefore, an event in the long process by which the cosmos emerged. It is as much a thing of the past as the revolt of the suffering gods. It constitutes no threat to man and its recurrence is

[29] We shall elaborate our views on the creation of man in *BASOR* 200 (1970) [reprinted as ch. 8 in this volume—Ed.].

[30] Lambert-Millard, 60–65. On lines 389ff. we would follow the suggestion (private communication) of Thorkild Jacobsen that in line 290 the *qadištum* is the mother after childbirth—Lambert-Millard, without comment: "Let the midwife rejoice in the prostitute's house" and that the whole passage deals, first, with a nine day celebration after childbirth in honor of the mother-goddess, then (299ff.) with the resumption of sexual relations. On this basis we would propose that in line 299 the date of the latter is given (*ina* UD X.KAM, "on the X day") and that in line 300 we restore *li-iḫ-ti-*[*pu*], "let the woman and her husband purify each other (themselves ?)." The Lambert-Millard reading has been rightly criticized by von Soden ("Als die Götter," 425–426, n. 32), but his own proposal, *liḫtī*[*dā*], "let them speak with one another," yields, in our opinion, a meaning much too unspecific for the context. The purification we propose could refer to rites freeing the woman of her taboo and the man of any pollution through contact with her. The use of the G stative of *ḫiāpum* in connection with love (KAR 158 rev. ii 11) and sex appeal (W. G. Lambert, *Or* 36 [1967] 122:96, 120; 124: 125) is certainly relevant, but a more general meaning, "fair, handsome" seems to have developed; cf. *namrum*, "shining" > "perfect, in excellent condition." However, attractive as Jacobsen's suggestion on *qadištu* in line 290 may be—and note the late variant *ḫarištu* , woman in confinement (Lambert-Millard, 62:15)—also to be noted are the Middle Assyrian evidence (E. Weidner, *AfO* 17/2 [1956] 268:11) associating the *qadištu* (*qadiltu*)-function with the midwife, and the Old Babylonian evidence for a *qadištu* serving as a nurse (see most recently, W. von Soden, *AfO* 18/1 [1957] 121).

[31] We assume that they are to be understood as remaining, even if they may not be mentioned explicitly in Enki's plans for the future; cf. Ea's speech in *Gilg.* XI 180ff.

unthinkable. But it is also a supremely important event, for it revealed to the gods their need of man. They should have known this before they suffered hunger cramps, for their own efforts at self-support had issued in the fateful impasse that led to man's creation. But unthinking, they had supported the foolish and irresponsible decision of Enlil. The Atrahasis Epic is an assertion of man's importance in the final order of things.

It is also a strong criticism of the gods, and in the case of Enlil one should perhaps even speak of polemic.[32] The attack on him is most evident in the speeches of Enki and the mother-goddess after the Deluge; as we have seen, the former accuses him of wanton destruction, and the latter charges him, so frequently called "the counsellor of the gods" (*mālik ilī*), of not having taken counsel (*mitluku*).[33] And throughout the epic Enlil cuts a sorry figure. He is not only "the counselor of the gods" but *qurādu Enlil*, "the warrior Enlil,"[34] an epithet he often enjoys, and yet when his house is besieged by the rebel gods, the only occasion he has to display his valor, he pleads with his attendant Nusku for protection, and cowers behind him in fear.[35] Confronted with the stubbornness of the rebels, he breaks into tears and would resign his office and go off with Anu to heaven.[36] Throughout the crisis he is singularly inept; it is Nusku, Anu or Enki who must sug-

[32] Where we differ from von Soden is mainly in holding that the poet's criticism is directed against the gods only as sources of disorder; hence anthropomorphic aspects of the divine such as holding assemblies, casting lots, etc., are not his target. Specifically, we do not believe that the first line of the epic speaks of the gods in general; they are clearly only the gods who toil (line 2) and whose corvee-labor is great (line 3). We agree, too, with Lambert ("New Evidence," 535) that von Soden does not prove that *awīlum* as a predicate means that tile gods had only some human characteristics, whereas *awilū* (pl.) or *awīlūtum* (abstract) would have implied they were simply men. On the other hand, we do not believe that to say some gods were men is "nugatory" or "nonsense" (Lambert, ibid.). A poet is permitted metaphor as well as simile, and in this case he quickly explains the deliberately bold identification by presenting the gods as laborers. It is this implied functional view of man that dominates the account of his creation. Nor, in our opinion, is the evidence as yet clear enough to assert that locative *-um* can mean "like" (see Lambert's latest arguments, ibid., 536). Hence, for the present at least, we would translate the opening line "When (some) gods were mankind."

[33] The *mālik ilī* references are listed in Lambert-Millard, 188. For Enlil who did not take counsel, see Tabl. III v. 42 (Lambert-Millard, 98–99).

[34] For references, see Lambert-Millard, 193.

[35] Tabl. I 85ff. (Lambert-Millard, 48–49).

[36] Tabl. I 168ff. (Lambert-Millard, 52–53).

gest courses of action. He also seems blind to what is evident to both Anu and Enki, the justice of the gods' complaint.[37] When he does act, as in the plagues and the Deluge, he is thwarted of his purpose again and again by the crafty Enki. And finally, when Enki attacks him after the Deluge, he cannot offer a single word in defense of himself and can only ask Enki to work out with the mother-goddess some new scheme of things. In brief, Enlil is seen as a power, with his legitimate domain on earth, but a power seriously flawed by fear, childish resentment, a certain obtuseness, and, above all, a wrath that can issue in completely irresponsible violence.[38]

But all the gods, with the possible exception of Enki, share to some extent in the poet's criticism. Anu is expressly mentioned by the mother-goddess, and she does not spare herself for her own part in the catastrophe that overtook her children.[39] No one, in fact, escapes her bitter reproaches, for all consented to the Deluge. And, though caution is in place here, one may wonder if the poet's criticism does not become contempt when he has the gods thirsty and suffering hunger cramps, then swarming later on like flies about Atrahasis' sacrifice.

Behind this criticism we should probably see with Landsberger the intellectual climate of "the Tablet House," the Babylonian "university."[40] It supposes an "enlightenment," assertive of man's place in the world and correspondingly critical of gods who, as the tradition of the Deluge proved, were capable of terrible folly. We cannot say, however, whether the Atrahasis Epic reflects in its attitude and in its particular expression of this attitude any specific political or social situation.[41]

We have lingered over the problem of understanding the Atrahasis Epic, to the apparent neglect of the main interest of the reader of *Bib-*

37 See the entire course of events (Lambert-Millard, 48–56).

38 This 'shadow side' of Enlil's character is not an invention of the poet; see T. Jakobsen, "Mesopotamia," in *Before Philosophy* (Harmondsworth, 1949) 157.

39 See Lambert-Millard, 94–101.

40 See "Scribal Concepts of Education," in *City Invincible* (eds. C. H. Kraeling and R. M. Adams; Chicago, 1960) 98, where Landsberger speaks of the ridicule and contempt for the old set of gods in the *Gilgamesh Epic,* among them Enlil, in which case the reference can be only to *Gilg*. XI. See also von Soden, "Als die Götter," 419.

41 Von Soden suggests ("Als die Götter," 429) that the background of the conflict between the laboring gods and the others is the severe burden of toil laid upon the incoming Semitic Amorites in the Ur III period by the older inhabitants; see also *Iraq* 28 (1966) 144–145.

lica, the relevance of the new discoveries for the Old Testament.[42] However, though we must leave the discussion of the latter question to others, it should be immediately evident that the results of our inquiry, if correct, heighten the contrast between the Mesopotamian and biblical traditions. Not only is the stress in the Old Testament on man's depravity as the cause of the Deluge still unparalleled, but the respective resolutions of the conflict are now seen to be completely different. In the particular form we have of the Mesopotamian tradition, the post-diluvian order represents a correction of an earlier imbalance in the cosmos, an adjustment necessary to achieve stability and to overcome an inherent disorder. The correction is the limitation of man's growth. Viewed in this light, Gen 9:1 ff. looks like a conscious rejection of the Atrahasis epic.[43] God's first words to man after the Deluge are a repetition of Gen 1:28, the command to be fruitful, multiply, and fill the earth. There is no going back on this command, for the problem of man lies elsewhere, in his evil inclination (Gen 8:21).

[42] For the present, see A. R. Millard, "A New Babylonian 'Genesis' Story," *TynBul* 18 (1967) 3–18. [See now ch. 7 in this volume—Ed.]

[43] Whether the contrast here noted, which is in P, was paralleled in the J account cannot of course be known. Obviously, too, we cannot prove that the contrast is a conscious one. Conscious or not, it is evidence of a completely different view.

CHAPTER 6

Some Considerations of Form and Interpretation in Atrahasis

praesenti tibi maturos largimur honeres

I.

If one breaks down *Atraḫasīs* into its several major units, sequences and configurations, and graphs them in terms of "discourse-time" (fig. 1),[1] one defines rather than simply experiences the poet's pace, its broad design and symmetries, and the varying emphases of his tellings. *Atraḫasīs* is in a sense two stories, two myths. The first, the Igigu-myth, is both a story in itself as well as the preface to the second, the Deluge-myth. It is told in ca. 320 lines: an introduction of 20 lines (I 1–20); then in ca. 150 lines (I 21–173) the narration of the crisis; then of its resolution, again in ca. 150 lines (I 174–ca. 320).[2] Here, as is evident, the poet assumes an audience as interested in the resolution—the creation of the first men, their composition, the origins of birth and wedding customs—as in the crisis and its drama. Viewed as belonging to the story that follows, the Igigu-myth is about the same length as the

[1] Here understood simply as the time taken in the telling; for a recent discussion of this much discussed term and certain theoretical difficulties, see N. Goodman, S. Chatman and B. Hernstein Smith, in *On Narrative* (ed. W. J. T. Mitchell; Chicago, 1981). All references to *Atra-ḫasīs* are to the edition of W. G. Lambert and A. R. Millard, *Atra-ḫasīs: The Babylonian Story of the Flood* (Oxford, 1969).

[2] The margin of error is ca. ± 10 and, in terms of the present discussion, negligible.

narrative on the plagues (ca. 30 + 310 lines). Together they bring us to ca. line 660 and close to dead center in a poem of 1245 lines. The Deluge story proper (decision, etc.) takes about 570 lines.

The second myth also begins with a short introduction of ca. 30 lines (I ca. 321–51), and then follow the plagues, the telling of each becoming longer and longer, but with a certain symmetry: the second is ca. 30 lines longer than the first, the third ca. 65 lines longer than the second.[3] The gradual expansion continues: the very long session of the divine assembly (ca. 175 lines), longer by far than any previous session.[4] And then the cataclysm itself, ca. 300 lines, about as long as the entire Igigu-myth or the narrative of the plagues: preparation for the storm, ca. 100 lines (III i–ii 47); the storm itself, ca. 120 lines (III ii 48–ca. iv [55]); the aftermath, ca. 95 lines (III ca. v [1]–vi 40). The resolution of the crisis is fairly brief, ca. 80 lines (III vi 41–ca. viii 10). Finally, the briefest of epilogues, 9 lines (III viii 11–19). The contours of this story, it is clear, are quite different from those of the first. It is dominantly a tale of crisis, a long, long crisis, and of an ever mounting tension, reaching its climax in screaming winds and wailing gods. The emphasis on the crisis and its several stages undoubtedly reflects the interest and delight of the audience in the frustrations and manifestations of power. However, it also provides an effective contrast with the resolution, which by its very brevity brings relief and a sense of order and measure—something that can be counted and contained.[5]

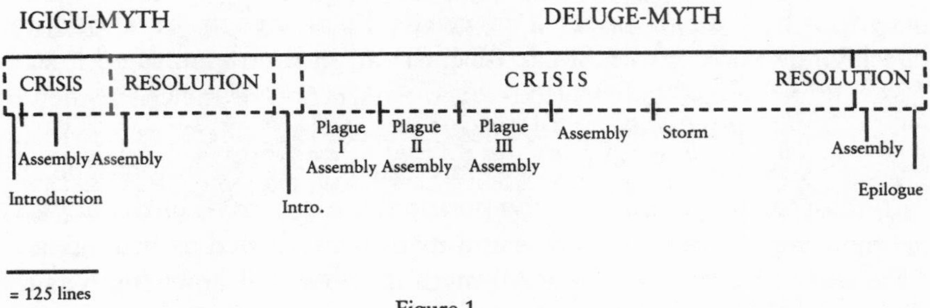

Figure 1

[3] Plague I = I 352–415; II = II i 1–ii ca. 36 (allowing 55 lines per column); III = II ii ca. [37]–v 25.

[4] Note that there are seven sessions of the assembly.

[5] Note the numbering as Enki spells out the various features of the new post-diluvian order (III vii 1).

2.

inūma ilū awīlum	3	When gods were man,
ublū dulla izbilū šupšikka	2:2	they bore the toil, the basket lugged.
šupšik ilī rabī-ma	3	The basket of the gods being large,
dullum kabit mād šapšāqum	2:2	And heavy the toil, the suffering was much.

The narrator's art in the introduction, aspects of which Wilcke has so ably described,[6] is nowhere more conspicuous than in these opening lines. The introduction brings us back to a point in mythic time when the gods had cast lots and then gone off to their respective realms, leaving Enlil in charge of the earth and forcing some gods to work for the rest. The poet, however, does not follow the order of events; he inverts them and begins immediately with the toil of the gods. He begins, too, with a metaphor, "when gods were man."[7] The effect of anachrony and trope is to thrust us *in medias res*[8] and into an anomalous and unstable situation, divine humanity and toil and pain. Of this will the poet tell first.

The paradoxical identity announced in the first line is reinforced by the assonance of *ilū-awīlum*, and in the following line it is echoed, in a

[6] "Die Anfänge der akkadischen Epen," *ZA* 67 (1977) 160–63.

[7] For a review of opinions on this controversial line see R. Oden, "Divine Aspirations in Atrahasis and in Genesis 1–11," *ZAW* 93 (1982) 199–200, and add H. Kümmel, "Bemerkungen zu den altorientalischen Berichten von den Menschenschöpfung," *WO* 7 (1973) 25–88; B. Groneberg, "Terminativ- und Lokativadverbialis in altbabylonischen literarischen Texten," *AfO* 26 (1978–79) 20; K. Oberhuber, Kraus AV (1982) 280–81. There is general, if not universal, agreement that the poet refers to the gods' doing the work that later was to be man's, but for reasons that escape us most interpreters choke at what seems an obvious metaphor. Groneberg, followed by M.-J. Seux, *RA* 75 (1981) 190–91, has argued that a noun may be used in the nominative to express comparison (e.g., Gilg. Y iv 8 *mimma ša īteneppušu šārum-ma*, translated as if *kīma šārim-ma*), and she renders the line by "Als die Götter wie Menschen waren." This obliteration of the distinction between simile and metaphor must be rejected (see *On Metaphor* [ed. S. Sacks; Chicago, 1979]). In our version (see already "Atrahasis: The Babylonian Story of the Flood," *Bib* 52 [1971] 59, n. 2 [above, p. 43, n. 32], and Wilcke, "Anfänge," 160, n. 12) *awīlum* is a collective, as in I 191, 197, and elsewhere (*AHw* 90, "auch koll."), and so its use as the predicate of a plural subject creates no grammatical difficulties (contra Oden).

[8] Anticipating briefly later classical models (*semper ad eventum festinat et in medias res*; *Ars Poetica* 148).

sense restated and defined. Likeness of sound creates, in context, a certain likeness of meaning: *ilū //(aw)īlum // (ub)lū // (du)lla // (izb)ilū.*[9] Lines 3–4 return to the *dulla* and *šupšikka* of line 2, but in chiastic order. By now, too, the metrical pattern is established: to 3-stress line 1 corresponds 3-stress line 3, and to 2-stress hemistich *ublū dulla* of line 2 corresponds 2-stress hemistich *dullum kabit* of line 4. Thus, the nouns of line 2 having been (so to speak) accounted for, the pause at the caesura in line 4 is especially heavy. It becomes a brief silence filled with expectation.

In the hemistich that follows there is a sudden and decided shift in the vowel pattern. After a long series of i-u vowels—eleven of each—but only six a-vowels, all short and none stressed except the last, just before the caesura (*kábit*), we now hear ā́-a-ā́-u, three a-vowels in succession, two long, both stressed, the first in a monosyllable. The difference is evident and creates, when "read with the ears" (Hopkins), a strong contrast and unmistakable prominence.

At this point, too, there is also a stylistic shift: the usual order of noun subject-predicate adjective, which is used in the previous two clauses, is inverted, so that full weight falls on *šapšāqum*. This is the emphatic word. It fills the blank that the sequence of synonymous parallelisms, *rabi // kabit // mād* and *šupšik // dullum // x*, creates, and *šapšāqum* becomes a kind of synonym of the latter two. The synonymity is reinforced by the correspondence in sound and line-final position: *šupšikka* (line 2) // *šapšāqum* (line 4). The marking of this hemistich is extremely heavy. The toil was pain, all pain.

3.

New joins in the Assyrian recension make an important contribution to the reading and understanding of I 128ff.: 128 *ma-an-nu-um-mi [be-el qá]-ab-lim* 129 *[ma-an-nu-um be-el ta-ḫ]a-zi* 130 *ma-an-nu-u[m ša ib-ni-a(m) t]ú-qu-um-tam* 131 *[qá-ab-lum i-ru-ṣa(-am) a-na ba-a]b* / K]Á

9 See J. M. Lotman, *Die Struktur des künstlerischen Textes* (Frankfurt am Main, 1975) 165ff. on repetition, but especially p. 189 (". . . in der Wortkunst ist *die Trennung von Klang und Bedeutung unmöglich*" [italics his]), pp. 194–95 (" . . . werden ausserdem . . . in der Poesie die Phoneme nicht nur zur bedeutungsdifferenzierenden Element, sondern auch zu Trägern lexikalischer Bedeutung. Laute sind bedeutungshaltig. Allein schon daher wird die lautliche (phonologische) Annäherung zu einer Annäherung der Begriffe").

[^{d}*e*]*n-lil.*[10] This speech, which is Enlil's message to the striking gods, is framed by [128] . . . *qablim* [131] *qablum* . . . , and consists of allusions to earlier speeches: 1) of the leader of the rebellion, I [61] *anumma tisiā tuqumtam* [62] *tāḫaza* (alliteration!) *i niblula qablam*; 2) of Nuska, I [81//83] *qablum irūṣa ana bābīka*; 3) and of Enlil, I [110] *qablum irūṣa ana bābīya*. Lines 128–30, in taking up 61–62, repeat the nouns in chiastic order, and in 131 *qablum irūṣa* . . . marks closure, as it does in the lines alluded to (cf. also *qablam* ending the speech in 62).

Thus, lines 132–33 are not part of Enlil's message (Lambert-Millard), and there is no reason to assume that they were repeated in lines 144–45.[11] Rather, they are the narrative link between Enlil's speech and its repetition by Nuska in lines 136–43, as already seen by G. Pettinato,[12] and lines 144–45 must be the narrative link between the message and the reply of the rebels.

[132] [^{d}*nuska* ip-te] ⌜KÁ⌝-*šu* [133] [ka-ak-ki-šu il-qé] i[l-li]k x x x ^{d}*en-líl* [134] [*i-na pu-uḫ-ri k*]*a-la i-li-ma* [135] [*ik-mi-is iz-z*]*i-iz t*[*e-e*]r-*tam ip-šu-ur,* "Nuska *opened* his *gate, His weapons took, marched to the sons of* Enlil. In the assembly of all the gods, He bowed, stood, the charge set forth." Lines 132–35 are the execution of the orders of 120–23.[13] The Assyrian recension begins with ^{d}*nuska annīt*[*a ina šemêšu*], "Nuska, on hearing this, . . . ," and]-⌜e⌝-*šu* seems a possible reading of the OB text. However, this epic formula is attested only in later sources,[14] and so the reading of Pettinato adopted here seems preferable. The reading of 135 is also Pettinato's.

[10] W. Lambert, "New Fragments from Babylonian Epics," *AfO* 27 (1980) 72–73 and, for further discussion, 74. The new text, especially the parallelism of *ša ibnâ* (pret.!) *tuqunta* with *bēl qabli/tāḫazi*, shows that the latter are not simply fighters/warriors, and confirm Lambert-Millard's initial understanding of the passage, i.e., Enlil wants the ringleader.

[11] W. von Soden, "Die erste Tafel des altbabylonischen Atram-ḫasīs Mythus," *ZA* 68 (1978) 60.

[12] Review of W. G. Lambert and A. R. Millard, *Atra-ḫasīs: The Babylonian Story of the Flood*, *OrAnt* 9 (1970) 78. Pettinato's contribution to the understanding of 132–35 has unfortunately been ignored.

[13] [121] *ka-ak-ki-ka l*[*e-qé* a-lik a-na mārī-ia] [123] *ki-mi-is i-zi-i*[z pu-šu-ur te-er-ta]-*ni*—despite the dactyl, perhaps better than [*a-wa-at*]-*ni* (Lambert, following von Soden), in view of 135 *tertam ipšur*, but also [157] *ap-šu-u*[*r te-er-ta-k*]*a ra-bi-tam* (Pettinato), and perhaps [116] *te-er-ta-k*[*a* lipšur rabītam].

[14] K. Hecker, *Untersuchungen zur akkadischen Epik* (AOATS 8; Neukirchen-Vluyn, 1974) 172.

The narrative link [144] *i-na* [. . .] x [145] *ib-ba-*[. . . ^{d}*en-l*]*íl* suggests no convincing restorations.[15] In the reply of the gods that follows, having in Enlil's message moved by allusion back to his fear, Nuska's warning, and the harangue of the rebel leader, we are now brought back to the very first lines of the myth: [149] ***šupšikku atru iddukniāti*** [150] ***kabit dullanīma mād šapšāqum***. We have come full circle, and when, as it seems, the justice of the charge is admitted,[16] we can go no further. A turning-point has been reached.

4.

After announcing the creation of man and receiving her new name Bēlet-ilī, Mami together with Enki enter the *bīt šīmti*, where man will be formed (I 249; cf. *En. el.* I 79–80). Here the OB text breaks off and is not recovered until line 277, except for a few signs and words at the end of lines 271–76. The broken passage, as in the later recensions, was undoubtedly concerned with the formation of man and certain prescriptions for women in childbirth. Then [277][*sa-as-s*]*ú-ra-tum pu-uḫ-ḫu-ra-ma* [278] [*wa-aš-ba*]*-at* ^{d}*nin-tu* [279] [*i-ma*]*-an-nu ar-ḫi*, "The birth-goddesses being gathered, Nintu was seated, counting the months."

For this scene there are parallels in the western epic tradition that to our knowledge have not been noted and are helpful in interpretation. In the Hittite Kumarbi myth, two passages are comparable. In the first, Kumarbi counts the months of his (!) pregnancy, apparently also seated,[17] and in the second, Ea is said to count the months of earth's pregnancy, and then "the tenth month arrived,"[18] in other words, *ešru arḫu illikam-ma* (I 281). But much more important is the passage in the

[15] A guess: [144] *i-na* [pu-uḫ-ri ^{d}we-e iz-zi-iz / it-be-m]a [145] *ib-ba*[al-ki-it te-er-ti ^{d}*en-l*]*íl*, "We stood / arose in the assembly, Rebelled against Enlil's charge." Cf. [157] *apšu*[*r tertak*]*a rabītam* [158] *na-a*B [. . . ib]-⌜bal-k⌝i-is-sí?

[16] By Ea in one OB version (p. 54, BM 78257:4), and by Anu in a later one (p. 52:177).

[17] H. Guterbock, in *Mythologies of the Ancient World* (ed. S. N. Kramer; New York, 1961) 175, "he sat down," as against A. Goetze, in *ANET*, 120b (bottom), "settled down."

[18] M. Vieyra, in R. Labat et al., *Les religions du Proche-Orient* (Paris, 1970) 546. For the Hittite material, see G. Beckman, *Hittite Birth Rituals* (2d ed.; Studien zu den Boğazköy-Texten 29; Wiesbaden, 1985) 1ff., and especially H. Hoffner, "Birth and Name-giving in Hittite Texts," *JNES* 27 (1968) 198ff.

Ugaritic myth of Aqhat where it is said of Dan'el, as he awaits the birth of his son, *yṯb dnʾil [ys]pr yrḫh*, "Danʾel was seated, counting her months."[19] Here, as is obvious, we have a virtual word-for-word correspondence, the only real difference being lexical, Akk. *manû* = Ug. *spr* (probably durative *yaspuru*). Moreover, it should be noted that in the Ugaritic myth, prior to the passage quoted, it is told how, after being childless, Dan'el receives the good news that a son is to be his, and he rejoices greatly. Then he returns to the palace, to be joined there by the *kṯrt* who had entered his house (*ʿrb bbth*). There they receive offerings for seven days, a period, it seems, of sexual union and conception, after which they depart and Dan'el begins counting.

Recalling that the *kṯrt* are elsewhere equated with *ᵈsassūratu*,[20] we seem to have a common narrative-scheme: A. announcement of good news and rejoicing; B. retirement to bedroom / workshop, accompanied by birth-goddesses; C. conception/formation of child; D. counting of months of pregnancy. In *Atrahasīs*, the incantations and pinches of clay seem to be the workshop version of the conception of the child.[21]

5.

Early in the narrative of the third plague we are told that Atrahasis was weeping daily, bringing *muššakku*-offerings every morning. There follows a slightly broken passage that Lambert-Millard read as follows: II iii [7][x] x-*a i-li ta-mi-ma* [8][*uz-na*] *i-ša-ak-ka-na šu-na-a-ti* [9][x x-

[19] *CTA* 17 (2 Aqht) ii 43–44. The Babylonian parallel supports the reading of the Ugaritic text and favors [*ys*]*pr* (Virolleaud) rather than [*ls*]*pr* (Herdner). The period in question is that of gestation (H. L. Ginsberg, *BASOR* 97 [1945], p. 4, n. 7), not of growth after birth (A. Caquot et al., *Textes ougaritiques: Mythes et legendes*, Tome I [Paris, 1974] 426).

[20] *Ugaritica* 5, p. 63, and see Caquot *et al.*, *Textes ougaritiques*, 384ff.

[21] In the Ugaritic myth, the birth-goddesses depart after a week, whereas in *Atraḫasīs* either they stay on or reassemble for the birth. If, as seems very likely, line 251 corresponds to the later SB version and reports on the gathered birth-goddesses ([251] *s[a-as-sú-ra-tum* . . . ; see S. Lieberman, *The Sumerian Loanwords in Old-Babylonian Akkadian* [HSS 22; Missoula, 1977] 474, n. 708), the repetition is noteworthy. Does the repetition structure the narrative, or is this an instance of *Wiederaufnahme*, lines 251–76 being a later (but OB) addition, so that in an earlier stage of the tradition the workshop-version was absent? For other instances of *Wiederaufnahme* in the epic tradition, see J. Tigay, *The Evolution of the Gilgamesh Epic* (Philadelphia, 1982) 75.

a] ^{d}*en-ki ta-mi-ma* [10] [*uz-na i-š*]*a-ak-ka-na i-na šu-na-a-ti.* They rendered, "He swore by [.] . . of the god, Giving [attention] to dreams. He swore by [. . .] of Enki, etc." Difficulties: 1. a bound-form ending in *-a* would be extremely rare; 2. the motivation of the hero's oath is obscure; 3. where Enki is associated with Atrahasis, he is not called simply "the god," but, with the possible exception of III i 49, either "his god" (I 365, 367; II iii 2, 11, therefore just before and just after the passage in question; Assyrian recension, p. 106:18–19 = 112:28–29;[22] p. 113:31), or "my god" (III i 42 // ^{d}*enki*); 4. with *uzna šakānu*, one expects *ana*, not *ina* (*AHw*, 1448). It is, therefore, much more likely that *il-i* is *ilī*, "my god," that Atrahasis is speaking, and that the one under oath is Enki. The conjunction of oath and dreams reminds one of course of the constraints placed on Enki before the Deluge and especially of Gilg. XI 19, ^{d}*nin-igi-kù* ^{d}*é-a it-ti-šú-nu ta-mì-ma.* Therefore, [*ṭēma*] *išakkana ina šunāti*, and perhaps [i-tam]-⌜ma⌝-*a*, "My god speaks to me, but being under oath, He must inform me in dreams" (*itammâ . . . tamīma* would be appreciated). In the OB version, then, it seems that by the third plague the gods (only Enki?) were under oath not to speak to mankind, which Enki evades by speaking in dreams, and that then, before the Deluge, even this loophole was closed, only to have Enki speak, not to Atrahasis, but to the wall of his house.[23]

6.

Since the Lambert-Millard edition two fundamentally opposed interpretations of this version of the Deluge myth have been proposed. According to one, man is in some way guilty and his guilt explains[24] and justifies Enlil's punishing plagues and his desperate attempt to destroy man utterly. According to the other, man is not guilty at all, and if he provokes "plague, famine and war" he does so innocently, simply a victim of his own powers of procreation. Ever more numerous, he is also, and necessarily, ever more noisy, ever more a nuisance, and finally an intolerable one, to a god desperately in need of sleep.

[22] See Lambert, "New Evidence for the First Line of Atra-ḫasīs," *Or* 38 (1969) 538.

[23] In Gilg. XI 186–87, as in Berossos, Ea admits simply to having caused Ut-napishtim to dream. Perhaps in the short version of the Deluge, which omitted the story of the plagues (cf. *Ugaritica* 5, No. 167), the delightful casuistry of speaking to the wall was lost.

[24] For a review of opinions, see Oden, "Divine Aspirations," 204–8.

In favor of the first view and against the second a number of arguments have been offered. In the latter category, one: overpopulation is not the issue because Enlil complains, not about numbers, but about noise.[25] Two: if overpopulation were the real issue, one would expect to find it presented as a problem elsewhere in Mesopotamian literature, whereas in fact the literature is silent on the subject.[26] Three: one cannot conceive the Mesopotamians not finding a crime to fit the punishment, a consideration only confirmed by the comparative evidence, especially the biblical and classical, that the Deluge was always conceived as a punishment for man's iniquity.[27]

Among the positive arguments, one: the *rigmu* of the gods outside the surrounded Ekur (I 77) is the cry of rebels, and it is this *rigmu* that the gods pass on to man at his creation (I 242); therefore, the *rigmu* of men that Enlil hears (I 356; II i 5) is also the cry of rebels protesting against their heavy labor as did the rebellious gods before them.[28] Two: Enki advises a bold *non serviam*, the refusal of all cult to the gods except to the one afflicting them directly, and the people carry it out (I 378–83 // 393–98; II ii 9–14). It is also to be the object of a loud *rigmu* in the land, which confirms the implications of rebellion in man's *rigmu*.[29] Three: *ḫubūru*, the other source of the annoyance of the gods, is not so much "noise" as "noisy activities," and therefore the displeasure of the gods must be explained not so much by the noise of men as by the nature of their activities, suggesting that man had gone beyond the modest role assigned him of working for the gods and was aspiring *ad altiora*, things not properly man's, a development not altogether surprising in one gifted with *ṭēmu*, the power to plan.[30] Four: endowed

[25] G. Pettinato, "Die Bestrafung des Menschengeschlechts durch die Sinflut," *Or* 37 (1968) 174–75.

[26] Von Soden, "Der Mensch bescheidet sich nicht: Überlegungen zu Schöpfungserzählungen in Babylonien und Israel," in *Symbolae biblicae et mesopotamicae, F. M. Th. de Liagre Böhl dedicatae* (ed. M. Beek et al.; Leiden, 1973) 358.

[27] Pettinato, "Bestrafung," 183.

[28] Pettinato, "Bestrafung," 186–87; Oden, "Divine Aspirations," 208–9; W. M. Clark, "The Flood and the Structure of the Pre-patriarchal History," *ZAW* 83 (1971) 185.

[29] Pettinato, "Bestrafung," 189; von Soden, "Als die Gotter (auch noch) Mensch waren," *Or* 38 (1969) 427. A. van Selms, in *Symbolae*, 541–48, speaks of "temporary henotheism."

[30] Von Soden, "Der Mensch," 353–55.

from his creation with the *ṭēmu* and *eṭemmu*, mind and spirit, of a rebellious god, man cannot help but be a rebel too.[31] Five: when Enki defends himself for having saved Atrahasis, according to Gilg. XI 180 he says, "On the sinner lay his sin, on the transgressor his transgression." From this it is to be inferred that sin and guilt were considerations in the decision to wipe out man.[32]

Neither singly nor cumulatively do these arguments add up to much of a case for the guilt of man and against overpopulation. Among the positive arguments, one: the Igigu-myth does seem in many respects the Deluge-myth in miniature or its extended metaphor: the sleeping Enlil awakened // the sleepless Enlil; noise of the Igigu // noise of men; the failure of Nuska's mission // the failure of the plagues and Deluge; the intervention of Enki and Mami, the creation of man // the intervention of Enki and Mami, the creation of a new order. In both myths, too, death in some way mediates and leads to life. But just to list the parallels is to show that there is also profound diversity within the likenesses. Whatever homologies one might set up from these elements, they would be expressions of analogy, not univocity.

Two: Enki neither advises nor is man guilty of a bold *non serviam*.[33] What Enki proposes is to divert all the offerings the people make each day to their individual *personal* gods to the god now afflicting them. That this is the plan, not boldly to confront all the gods and cut off their cult, fits with the use of the pronominal suffix ("your gods," not "the gods"), the nature of the offering, the nature of the sly source of the plan, and is required by two facts: one, the plan calls for secrecy and Enlil does not understand why he is failing; two, at the end of the myth, when the gods suffer hunger cramps and discover their need of men, this is clearly a completely new experience, a deprivation they had never known before. And the loud *rigmu* with which this plan is to be promulgated is nothing more than the cry of the heralds and says

[31] Oden, "Divine Aspirations," 202, 210.

[32] Pettinato, "Bestrafung," 199, and Oden, "Divine Aspirations," 204–5, and cf. A. Heidel, *The Gilgamesh Epic and Old Testament Parallels* (Chicago, 1949) 225, 268.

[33] For greater detail see *Bib* 52 (1971) 54–55 [pp. 36–38 above]. The *masḫatu*-offering that Enki prescribes belonged to the cult of the personal god, at least in later times (Lambert, *Babylonian Wisdom Literature,* 38:20, 74:51). Was the afflicting god also to be embarrassed by the prayer to the personal god of later times, "Protect, protect" (*uṣur, uṣur*; see Craig, ABRT I 27 K.883:10)?

nothing whatsoever about the character of the *rigmu* that so disturbs Enlil.[34]

Three: there is of course no logical connection between noisy activities and man's overweening ambitions, and it is read into the text on the grounds that the myth begins with gods who are a little less than divine and with men who are or aspire to be a little more than human. All of which is rather asserted than argued. *Gratis asseritur gratis negatur*. We read simply, but not, we trust, either naively or superficially: what is specific about *ḫubūru* is noise, and it is the noise that disturbs, whatever the activity producing it might be. And *ḫubūru* parallels *rigmu*, and they both explain the fatal fact: Enlil can't sleep.

It should be added that considerations of intertextuality make sinful *ḫubūru* and *rigmu* no more plausible. In the culture, the *rigmu* of men may, like the work-song, be evidence of life, and its absence evidence of destruction.[35] There is no *ḫubūru* in the stillness of the night.[36] or in the silence of death and desolation.[37] And in the mythic tradition, as is well known, there are the cry (*rigmu*) of the young, zestful gods that keep old Apsu awake (*En. el.* I 25), the noise of the numerous people depriving of sleep the Anunnaki, who as denizens of the underworld are lovers of absolute silence (*rā'im šaḫrarti*),[38] and the noise of many people whom Erra may take it into his head to destroy—and occasionally does.[39] Old gods, underworld gods, the head of the underworld

[34] See *AHw*, 1177, and correct *Bib* 52 (1971) 54, n. 1 [above, p. 36, n. 10].

[35] Streck, *Asb.* 56 vii 101ff.

[36] *ḫabrātum nišū šaqummā*, "the noisy people are still" (von Soden, *ZA* 43 [1936] 306:3).

[37] J. Finkelstein, "The So-called 'Old Babylonian Kutha Legend'," *JCS* 11 (1957) 86 iv 5 (cf. 16). In this and the following lines there is a description of absolute destruction, the obliteration of all distinctive features, everything having become like everything else (*mitḫāriš kalîš uštēmi*) and the land as if it had never existed (*kīma lā nabšî kalâša ussaḫḫir*). Consistent with this is *ḫubūru* // *ṭēmu* as characteristic of (civilized) life, not as "(böses) Treiben, Aufstand" (Pettinato). Cf. the silence in the Eridu lament (M. Green, *JCS* 30 [1978] 132:9–10, and see her remarks and the parallel cited, 142); as plague breaks out, the wide streets, once the scene of playing, filled with silence (W. Hallo, Kraus AV [1982] 98 ii 13); the stock expression in descriptions of devastation, *šakin qūlu*; etc.

[38] Cagni, *Erra* I 81.

[39] Ibid., I 41, 73, 82; IV 68.

and his cohorts, the Evil Seven—such are those who hate din and cry, divine or human. None of this suggests human guilt in *Atraḫasīs*.

Four: a likely hypothesis perhaps, but not borne out by the facts.

Five: Enki's speech suggests the very opposite of what is claimed: in sending the Deluge Enlil never considered distinctions of guilt and innocence, and therefore could attempt to destroy man utterly. It is Enki who introduces the vocabulary of sin and guilt, considerations unknown in the myth up to this point.[40]

The criticisms, one: the distinction between noise and numbers is specious. The obvious story is that "the human race multiplied and their noise became such that Enlil—still on earth—could not sleep."[41] The Assyrian version could not be clearer when it has Enlil, after the failure of the first plague, cry out to the gods, "Afflict them no longer with Namtar. The people have not decreased, they have increased more than ever."[42] Two: overpopulation is not a problem recognized in Mesopotamian literature because the literature reflects post-diluvian conditions. According to Gilg. X vi, as Jacobsen and Lambert have shown, the mortality man is now subject to was a post-diluvian innovation, and Lambert has also argued convincingly that *Gilgamesh* here depends on *Atraḫasīs*.[43] Given this insight, all the pieces of the puzzle fit: one understands the magnitude of the chaos of man's ever increasing numbers and can concede the wisdom, the necessity, of the existence of death.

Three: the Mesopotamians were quite familiar with disasters that were, in their lack of discrimination, beyond considerations of good and evil and unrelated to human guilt. Such were political catastrophes, local or national, determined by inscrutable gods and bewailed in lamentation. Thus, the storm that destroyed Eridu was "a storm possessed of neither kindness nor malice, familiar with neither good nor evil."[44] Of such a storm the Deluge was the prototype. And, it might be added, in its implications of mystery and tragedy such a

[40] See *Bib* 52 (1971) 57, n. 1 [above, p. 40, n. 24].

[41] Lambert-Millard, *Atra-ḫasīs*, 9.

[42] See Lambert, *AfO* 27 (1980) 74. Namtar has proved ineffective, and so the puzzled Enlil is about to shift to famine to lower the population.

[43] T. Jacobsen, in *Death in Mesopotamia* (ed. B. Alster; Mesopotamia 8; Copenhagen, 1980) 20–21, and Lambert, ibid., 54–58.

[44] *JCS* 30 (1978) 127:20, and see Green's remarks and the parallels cited, ibid., 145.

storm goes far deeper than so-called moral universes in which evil is necessarily punishment, in which, therefore, the good are blessed and the wicked chastised—Oscar Wilde's definition of fiction.[45]

[45] Oden, "Divine Aspirations," 209–10, adds two more arguments: (1) comparative mythology shows that loud noises are attributes of the divine, and therefore man's noise takes him out of his proper sphere; (2) "the shouting/noise of Sodom and Gomorrah" (Gen 18:20) is the perfect semantic parallel to *rigmu* and clearly an instance of criminal noise. As to (1), it may be readily granted that there was something divine about the people's din—measureless, chaotic, a bull's roar like the Deluge itself (I 354; II i 3; II1 iii 15)—but that does not make it a crime. As to (2), in our opinion the *zᵉʿāqā* is not at all comparable to *rigmu* either in *Atraḫasīs* or in general, for it is a cry of distress, a cry for help, often to those legally bound to assist (vassals of a common suzerain in EA 366:24) and, in the case of Genesis, the rest of the legal community failing, to the ultimate custodian of the community and its law (cf. *iʾūtu* = *ḫablu*). The cry itself was probably "violence!" (*ḥāmās*); cf. Hab 1:2. Therefore, God must descend to verify whether the cry against the cities is true, whether they have acted "according to the *zᵉʿāqā*" (following verse).

CHAPTER 7

A Mesopotamian Myth and Its Biblical Transformation*

In his *Das sprachliche Kunstwerk*, Wolfgang Kayser notes as a basic characteristic of the epic the leisure with which the poet moves through his tale. In support of this observation he cites a letter from Schiller to Goethe in which he wrote: "The purpose of the epic poet is present at every point of his movement. Hence we do not hasten impatiently to an end, but linger with love at every step."[1]

It is with Schiller as my guide that I speak. My subject is a myth which is familiar to all of you in both in its Mesopotamian and biblical forms—the Deluge myth. As you also know, despite almost a century of study of the interrelationship between the two, the subject is by no means closed. It was only five years ago that we recovered the Mesopotamian myth in a form which allows us for the first time to appreciate its full scope and to trace its plot in its classical expression. Since that time, of course, a number of studies have appeared by both Assyriologists and biblical scholars—I know I have not seen all of the latter group—but no one would deny that most fundamental problems of interpretation still exist. And so what I would like to do now is to assess the situation, examine the basic issues, present my own views,

* Lecture delivered to the Catholic Biblical Association, 1974. All references to the Atrahasis myth are to the edition of W. G. Lambert and A. R. Millard, *Atra-ḫasīs: The Babylonian Story of the Flood* (Oxford, 1969).

[1] W. Kayser, *Das sprachliche Kunstwerk* (Bern, 1948) 351.

some old, same new, about the Mesopotamian myth, and finally, after venturing onto ground where I feel less secure, the question of its biblical transformation, to have in the discussion which follows the advantage of your clarifications and corrections. However, all this in the spirit of Schiller—*mit Liebe verweilen*. Sharing as we do a love of ancient texts, let us linger a while over one of them.

I propose to move through the myth, following the thematic structure I have outlined on figure 1 (above, p. 47). One or two preliminary remarks. The structure as graphed is tentative; it certainly needs refinement and clarification. Also, the rather frequent appearance of *circa* in the distribution of lines reflects a broken text; however, the margin of error is always fairly small and far our purposes negligible, as we are not suggesting that the poet was guided by any concern for mathematical niceties.

What is most obvious in the structure as a whole is a considerable symmetry. A short prologue is balanced by a short epilogue. The Igigi-myth at the beginning is just about the same length as the section on the plagues that follows. The telling of both of them, which in any reading of the text is in some sense prefatory to the Deluge, brings us to about dead center in the poem—about line 660 in a poem of 1245 lines. Each telling of the several plagues gets longer and longer, but again with a certain symmetry. The expansion continues, first the longest by far session of the divine assembly, next the longest single section of the entire myth. Then the resolution, which is relatively brief. The contour here is roughly the same as we find in each of the plagues. Finally, note the distribution of the occasions when Enlil initiates discussion in the divine assembly: twice in the Igigi-myth, three tines in the plague-section, twice in the Deluge-section—seven times in all. All of which of course does not just happen. In the macrostructure we are already aware that we are dealing with a work of verbal art.

The prologue is quite brief, just sixteen lines. It brings us back to a point in mythic time, *in illo tempore*, when the gods had cast lots and then gone off to their respective realms, with Enlil left in charge of the earth. In this order of things certain gods called the Igigi were required, as we are told, to labor for the others.

But the poet does not follow the order of events; he inverts them and begins with a description of the toil of the gods. From the first lines, he thrusts us into a world of sweat and intolerable pain. It is of this that he would first sing.

The prologue is not without its difficulties, some of them quite serious, and they have provoked considerable discussion, some of it quite heated. Here I can only state my own opinion on the meaning of the first four crucial lines.

inūma ilū awīlum
ublū dulla izbilū šupšikka
šupšik ilī rabīma
dullum kabit mād šapšāqum

When gods were man,
Bore toil, carried basket,
The god's basket was large,
So the toil was heavy, great the misery.

The obvious crux is the first line. Most scholars deny the predication my translation assumes, and for obvious reasons. I think the poet begins with a bold metaphor, or perhaps more exactly, a redefinition of the term "man": man is understood in terms of function, he is a servant of the gods. The paradoxical identity, which the similarity and diversity of the two nouns—*ilū* // *awīlu*—only emphasizes, is restated in the following line and re-sounded in *ublū* and *izbilū*.

All now moves towards the assertion that this relationship was one of misery and pain. At the end of the second line, After a consonantal pattern of all sonants (1 n, 2 m's, 2 b's, 1 d, 1 z, 6 l's), it shifts to all surds (2 š's, 2 k's, 1 p). *šupšikka* is marked: the sound-contrast is heightened by line-final position.

Lines 3 and 4 return to the *dulla* and *šupšikka* of line 2, but in chiastic order. By now, too, the metrical pattern has been established: to the 3-stress line 1 corresponds line 3, to the two stress half-line *ublū dulla* in line 2 corresponds the two stress half-line *dullum kabit* in line 4. Thus the pause at the caesura in line 4 after the chiasm is a brief silence filled with expectation.

At this point there is a sharp shift in the vowel pattern. After a long series of i and u vowels—eleven of each—with only four a vowels, all short, none of them stressed until the last one, just before the caesura (*kabit*), we now hear ā-a-ā-u, three a-vowels, two of them stressed.

There is also a syntactical shift: the order of subject-predicate-adjective in the two previous clauses is inverted. Thus full weight falls on the subject—*šapšāqum*. The sound-correspondence—*šupšikka* and *šapšāqum*—and line-final position correspondence create a kind of identity. The effect of these lines is to tell us that toil and tools meant pain, nothing but pain.

The poet then moves on to naming the establishment that imposes all this: Anu father and king, Enlil warrior and counselor, Ninurta the overseer, and Ennugi the sheriff. He will soon cite these lines once more.

The Igigi begin their labors. The narrative is brief, just twenty lines. Then the theme of the opening lines returns: we hear of the basket, the heavy toil which the gods carry night and day. The crisis has begun. At first the Igigi think of appealing to the overseer and bringing Enlil himself to the scene to see what they have to bear. But another voice speaks out and dissuades them from such peaceful measures which, apparently alluding to earlier efforts, he says have already proved ineffectual. Violence is needed. The mob is persuaded, they throw their tools into the fire and advance in the dead of night against Enlil's residence. Awakened by his chamberlain Nusku, and frightened by the rebellious mob outside, Enlil hastily summons the gods of the universe and puts before them his problem. At the sky-god's advice, Enlil dispatches Nusku to demand that the rebels hand over the instigator of the rebellion, but tells him first to observe the formalities of prostration and then—and Enlil cites the prologue—to announce who sent him: their father Anu, their counselor warrior Enlil, their overseer Ninurta, and their sheriff Ennugi. This Nusku does, but the rebels also cite the prologue:

> Is the basket to kill us?
> Heavy is our toil, great the misery.

And they refuse to name their leader, asserting solidarity in their common decision.

When Nusku returns with this news to the assembly, Enlil weeps and, turning to the sky-god, says he wants to go away with him to heaven. The crisis is only intensified by Anu or Enki—versions differ—replying, like the rebels, with a citation of the prologue and an admission of the justice of the rebels' complaint:

> Why do we blame them?
> Heavy is their toil, great their misery.

With this citation of the prologue, and the rebels' viewpoint shared by the other gods, the impasse seems total.

Now it is that the wise and ever-resourceful Enki intervenes with a new idea: the creation of man. A god is slaughtered, presumably the rebel leader—we will return to the obvious difficulty in a moment—Enki and the birth-goddess collaborate in forming man from the slain god's flesh and blood, and man is finally born. In gratitude for what she had done in freeing them from their toil, the gods give the birth-goddess a new name, her supreme title, "Mistress of all the gods."

In my opinion, we are dealing here with an originally independent myth. The clearest indication of this is towards the end. The god has been killed, the birth-goddess has done what Enki has instructed her to do, and she summons the gods to tell them she has *completed* the task they gave her, she has imposed their toil on man—another allusion to the prologue—and she has achieved their liberation. It is then that they fall down, smother her feet with kisses, and give her her new name. The language and the whole feeling of the narrative movement tell us that this is the end.

But it is not the end! There are still about eighty lines—man's creation is not finished, we learn, his birth is yet to come, there are rites to assure its success and they are prescribed for the future, and there is a long section about marriage. All this reveals a new focus of interest, man's fertility, and this, as we shall see, is to be the central issue in the Deluge-myth that follows. In other words, our problems begin precisely where the narrative is oriented towards the next myth. So I would argue that the original Igigi-myth ended with the etiology of the goddess's title, "Mistress of all the gods." In this myth, man is the solution to a problem, not the beginning of one. (A structural note: the resolution of the crisis would be considerably shorter, and the myth would assume a more normal contour.)

There is also evidence that the Igigi-myth has been telescoped. We have already heard the rebel-leader refer to earlier futile negotiations, which suggests the possibility of a longer version in which these negotiations were recounted. There are also a number of small inconcinnities, little discordances in the narrative, but a truly serious one is the appearance of the strikers in the assembly after man is made expressing their gratitude to the goddess. How did they get there? How were they informed that their demands were being met? There is a break of only six lines in the text to account for all this. So I think the myth has been shortened—the poet's audience knew the full version and could fill in the gaps—and given a length befitting its new function, the first stage of a now new and longer myth.

In its new context, lacking its original finality, it changes its meaning somewhat. In its independent form I would classify it as a myth about evil, under the type of drama of creation. Here I am adopting the typology elaborated by Paul Ricoeur in his *The Symbolism of Evil*, and since we shall make use of this typology again, let me outline briefly Ricoeur's position.[2]

The first type of myth about evil is what he calls the drama of creation. In this the origin of evil is coextensive with the origin of things; it is the chaos with which the creative act of the god struggles.

The counterpart of this view of things is that salvation is identical with creation itself; the act that founds the world is at the same time the liberating act.

In the second type we meet the idea of a fall of man that arises as an irrational event in a creation already completed. The counterpart of a schema based on the notion of a fall is that salvation is a new *peripateia* in relation to primordial creation; salvation unrolls a new and open history on the basis of a creation already completed and, in that sense, closed.

A third and intermediate type he calls tragic. Behind it is an implicit and perhaps unavoidable theology: the tragic theology of the god who tempts, blinds, leads astray. Here the fault appears to be indistinguishable from the very existence of the tragic hero, and salvation consists in a sort of aesthetic deliverance issuing from the tragic spectacle itself, internalized in the depths of existence and converted into pity with respect to oneself. Salvation of this sort makes freedom coincide with understood necessity.

A last type is that of the exiled soul. Salvation is liberation from the body.

Under this typology, as I think is evident, the Igigi-myth belongs to the first type, the drama of creation. For though it does not bring us back to earliest origins and the earliest stages of cosmic struggle, it still betrays a view of reality in which evil is inherent in the origins of

[2] P. Ricoeur, *The Symbolism of Evil* (trans. E. Buchanan; Boston: Beacon, 1967) 172–74.

being. The beginnings of the Igigi coincide with toil and pain, and the latter are excessive and unjust. The situation is unstable and violent, and violence is conquered by violence. We have here a fragment of essentially the same epic of being that we find, for example, in *Enuma eliš*. There is a difference of course: here the saving, creative act is one of intellectual rather than physical force and it is this that creates man. Final and saving act in the original myth, it is now to become an intermediate act and acquire a new ambiguity.

To return to our structure. Between the resolution of the Igigi-myth and the first plague, the text is badly broken. Just enough is preserved to indicate that man is establishing himself on earth, acquiring new tools and performing his service for the gods. The peaceful interlude ends at line 352:

> Not 1200 years passed.
> The nation was extended, the people multiplied.
> The nation was bellowing like a bull.
> By their din was the god afflicted.
> Enlil heard their cry
> As he addressed the great gods:
> "A burden to me has become the cry of man,
> From their din I am ever sleepless."

These are crucial lines in the interpretation of the myth; they will be repeated again before the second plague, and I think we may safely assume they also introduced the third. To their meaning we shall return in a moment.

Then Enlil goes on. He has the assembled gods agree to the sending of sickness upon mankind. His proposal takes only four lines; it seems almost perfunctory. He is unaware of the opposition he is to meet in the sly Enki, the father of mankind.

Though he must have been mentioned earlier, the human hero of the Deluge myth, Atrahasis, now makes his first appearance in our text. We find him complaining to this personal god Enki of the sickness ravaging mankind. His master tells him to send a message to all the people:

> Do not reverence your gods,
> Do not pray to your goddess.

Again two crucial lines. Instead, the people are to concentrate their cult on the god of sickness who is afflicting them. Embarrassed by their gifts, he will soon give them relief. And this is the way things work out.

We come to the second plague. Again the cry and din of man, again the sleepless god. But now Enlil is not so casual. His proposal, a beautifully structured text and almost a parade example of what Roman Jakobson calls "the poetry of grammar," now takes at least twelve lines and probably several more. Essentially, he orders a drought. But again Enki intervenes with essentially the same advice, and eventually with the same success.

So Enlil needs a third plague. The text at this point is very badly damaged. We can only be sure of Enlil's mounting fury, and the increasing severity of the plague, and man's eventual deliverance, thanks once more to Enki.

Enough is enough. Enlil decides to annihilate man. Again the text is badly damaged, but it is evident that the discussion in the assembly must have been a long and bitter one. The fact that Enlil is accused after the flood of not having taken counsel, can only mean that he refused to listen to the advice or objections of others and bullied the assembly into finally agreeing with him.

The part that follows hardly need be recalled, it is so familiar to everyone. Enki evades his oath of silence, instructs his servant Atrahasis to build a boat, and tells him of the impending disaster. Atrahasis obeys. As the dread moment approaches, and a feast goes on about him,

> He was in and out; neither sitting nor crouching,
> His heart broken, he was vomiting gall.

The storm god roars, tears the ship loose, and chaos breaks upon the world. Description of howling winds and washed up corpses alternate and blend with the wild wails of the birth-goddess's grief. But Atrahasis is saved.

As the gods gather about his sacrifice, Enlil spots the boat and is furious. The finger is pointed at Enki. He admits his responsibility but lashes back at Enlil for destroying indiscriminately, just and unjust alike. This seems to chasten Enlil somewhat; at least he tells Enki and the mother-goddess to put their heads together and find same workable compromise. This they do, and so far as we can see, what they come up with is exclusively, or at least primarily, a series of measures to check overpopulation: in the new order there will be sterile women, there will be a demon who snatches babies from their mother's lap, there will be religious institutions of women who forego marriage.

Then the text becomes very fragmentary. In the break, we may surely assume that Atrahasis was rewarded with immortality. The text becomes intelligible again only in the last few lines. Someone, apparently a god, urges the Igigi to praise the great deeds of Enlil. Then, in the last line, I believe the poet himself speaks. It is simple and solemn: "I have sung of the deluge to all peoples. Hearken!"—So ends this remarkable myth.

How shall we interpret it? In other words, why the plagues, why the deluge? Obviously, now that we have the full tale, we can no longer speak of the caprice of Enlil and the other gods which the abbreviated version in Gilg. XI suggested. Certainly Enlil had provocation. The question is, Was he justified? If so, in what sense? If not, why not?

Among Assyriologists who have addressed themselves to these questions—and among a number of others whom I have talked to—most seem to side with Enlil, either from the very beginning or in the course of events. They find his action ultimately ethical, and in the deluge they see a judgment on sinful man. Or—minimalist position—it is claimed that the motivation for the plagues and deluge remains somewhat obscure, but certainly the mankind that follows Enki's advice, "Do not reverence your gods, do not pray to your goddess," has its fist raised against the gods and punishes them for punishing him.

Allow me to quote a recent statement on this whole problem, that of Professor Kilmer, and gloss it as I go along. She begins:

> It should be noted . . . that previous interpretations have revolved around the line concerning the "noise" of mankind, and the noise itself has been taken to be man's offense, whether considered as innocent noise, or as representing rebelliousness. This has been true especially because the same motif of noise is found in the Creation Epic, there said of the minor gods. However, in view of the whole poem now before us, I believe that our understanding of man's offense must be based primarily on his numerical increase, and only secondarily on his noisiness, which may be regarded as the natural consequence of the many lively beings,

not to mention the poetic imagery intended by the poet, from which one can imagine the god holding his hands over his ears against the din.[3]

Agreement.

It is only with regard to the subsequent noise that one might, with Professor Pettinato of Heidelberg, in a recent and comprehensive study, identify the noise with the noise of rebellion. Prof. Pettinato's argument is that the word "noise" implicitly signifies rebellion, that man must have refused to do the very work for which he was created, and thus was punished by the Flood. But, if we follow the text, the first plague is sent without work refusal as a reason. We may say only that after the plagues man may have neglected his usual work duties. It is nowhere stated in the text, however. Man gives instead intensified worship toward the deity in charge of the particular pestilence at hand . . .[4]

(1) The word far noise—our "cry"—does not *denote* rebellion. Look at *AHw, sub voce.*
(2) In context, it does not *connote* rebellion. To find this sense implicitly one must with Pettinato flaunt the plain evidence of the text and deny a connection between man's numbers and the noise. One must also ignore the conclusion of the myth which solves the problem of man by reducing his numbers.
(3) "We may say only that after the plagues man may have neglected his usual work duties. It is nowhere stated in the text, however." Then why should we allow for it? If it is not in the text it is irrelevant for interpretation.
(4) The motive therefore of Enlil, insofar as it is the noise of mankind, is not an ethical one.

The human hero of the epic first appears after the first attack on man. He, Mr. Atra-Ḫasīs, complains to the friendly god Enki that mankind cannot withstand such hardship, and he asks for advice. Enki suggests that mankind forego the usual prayers and devotions to the usual gods. . . .[5]

[3] A. D. Kilmer, "The Mesopotamian Concept of Overpopulation and Its Solution as Reflected in the Mythology," *Or* 41 (1972) 167.

[4] Ibid.

[5] Ibid.

If this were the sense then I would have to admit that here is "practically a declaration of war against the gods,"[6] or at least a picture of man punishing them. A show of hybris.

I have expressed my opinion on this advice of Enki's elsewhere:

> The unlikelihood that the people are to be told to cut off all cult to the gods with the exception of Namtar and Adad, should at least be suspected in view of the one who gives the advice. It is the clever, wily, devious Enki. This is the god who evades his oath and warns Atrahasis of the final impending disaster by speaking, not to him, but to a wall. He is the one who in the face of revolt does not think of arms but conceives the new thing, man. It is he, too, who finds the compromise that establishes the postdiluvian order. This is not a god of bold confrontations. He is the sly diplomat, and it would be completely out of character if he were to urge a kind of showdown of power, and a necessarily futile one to boot.
>
> Furthermore, why bother bribing Namtar and Adad, and why insist that the latter act so stealthily, if there is to be an open rebellion which will force Enlil to relent. Not only is there not the slightest indication that Enlil ever felt compelled to reconsider his decisions, but when the gods suffer hunger cramps in the days of the Deluge, this seems a completely new experience for them. . . .
>
> All of these problems disappear with the observation that the text speaks of "*your* gods" and "*your* goddess," not simply of gods and goddesses. As almost countless examples show, this is the usual way of referring to personal gods. If the poet had wished to include all the gods, he would almost certainly not have used the pronominal suffix; hence, apart from all the difficulties that a reference to the entire pantheon causes here, it is not in itself a very probable reading of the text. Obviously, too, in our view Enki's counsels are duly clever and devious.[7]

I still hold to this view.

> We know that the problem of overpopulation continues . . . (The gods try different methods of decimating the population.) At the same time, and with each successive attempt, mankind becomes more distressing, more rebellious, and even more physically repulsive to the gods.[8]

[6] G. Pettinato, "Die Bestrafung des Menschengeschlechts durch die Sintflut," *Or* 37 (1968) 189: "praktisch eine Kampfsansage an die Götter."

[7] W. L. Moran, "Atrahasis: The Babylonian Story of the Flood," *Bib* 52 (1971) 54 [above, pp. 37–38].

[8] Kilmer, "Mesopotamian Concept," 168.

In the passages that follow, cited as proof of these assertions, I ask you to look, beyond the vivid description of famine, for the slightest indication that man has become distressing and physically repulsive to the gods, not to say rebellious.

The third year came
And their features were altered by hunger.
Their faces were encrusted, like malt,
And they were living on the verge of death.
Their faces appeared green,
They walked hunched in the street.
Their broad shoulders became narrow,
Their legs became short,

Later version:

When the second year arrived
They suffered the itch.
When the third year arrived
The people's features were distorted by hunger.
When the fourth year arrived
Their long legs became short,
Their broad shoulders became narrow,
They walked hunched in the street.
When the fifth year arrived
Daughter watched the mother's going in,
But the mother would not open her door to the daughter.

"Then, the offense most repugnant to the gods took place:"[9]

When the sixth year arrived
They served up the daughter for dinner,
They served up the son for food . . .
One house consumed another.

Here certainly is a picture of extreme human suffering leading to sheer desperation—cannibalism in one's own family. But offense to the gods? Rebelliousness? Where are these in the text? As Professor Kilmer notes, the ineffectiveness of the plagues established, Enlil's only words are:

[9] Kilmer, "Mesopotamian Concept," 169.

> But the people are not diminished,
> They have become more numerous than before.

Not a word about how repulsive they are, how rebellious they are.

I have belabored this point, I know, but it is, you will agree, absolutely basic to understanding both the Mesopotamian myth and its biblical transformation. In my opinion there is not a shred of evidence in the Deluge myth—or to speak more cautiously, in the text we have—for man's rebelliousness or sinfulness. Recall, too, two more facts: (1) Enki charges Enlil with an indiscriminate slaughter that ignored the ethical dimension; (2) the solution to the problem of man is completely a-ethical. And finally to anticipate a bit, recall what all of you know so well: in the biblical version of the myth, the ethical motives for the Deluge derive from the personal comments of the Yahwist and Priestly Writer. This does not prove of course that such motives were never in their source or its tradition at some time, but it does fit with all we have said, and it is something that those of a contrary view should advert to and explain.

I have elsewhere expressed the view that the Deluge myth is an etiology of the human condition in which man experiences, in the deepest level of his being, forces in a tension that allow him to be, but not without measure. I have also stated that the myth implies a consciousness of the importance of man's role in the universe, for if he needs the gods, they also need him.

But following Ricoeur's typology as outlined above, I believe one should say more. Ending as it does in an apparently final and established order, salvation achieved, the Deluge myth belongs in some sense to the drama of creation type. Violence (the din of man) is overcome by violence (the Deluge), though as in the Igigi-myth, intelligence also makes its contribution.

But in this myth I think we also find something approaching the tragic—both a tragic anthropology and a tragic theology. A tragic anthropology because man first appeared in an order of things in which necessarily and due to forces beyond his control he was drawn into and was responsible for an evil that approached the chaotic. He acquired a kind of guilt simply by being, and its very inevitability gives it a tragic dimension. There is also a tragic theology: behind the procreative forces leading to his destruction were the gods Enki and the birth-goddess. From one point of view, they act as blind forces, and this blindness they give to man. They—especially Enki—really lead men astray, and they bring man into a terrible confrontation with the master of the world he lives in.

I believe it all belongs to the same tragic world that we find in the lamentations over national disaster, like *The Lamentation over the Destruction of Ur*. Had others recognized the existence of this world they would not have felt compelled to find some sin to explain and justify Enlil's treatment of man. The tragic world of the lamentations is not the rational one in which God is always holy and innocent, and man attributes evil to his own sins, known or unknown—thus escaping the terrifying possibility that evil is simply absurd, the tragic vision, or the even more terrifying one that it comes from God. In the lamentations, no enemy is cursed, no sin is confessed, known or unknown. The people mourn, beg for deliverance, and pity themselves. They achieve salvation in the acceptance of necessity, the inscrutable and unalterable decision of the gods.

The Biblical Transformation of the Myth

I think Speiser has stated well the nature of the general relationship between the Mesopotamian and Hebrew myths. After noting the correspondences between the accounts of the Deluge in *Gilg*. XI and Genesis, which he calls "inescapable proof of basic interrelationship," but taking into account also a number of differences, he concludes: "It is thus clear that Hebrew tradition must have received its material from some intermediate, and evidently northwesterly, source, and that it proceeded to adjust the data to its own needs and concepts."[10]

However, he was writing solely about the Deluge. What about all the rest, the plagues and the Igigi-myth? We cannot assume that the Deluge myth circulated only in the form in which we have been studying it. This is evident in itself and has been confirmed by a fragment at Ugarit, which seems to confine itself to the deluge and the fate of its miraculous survivor.

Gen 9:1ff. (P) may imply knowledge of a longer version. "God blessed Noah and his sons and said to them, 'Be fertile and increase

[10] E. A. Speiser, *Genesis* (AB 1; Garden City: Doubleday, 1964) 55.

and fill the earth.'" These are the first words addressed to Noah after God has accepted his sacrifice. Certainly they witness to an interpretation of the Deluge completely alien to the Mesopotamian view; they reject man's numbers as irrelevant to the understanding of crises in either the antediluvian or post-diluvian orders. But are they a conscious rejection? Since the time after the flood introduces a new era, the Priestly Writer could well repeat, with no reference to or knowledge of Mesopotamian myth, the first command to man in Gen 1:20, thus emphasizing the same basic understanding of man's role in the universe before going on to the innovations of the new era.

Similar doubts attach to the Yahwist account. The Yahwist introduces the flood-section in Gen 6:1 with the remark, "Now when man began to increase on earth . . ." (*wayhî kî hēḥēl hā'ādām lārōb*). Here is the population motif. Then in 6:5, when the divine judge makes the verification that must precede his announcing sentence on man, the *lārōb* of 6:1 is echoed in the *rabbâ* of "And Yahweh saw that great (*rabbâ*) was the evil of man." Mankind is a *rōb*, but it perishes only because its wickedness is (so to speak) a *rōb*.

But again, is this opposition intentional in the sense of a rejection of Mesopotamian myth? It may be, but: (1) I think the Yahwist needed the population motif in any case, to avoid the appearance of the Deluge being an "overkill"; (2) there is nothing that implies either overpopulation, or excessive noise, specific traits of the motif in the Mesopotamian tradition.

And the Igigi-myth? Of course not, you say, and I agree. But note one curious fact: the most blatant piece of mythology in the whole Bible occurs in 6:1–4, the introduction to the Deluge, and it recounts what was undoubtedly for the Yahwist an abomination and proof positive of human iniquity, the intersecting of the divine and human. Could we possibly have here a faint reflection of a tradition of the Deluge myth which once began, "When gods were man"?

Amidst all these *non liquets*, there is of course, providing I am right about the Mesopotamian myth, one luminous certainty: a radical transformation, in accordance with the biblical view of the god-man relationship, of the motivation for the flood.

There is also another difference between the Mesopotamian and Hebrew myths, and one perhaps not less profound. We have seen an element of tragedy in the Mesopotamian myth, but it was muted tragedy, for all seemed to end well. Darker possibilities—of the kind actualized in the Erra myth—certainly are pushed to the background and are at most hinted at in the final "Hearken!"

How different the Genesis account! For sheer tragedy and sense of the inevitability of evil I know nothing to match Yahweh's first reflections, as the flood is over and the just man offers his sacrifice: "Never again will I doom the world of man, since the devisings of man's heart are evil from his youth." We have hardly tasted the savor of that sweet and reassuring "never again" and it turns to sand in our teeth as we realize that it has nothing to do with the sorry spectacle of human evil. This, we hear, is fated to go on as before. The promise that the cosmos will never again be involved and that the rhythm of days and seasons will go on uninterrupted does little to alleviate our shock and disappointment which, if it is not to be turned into despair, must become tragic resignation.

In fact, it seems to me that, in final analysis, the deluge makes a lot more sense in Mesopotamia than in Israel. It makes sense for one god to be hostile to man, another on his side, for one god to attempt to destroy him and another to save him, for the first god to consent to man's survival when the other agrees to remove the motive for destruction. But in a monotheistic world, even one of divine regret and sorrow over an earlier decision, the Deluge might make sense if it were eschatological, a final separation of the just and the wicked, or if it led to a new era that at least began with the possibility that the cause of the Deluge had been removed or at least significantly diminished. But in the Bible, it is not the one and it does not do the other. In the Deluge, it seems to me, the face of God grows dark and we are confronted with a terrifying ambiguous power, more terrifying than any Enlil, for there is no power to check him.

CHAPTER 8

The Creation of Man in Atrahasis I 192–248

The most important single witness to Babylonian speculation on the origins and nature of man is the description of his creation in the first tablet of the Atrahasis Epic, especially lines 192–248.[1] However, these fifty-six lines, where so much is new, are—not surprisingly—a tissue of cruces, major and minor. In the remarks that follow we hope to solve some of them, or at least (we refer to the most serious crux of all, lines 214–217 // 227–230) to define for the first time the full scope of the problems involved.

The distinction of lines 192–248 is not arbitrary; they constitute a unit, thematically and structurally. They are concerned with the first stage in the creation of man, beginning with the request of the gods to the birth-goddess to form man, and ending with their renaming her, in gratitude for what she had done, "Mistress of all the gods." What follows is another stage; the scene shifts, and Enki and the birth-goddess retire to "the house of destiny,"[2] where with other activities they continue the process of man's formation.

Reflecting the thematic unity is the structure:

[1] We follow the lineation of W. G. Lambert and A. R. Millard, *Atra-ḫasīs: The Babylonian Story of the Flood* (Oxford, 1969).

[2] This seems to be a designation of the room where the child is born; see the passage translated by Jacobsen, *Proceedings of the American Philosophical Society* 107/6 (1963) 475, n. 6 = *Toward the Image of Tammuz and Other Essays on Mesopotamian History and Culture* (ed. W. L. Moran; Cambridge, 1970) 322.

	narrative	(2)		192–193
A gods	speech		(4)	194–197
	narrative	(2)		198–199
B birth-goddess	speech		(4)	200–203
	narrative	(2)		204–205
C Enki	speech		(12)	206–217
	narrative	(12)		218–230[3]
	narrative	(6)		231–236
B' birth-goddess	speech		(6)	237–243
	narrative	(2)		244–245
A' gods	speech		(2)	246–248

Though this concentric structure, which gives formal expression to the pivotal importance of Enki's speech, the longest and, for the nature of man, the decisive intervention, merits detailed analysis, it must suffice here to call attention to the additional evidence of the unity of the passage in the relationship of the final lines to the opening narrative.

192–193 *iltam issû išālū*
tabsūt ilī erištam Mami
246–248 *panāmi Mami nišassīki*
inanna bēlet kala ilī lū šumki

As is clear, lines 246–248 harks back to lines 192–193 and is a kind of *inclusio*. Note *Mami, ilī*, and the two forms of *šasû*. The effect is not only to round off the whole passage, but to contrast effectively the change of status from merely *tabsūt ilī*, "midwife of the gods," to *bēlet kala ilī*, "Mistress of All the Gods."

In the first speech a minor problem is the translation of 197, *šupšik ilim awīlum liššī*, which has been rendered, "Let man carry the toil of

[3] Here and in lines 237–243, 246–248, we follow Lambert-Millard in the verse count. The distinction of two narrative sections at 218–230, 231–236, is based on the relationship of 218–230 (execution) to 206–217 (counsel), and the transition-marker at 231, *ištūma* ("Right after . . ."). The symmetry of the entire passage is striking, especially the balance between speech and narrative beginning at 206ff. It is probably the explanation why in 218ff. the description of the execution, which in general corresponds word for word with the advice of Enki, omits all reference to 209, 212–213; having to report the consent of the gods (218–22) and yet apparently wishing to balance speech and narrative, the poet had to omit something.

the gods." This version is undoubtedly influenced by *šupšik ilī* in I 3 and *šupšikkakunu* in I 241, both of which associate the corvée with the gods who toil. Against it are the sg. number and—decisively, in our opinion—the structure of the quatrain:

attīma šassūru	:	*bāniat aiwīlūti*	A -B
binīma lullâ	:	*lîbil abšānam*	B'-C
abšānam lîbil	:	*šipir Enlil*	C'-D
šupšik ilim	:	*awīlum liššī*	D'-E

The beginning of each line takes up, by repetition or a form of synonymous parallelism, the end of the previous line. This is patent in B-B' and C-C', which therefore clarify the relationship of D-D': *šipir Enlil* = *šupšik ilim*. Here interest is not in the corvée as once having been the lot of some of the gods, but in defining the authority under whom it will be borne. In this respect, with the creation of man nothing will be changed, and if this is made explicit, it is perhaps to reject by implication the resignation which, in his pique at the attitude of the striking and rebellious gods, Enlil had offered shortly before (I 170–171).

The goddess directs her reply to the *attīma* and its possible implications of her self-sufficiency. To the "*Thou* art" she begins her answer with *ittiyāma lā*, "By me alone not . . . ," and then piling up the emphatic *ma*'s (*Enkīma*, *sūma*) she insists on the necessity and nature of Enki's contribution:

ittiyāma lā naṭu ana epēši	By me alone he definitely cannot be fashioned.[4]
itti Enkīma ibašši šipru	For Enki alone there's a task at hand.
šūma ullal kalāma	He alone can purify everything.
ṭiṭṭam liddinamma anāku lūpuš	The clay he must give me that then I myself may fashion.

[4] "It is not possible for me to make things" (Lambert-Millard) would be *ittiya lā naṭu epēšum*; besides, in context it does not make sense (see the last two words of the strophe). For *lā*, "definitely not," see *AHw*, 521a; for *epēšu*, "to fashion" (rare), cf. I 289 (*anākūmi abni ipušā qātāya*). A bit differently J. Bottéro, "Antiquités Assyro-Babyloniennes," *Annuaire de l'École pratique des hautes Etudes: IVe Section* (Paris, 1967–1968) 11: "A moi seule, la chose n'est point realisable."

Since Enki in the following speech distinguishes his role as purifier from that of provider of clay, this is more likely to be the mind of the goddess.[5] But why does she think his powers of purification will be required at all? To answer this question we must go on to Enki's address to the divine assembly.

Enki says:

ina arḫi sebūti u šapatti	On the new-moon, seventh and fifteenth days
tēliltam *lûšaškin rimka*	A purification let me institute—a bath.
ilam ištēn liṭbuḫūma	The leader-god let them slaughter, then
lîtellilū *ilū ina ṭībi*	Let the gods purify themselves by immersion.
ina šīrišu u damīšu	With his flesh and his blood
Nintu(r) lîballil ṭiṭṭa	Let Nintur mix the clay.
ilumma u awīlum	Let the god himself and man
libtallilū *puḫur ina* ṭiṭṭi	Be mixed together in the clay.
aḫriātiš ūmī uppa i nišme	For all days to come let's hear the drum.
ina šīr ili eṭemmu libši	In the flesh of the god the ghost shall remain.
balṭa ittašu lišēdīšūma	Let her inform him while alive of his token, and so
aššu lā muššî eṭemmu libši	That there be no forgetting, the ghost shall remain.

As in the preceding speeches, the basic unit is the quatrain. But, whereas there the formal unity was achieved by either the chain-like construction of A-B, B'-C . . . , or the repetition of the particle *ma* with the first word or phrase (note also *ana epēši* [1] . . . *anāku lūpuš* [4]), here another device is employed: the repetition in the fourth line of a word(s) or a phrase in the second line—

tēlitam	*lîballil ṭiṭṭa*	*eṭemmu libši*
lîtellilū[6]	*libtallilū . . . ṭiṭṭi*	*eṭemmu libši*

Structurally, too, the first two quatrains are very similar: first line, a prepositional phrase introduced by *ina*; second line, second and third

[5] Cf. W. von Soden, *Or* 26 (1957) 312. Contrast Lambert-Millard, *Atra-ḫasīs*, 57.

[6] Note that *tēliltum (taprist)* is the *nomen actionis* of the D-stem.

words, volitive plus noun-acc.; third line, first word, a form of *ilum*; fourth line, first word Dt prec. 3 m. pl. (note too similarity of *lîtellilū* // *libtallilū*), final phrase—like the beginning of the strophe—another prep. phrase introduced by *ina* (and again note similarity of *ina ṭibi* // *ina ṭiṭṭi*). This parallelism of the first two strophes sets them off from the third, which thus receives special marking.

In the first strophe the last two lines have been thought to mean that the god is to be slaughtered in order that the gods may be purified, thus implying that they are to be cleansed in the blood of the slain god.[7] This cannot be right. The structure rules out the possibility of any doubt that the gods are to bathe according to the rite established by Enki, and the god of fresh-waters, and therefore the purifier *par excellence*, does not invent a "blood-bath." Not even exceptionally. There is no evidence that, in Mesopotamian thought, blood was ever believed to be endowed with magical cleansing powers.[8]

As to the purpose of the ablutions, which are presented as necessary once the god is killed, it must be more than to wash off the spatterings

[7] Lambert-Millard, *Atra-ḫasīs*, 58. Similarly, von Soden, *Or* 26 (1957) 309, but on the basis of a defective manuscript.

[8] See A. L. Oppenheim, *Ancient Mesopotamia* (Chicago, 1964) 192, 365, n. 18. If the poet here explains the origins of ritual bathings of the gods, this would be another argument against a "blood-bath." The 1st, 7th, and 15th were three of the most sacred days in the monthly calendar. Ritual bathings (Sum. a.tu$_5$.a = Akk. *rimku*) of the gods are attested for the beginning of the month in the Ur III period; see B. Landsberger, *Der kultische Kalender der Babylonier und Assyrer* (Leipziger Semitistische Studien 6/1–2; Leipzig, 1914) 70, n. 4, and A. Goetze, *JCS* 9 (1955) 21. They can be inferred for the OB period, at least at Mari, from *ARM* I 10, in which Šamši-Adad says he is waiting for "the (ritual) bathing and the *eššešu*-feast"; the latter occurred on the 1st, 7th, and 15th—possibly, too, on the 25th (see *CAD* E, 373b)—but since the letter was sent on the 30th of Tammuz, reference is probably to the first date. To our knowledge, there is no evidence for such bathings on the 7th or 15th, though they may perhaps be inferred from our passage. Another possible contact between the Atrahasis Epic's "chronology" and the monthly cultic calendar is suggested by the fact that the 26th of the month is the one for *nadê libitti (ša Ea) Dingir-maḫ,* "setting the brick (of Ea and) Dingir-maḫ"; see Landsberger, *Kalender*, 140–141, and, with the omission of Ea and minor variants, J. Nougayrol, *JCS* 1 (1947) 333:9', and D. J. Wiseman, *Iraq* 31 (1969) 179:85'. The brick is undoubtedly the birth-brick, which plays a rather prominent role in the account of man's creation. Now, if we put the mixing of the clay to create man on the 16th and allow 10 days as the equivalent of the 10 months that are counted till man is born (I 280ff.), we arrive at the 25th or 26th of the month, depending, on whether we start with the 16th or 17th. The coincidence seems too close to be fortuitous.

of blood. Apparently all the gods must bathe, and the magical powers that are Enki's alone are required. Hence the pollution must be the defilement resulting from the common association with, and responsibility for, death.[9]

The phrase *ilam ištēn* is difficult.[10] "The leader-god" may be a bit bold as a translation, but it is, we believe, the right interpretation.[11] Enki's words cannot be dissociated from Enlil's demand, which begins the discussion leading to the decision to create man, that *ilu ištēn* be summoned and punished, and here it seems that he speaks specifically of the rebel leader.[12] Moreover, the one whom at Enki's advice the gods

[9] See also *CAD* B, 42a; Bottéro, "Antiquités," 118; G. Pettinato, review of W. G. Lambert and A. R. Millard, *Atra-ḫasīs: The Babylonian Story of the Flood*, *OrAnt* 9 (1970) 79. Whether one should speak of murder, as Bottéro does, depends on who is killed; on this problem see below.

[10] Lambert-Millard, *Atra-ḫasīs*, 39, "one god"; Lambert, *Compte rendu de l'onzième Rencontre Assyriologique Internationale* (Leiden, 1964) 101, "a certain god." If by "certain" is meant that the identity of the god is known but is to remain nameless, we are in substantial agreement.

[11] More cautiously, "the one god." Supporting the possibility of the "leader-god" (cf. also *En. el.* VI 13) is *ištēn* in the meaning "foremost" (most probable example, *ištēn eṭlum*, *Gilg.* P iii 36); cf., too, Sum. dili, lit. "one" = *gitmālu*, "noble, perfect."

[12] I 173 (see also Lambert-Millard, *Atra-ḫasīs*, 54, K. 8562 ii 9): *ilu ištēn šisīm[a l]iddûšu* UD-*ta*, "Summon the leader-god so they [the Anunnaki] can . . ." Assuming that the Assyrian recension here faithfully reflects the OB source, against Pettinato, "*Atra-ḫasīs*," 78–79, who believes that Enlil here speaks of his replacement, we follow Lambert-Millard in taking this as a demand for punishment. Since in K. 8562 Anu is apparently willing to pass on this demand to the rebel gods, we cannot see him agreeing to Enlil's abdication, to say nothing of replacing him with one of the strikers. Since the gods from the beginning had sought the main rabble-rouser (I 128–133, 140–145), Enlil's honor would hardly allow him to back down before the refusal of the rebels to disclose their leader's identity, and to settle for just any victim. It may be objected that when Enki speaks there is no indication that the position of the rebels had become any less adamant. However, there is a break before I 189, and here there may have been some brief indication that the strikers had modified their stand or could be safely assumed to do so if the sacrifice of their leader meant their being released from their labors forever. Note that when the senior members among them come to spit on the clay they seem quite familiar with the whole situation (I 233–234). Furthermore, K. 8562 reports a second embassy to the rebels, and in all probability this is either an elaboration of the Old Babylonian tradition, or makes explicit what was there simply assumed. What Enlil wants done to him is another question. If the expression is related to OB *damtam šapākum* (so Lambert-Millard), then he literally calls for a burial-mound to be heaped on him (see A. Westenholz, *AfO* 23 [1970] 27–31), which seems an odd way to demand his execution. Read *liddûšu bír-tam*, "so they can throw him in chain(s)?"

put to death is the chief culprit. This explains why he is characterized as *ša išû ṭēma* (I 223), and later is said to have been slaughtered *qādu ṭēmīšu* (I 239). In the first instance, unless the statement is ironical—and then it would also fit the rebel leader—the meaning can hardly be simply that he had sense or judgment, as if in this respect this obscure god was distinguished from, or surpassed, the other gods. If *ṭēmu* is characteristic of him, it can only be in a specific case or role, and since the latter also explains his death, it is most easily understood of the part he played in the rebellion. It is he, we submit, who was "the god who had the scheme" to overthrow Enlil, and it is this scheme that is effectively ended with his death; he dies "along with his scheme."[13]

Having treated his role as purifier, in the next strophe Enki takes up what the birth-goddess is to do with the clay that he is to give her. The problem is the expression in the last two lines, which seem to have man enter into his own composition. To answer this difficulty it has been suggested that "man" be taken to refer to the clay, the component in man that distinguishes him from the gods.[14] But then how are we to explain "in the clay," which in this review is redundant? The solution, we believe, is that god and man are viewed as being both in a sense end-products. When the goddess finishes mixing the clay, both god and man will be present, but completely fused and compenetrating each others.[15] The poet's stress on the presence of the *god—ilum-ma—* perhaps reflects the fact that man will be made not just from the god's blood, but from his flesh as well. This novelty is connected with another otherwise unparalleled feature that we meet in the next strophe—the ghost.

[13] The argumentation is ours, but we owe the interpretation to Thorkild Jacobsen, whom we would here thank for the many hours he has discussed Atrahasis with us. For other views, see Lambert-Millard, *Atra-ḫasīs*; von Soden, "'Als die Götter (auch noch) Mensch waren': Einige Grundgedanken des altbabylonischen Atramḫasīs-Mythus," *Or* 38 (1969) 424; Bottéro, "Antiquités," 119–120; Pettinato, "*Atra-ḫasīs*," 80.

[14] Lambert-Millard, *Atra-ḫasīs*, 22.

[15] For the object of *balālu (bullulu)* as the end-product rather than an element in the mixture, see I 231; *šikaram balālum*, "to mix beer" (*CAD* B, 40b); and *CAD* B, 40 1.2' (mixing clay or mortar; see Richard S. Ellis, *Foundation Deposits in Ancient Mesopotamia* [Yale Near Eastern Researches 2; New Haven, 1968] 30, n. 131). in the light of these last examples, perhaps the flesh and blood of the god should be compared with the precious substances like wine, honey, ghee, etc. that are occasionally mixed with building-clay, Bottéro, "Antiquités," 118, ". . . du dieu et de l'homme / Se trouveront mêlés. . . ."

Before attempting to identify this ghost or to resolve any of the ambiguities of the third strophe, we must consider the structure, for, as we remarked in the beginning, it makes clear the full task of the interpreter. Guided by it we may assert that the first line of the strophe may not be treated apart from the lines that follow. As in the case of the opening lines of the first two strophes, it must be integrated with the following line, and these two lines with the next two. The four lines are a unit and must be interpreted as such.[16] This is the real problem of the third strophe.

Confirming this unity is the considerable number of passages that associate expressions like "for all days to come" *(aḫriātiš ūmī)* and "not forgetting" (*lā muššî*).[17] Especially important is *Enūma eliš* V 76 where Marduk, after fashioning the images of the monsters who had supported Tiamat and placing them at the Bab-Apsi, declares: *[aḫ]râtaš lā immaššâ šī lū ittu*, "In the future it shall not be forgotten—this (the images) shall be the token." Note: *aḫrâtaš / aḫriātiš ūmī* (line 1), *lā immaššâ / lā muššî* (line 4), and also *ittu / ittašu* (line 3). In view of this passage also relevant is *ARM* X 141: 25–28: *lū ittum inūma šamû iznunu ḫussinnīma lā tamaššenni*, "This is to be a token: When it rains, recall me to mind so you will not forget me."

These last two passages not only confirm the inferences we based on structure, but indicate that the token that is mentioned is a memorial. Context and the parallel from *Enūma eliš* then make it clear that the memory that is to be kept fresh is ultimately that of the dead god; it is his story and its significance that are not to be forgotten. Furthermore. as the parallel passages show this sign should be something perceptible like the images or the rain storm. In context there is only one possibility: the sounding *uppu*.

Whose, then, is the ghost: is it man's or the god's? So far only the first possibility has been considered.[18] This would certainly be legiti-

[16] This has not been recognized. In Lambert-Millard at least the first two lines are treated as a unit.

[17] We may refer simply to the entries *aḫrâtaš, aḫrâtu,* and *aḫrītiš* in *CAD*. Note that in all cases there is question of the indefinite future; this rules out Pettinato, "*Atra-ḫasīs*," 79.

[18] So Lambert-Millard, *Atra-ḫasīs*, 22, 152; von Soden, "Als die Götter," 424, n. 1 ("das Schicksal sterben zu mussen"); Bottéro, "Antiquités," 119 ("une durée comparable à l'immortalité divine"); Pettinato, "*Atra-ḫasīs*," 79 ("la contingenza dell'essere umano").

mate if there were clear outside evidence establishing the ghost's identity; or if on this hypothesis, and this hypothesis alone, the text made satisfactory sense; or, finally, if the concept of a god's ghost were demonstrably alien to Mesopotamian thought. However, none of these alternatives is verified. No such evidence exists; the difficulties with the hypothesis are either conceded or are evident,[19] and the idea that dead gods, like dead men, survived as ghosts is not only in accord with the profoundly anthropomorphic conception of the divine in Mesopotamia, but is actually attested.[20]

The possibility, therefore, that the ghost in question is the god's must be seriously entertained. It is supported, we believe, by several considerations. The first is context. The previous two strophes are concerned, in one way or another, with a death. Then, in the third strophe, a ghost is mentioned. Nothing prepares the reader (hearer) for a radical shift of interest from the creation of man for the service of the gods to his mortality and his afterlife. The reader naturally associates the ghost with the death—the only death—he has just heard so much about.

Secondly, this ghost is somehow to cooperate in keeping fresh the memory of the dead god. Who is more likely to be given this task, the ghost of man or of the god himself?

Thirdly, if the ghost is man's, then in the corresponding narrative one must assume that the poet very briefly abandons his narrative about the events concerned with man's creation, looks into the rather distant future, and tells us that man's ghost actually did come into existence. While such a prolepsis may be possible, it is undeniably awkward, and any solution that avoids it is—*ceteris paribus*—certainly to be preferred.[21]

[19] Lambert-Millard, "very perplexing"; Bottéro, "laconique et difficile." Why (so Pettinato) a ghost should be needed to remind man of the misery of his lot, and why the very fact of death does not suffice for this, is not clear.

[20] *KAR* 307 (E. Ebeling, *Tod und Leben nach den Vorstellungen der Babylonier* [Berlin, 1931] 28ff.). The ghosts are of Enmešarra, Anu, Enlil, and Tiamat. The first is well known as an underworld deity. For Anu as a dead god, see perhaps *Sumer* 13 (1957) 117, pl. 25:14'ff.; according to *CT* 46, No. 43 perhaps Ninurta deposes Enlil. Note also the place of Anu and Enlil in Hittite god-lists among the old, deposed gods.

[21] If the reading of line 227 in Lambert-Millard, *Atra-ḫasīs*, 58, namely [. . . *iš-mu*]-⌜*ú*⌝, is correct, then the prolepsis is clear. However, the traces by no means make *ú* certain, and the only preserved reading is *ú-še-eš-m*[*e*] (K. 14967, Lambert-Millard,

On the hypothesis then that the ghost is the god's we make the following observations on the individual lines.

Line 1: we accept the view that *uppu* here refers to a kind of drum.[22] However, unless we are to assume a very abrupt transition, we must ask what in either of the first two strophes implies the use of a drum. To our knowledge there is no evidence associating the *uppu*-drum with the preparation of potter's clay, but its use in rites of lamentation would fit well with the death of the god.[23] The allusion we suggest to the first strophe receives some confirmation from the way that the reference to time in "for all days to come" is reminiscent of "On the new moon . . ." Perhaps, too, as in the first strophe, we should see here an etiological interest, this time in the origins of the *uppu*-drum in the cult.

Line 2: obviously something extraordinary is provided for here, but for what? The verb *bašû* is ambiguous, and Enki could be proposing either the very existence of a ghost ("let there be present"), an unusual place ("in the flesh of the god"), or the ghost's remaining in the body contrary to normal practice. Though any of these possibilities is compatible with our overall understanding of the strophe, we opt for the last. We have already seen reasons for doubting that a dead god would not be thought to survive as a ghost, and the flesh of the god seems to have been introduced into the composition of man precisely to account for the existence of a ghost. Normally, too, ghosts did not remain in the corpse, but until proper burial roamed about and then went to the underworld. We thus understand the second line to be a special fiat required to keep the ghost within the god's flesh.[24]

Line 3: *balṭa* we refer to the god "while alive." If understood of man, as has been done so far, again the difficulty of a prolepsis arises in the

---

Atra-ḫasīs, pl. 5), "she (the birth-goddess) had the *uppu* heard for all days to come," which may mean no more than that by her action she provided for this.

[22] *Uppu* in the sense of "hole, pit " probably occurs in Lambert-Millard, *Atra-ḫasīs*, 84 vii 37 (see von Soden, "Als die Götter," 430, and to the list of occurrences add Scheil, *RA* 15 [1918] 179 vii 4, *li-tu-ur up-pi-iš-ša*).

[23] See G. Reisner, *Sumerisch-babylonische Hymnen* (Breslau, 1898) 47:14–15, and cf. balag ír.ra in line 6.

[24] The lexical passage (*CT* 19, 36, S. 6:17, Nabnītu) that defines the formula for release of the breath of the dead as *edēpu ša eṭemmi*, "to blow away, (said) of a ghost," we do not consider sufficient evidence to postulate a belief that ghosts remained confined in the body until freed by the magic formula.

narrative section. We also go our own way in considering the birth-goddess the subject of the verb. This is the only possibility consistent with our interpretation of *balṭa*. But there are other reasons, too. First, apparently this is the way the verb is understood in one Assyrian recension.[25] Second, an arbitrary sign like the sounding-drum requires a proclamation like that of Marduk in *Enūma eliš* or of the girl in the Mari letter. Third, such a proclamation by the goddess would best explain how she can say later on (I 240 ff.), when as yet man is but an unformed mass of clay, that she has freed the gods of their toil and imposed it on man. If, when she says this, within this mass there is also present a ghost who because of her knows why he is there and exactly what man is for, her claim makes much better sense.

Line 4: an explanation of the D-form *muššî*, escapes us.[26] In any case, the ghost remains after the god's death to insure that the knowledge communicated to him is preserved.

To sum up by way of paraphrase: In the future we should go on hearing the drum that will sound in the lamentation rites for the dead god. Accordingly, the ghost of the god is to stay behind in the flesh of the god. Explanation: the birth-goddess shall inform the god while he is still alive that the sounding-drum is to be his token, i.e. the drum is to be sounded as a memorial of his death and the story behind it. Then, the god's ghost is to remain to see that the token—the sound and its meaning—is not forgotten. Thus shall the gods provide that man is kept ever mindful of his purpose, and perhaps also warned of the possible consequences of rebellion.[27]

This exegesis, though in our opinion not without its merits, also has its problems. Our explanation of the *uppu* is not completely convincing, not even to us; the connection between the drum and the ghost seems somewhat artificial. Hence the attractiveness of Jacobsen's sug-

[25] Referred to above, n. 21. In this manuscript the second line of the quatrain is omitted in the narrative section; an haplography occasioned by the repetition of *eṭemmu libši* is not likely, since in this case the third line should also have been dropped. Thus in this text the *eṭemmu* has not been mentioned when one come to *ušēdīšūma*.

[26] This is the only context passage for *muššû;* the evidence of the texts is equally ambiguous. We suspect a pluralic-D, but cannot prove it.

[27] Landsberger, "Einige unerkannt gebliebene oder verkannte Nomina des Akkadischen," *WO* 3 (1964) 72, suggests that *ittu* in *En. el.* V 76 serves as a warning as well as a memorial.

gestion (oral communication): *uppu* is also to be understood metaphorically of the heart—this is the "drum" that will sound "for all days to come," as the ghost beats within.[28] "But hark! My pulse like a soft drum / Beats my approach, tells thee I come" (Bishop Henry King, *The Surrender*).

Another problem is the ghost as a source of knowledge. In our view, we are certainly to imagine him present in the original seven pairs of men as a kind of innate knowledge. But this knowledge articulated and communicated, what does he do then, except perhaps to beat within man's heart? Perhaps nothing, but then perhaps, too, the poet saw in the ghost within the explanation of an enigma—man's religious impulse, the inner urging he experienced to submit to the yoke of the gods and to satisfy their needs. Perhaps.[29]

[28] There is a part of the body called *uppu* (*MSL IX* 10: 115, 37:58–59), but it seems to be somewhere in the intestinal tract.

[29] To other problems in the text—the name of the god (line 223), the precise significance of the spitting (line 233–234), and the meaning of the verb *ta-as-ta-aḫ-DA* (line 242)—we can contribute nothing.

CHAPTER 9

Puppies in Proverbs—From Šamši-Adad I to Archilochus?

Among Professor Ginsberg's many outstanding contributions to biblical and Near Eastern studies is his work on Qoheleth. As a token of esteem and admiration I offer this Assyriological gloss on the wisdom of the Preacher, *ʿēt lāledet.*

In *ARM* I 5, a letter in which Šamši-Adad writes to guide Yasmaḫ-Addu during a military crisis, he warns his son and his followers against acting like the bitch of the ancient proverb, ***kalbatum ina šu-te-*****B*****u-ri-ša ḫuppudūtim ūlid*** (11–13). As the recent discussion by A. Finet makes clear, this bit of popular wisdom still poses problems.[1] The bitch gave birth to a litter, but what is wrong with them, and why? The first question has been given various answers (blind, lame, dead, etc.). Finet's opinion is that ***ḫuppudu*** certainly refers to some serious defect of vision, but he also maintains that a number of possibilities remain. He mentions squint-eyed (***bigle***), one-eyed (***borgne***), and blind (***aveugle***), and his own preference, though he does not explain why, is for the second (". . . a mis bas des borgnes").

And then the problem of why. The infinitive ***šu-te-*****B*****u-ri-ša*** has been derived from: ***ebēru***, "to cross," and understood of being mated (Driver) or promiscuous gadding about (Bauer, *CAD*); ***epēru***, "to provide with rations," and understood of preoccupation with food, either fighting for it (von Soden), or searching for it (Lambert, Aro), or

[1] "Citations littéraires dans la correspondance de Mari," *RA* 68 (1974) 43–44.

simply overeating (Gordon); *šebēru*, "to break," and understood of physical injury (Finet).[2] Within this broad divergence of opinion, however, there is a consensus on one point. It seems generally agreed that Šamši-Adad cites the proverb to show his disapproval of the activities of Yasmaḫ-Addu and his cohorts as described in the previous lines.

I read the lexical evidence and the letter quite differently. First of all, *ḫuppudu* certainly does not mean "squint-eyed." Decisive is the new, improved, reading of OB Lu, Rec. B v 2 (*MSL* XII 183); lú-igi-nu-gál = *ḫu-up-pu-du*.[3] Sum. "eyeless" removes strabismus from consideration. There is also B. Landsberger's revised reading of Ḫḫ XIV 23–25 (*MSL* VIII/2 8): muš-igi-nu-gál = *pu-uḫ-ma-ḫu*, muš-igi-nu-gál = *up-pu-dum*, muš-igi-nu-tuk =."[4] Squint-eyed snakes speak for themselves, and Landsberger's identification of the "blind snake" as the Typhlops (or at least a member of the Typhlopidae) is convincing.

Said without qualification, the blindness is to be understood of both eyes. This must be the usual sense of IGI.NU.GÁL in administrative documents, for the skills of those so qualified suggest total blindness.[5] Moreover, in *ARM* VII 183 IGI.NU.GÁL contrasts with *nāṭilum*, "seeing" (Bottero: *aveugle* versus *non-aveugle*). It may also be noted that the equation lu-igi-nu-gál = *ḫu-up-pu-du* is embedded among nine entries in which reference to both eyes is explicit (*ša īnāsū* . . . , "whose eyes are . . ."); in this context, were *ḫuppudu* to be understood of only one eye, we would expect lú-igi-aš-nu-gál.[6] A final and, in my opinion,

[2] G. R. Driver, *WO* 2, 19; T. Bauer, *JNES* 16 (1957) 258 n. 7; *CAD* E, 13b, K, 68a; W. von Soden, *Or* 21 (1952) 76, and *AHw*, 223b; W. G. Lambert, *Babylonian Wisdom Literature* (Oxford, 1960) 280; J. Aro, *StudOr* 26, 238; A. Finet, see above, n. 1.

[3] The earlier reading was l[ú-igi-b]al; see *CAD* H 240b, but note, too, that Rec. A also has a new reading (see below). cf.igi-gál = *dagālu, naṭālu* (see dictionaries).

[4] In *Die Fauna des alten Mesopotamien* (Leipzig, 1934) 2, Landsberger read *up-pu-tum* and etymologized (64) "umwölkt." This reading is retained by *AHw* (sub *puḫmāḫu*), but one can hardly separate *ḫuppudu* and *uppuDu*, both meaning "blind"; cf. the variant *uppuṭu*.

[5] At Chagar Bazar, see O. Loretz, AOAT 3: Šamaš-ublam, an *atkuppu* (7 ii 7; 45 ii 2; 52 i 4); Šewiniri, one of a group of female millers (^{munus}*ṭe*$_4$*-i-na-tum*, 41/44: 29); Talbarra, Kilumšaya, Šeḫlipkanazi, three women listed after the *ṭēʾināt išparātim* (7 iv 3–5; 42 iv 18–20; 45 iv 346); Lušallim (7 ii; 42 iii 18), no profession indicated; see also 53: 10(?), 11–12. The manual skills of working with reeds and milling fall within the competence of the blind. See also J. Bottéro, *ARM* VII, 324, and perhaps E. Szlechter, *Tablettes* 151:3, PN (fem.) IGI.NU.<GÁL> to be trained as a singer [cf. J. Renger, *ZA* 9 (1969) 184]. On the synonymous igi-nu-duḫ of earlier periods, see I. J. Gelb, *JNES* 32 (1973) 87, and *Festschrift A. Salonen* (StudOr 46) 59–60, 69–70.

[6] Even *īn quqānim* (iv 45) and *īn* x (47) may be said of both eyes; cf. use of sg. bound-form for both sg. and pl. when context makes number of referent clear.

of itself decisive consideration is this: the blindness of puppies affects both eyes.

That the affliction of the bitch's litter which Šamši-Adad speaks of is the congenital inability of puppies to see in the first days and even weeks after birth was first proposed by T. Bauer.[7] About the same time E. Gordon independently came to the same conclusion, and this view now seems to be shared by *CAD* and *AHw*.[8] The strongest argument in its favor is common sense. Among the domesticated animals, this weakness is a very striking and almost unique feature of the puppy.[9] Of what other blindness is popular wisdom likely to speak? And how better refer to it? As we shall see, even the Greeks, who are supposed to have had a word for everything, simply said that the bitch brings forth *typhla*!

It is perhaps redundant to add that, in both Akkadian and Sumerian sources, this blindness is spoken of. In both, it is the source of simile; in the latter, it is probably also the subject of proverb.[10]

Another line of argument, first suggested by E. Gordon, may also be noted.[11] He could cite the Italian proverb *cagna frettolosa fa catelli ciechi*, "the hasty bitch produces blind puppies," and its almost literal equivalent in Turkish.[12] The latter he considered especially important

[7] This is inferred from the translation, "Eine Hündin, die sich überall herumtreibt (diese Übersetzung erfordert der Kontext) wirft (nur) blinde (Junge);" see above, n. 2.

[8] E. Gordon, *JCS* 12 (1958) 69–70; *BiOr* 17 (1960) 139 n. 123; ibid., 11; *CAD* K, 68a (inferred espacially from the translation "gives birth"); *AHw* 768 sub *nāṭilu* (inferred from the equation of *ḫuppudu* with *lā nāṭilu*).

[9] Cats suffer from the same affliction (see below, n. 12).

[10] "If a ewe has given birth to a lion and its eyes are closed like those of a puppy (*īnāšu kīma mīrāni katmā*)" (*CT* 27 23: 14 in E. Leichty, *TCS* 4 76:38); the young scribe opening his eyes "like a puppy" [ur-gi$_7$-tur-gim; W. Heimpel, *Tierbilder in der sumerischer Literatur* (Rome, 1968) 358, reference from T. Jacobsen]; cf. also the riddle in *UET* VI/2 340–341 of the house which one enters blind (igi-nu-gál, var. igi-nu-bad) and leaves seeing (igi-ni-gál, var., igi-bad) and its solution: the eduba; the proverb of the bitch(?) weakening herself(?) and therefore the whelps have unopened eyes [igi nu-bad-bad-rá; E. Gordon, *JCS* 12 (1958) 69].

[11] *BiOr* 17 (1960), 139 n. 123; ibid., 151. Gordon was familiar only with Archer Taylor's *The Proverb* and not the complementary *Index* (original edition, Helsinki 1934; reprinted together with *The Proverb* by Folklore Associates in 1962; also *Folklore Fellows Communications* No. 113). It is in the *Index* (15) that I found the leads to the sources cited in the following notes.

[12] For the Italian proverb, see Albert Wesseiski, ed., *Angelo Polizianos Tagebuch* (1477–9) (Jena, 1929) 190, with a host of references. Beside the variant forms, note the cat's replacing the dog.

because, though its source dates from the fifteenth century A.D., geographically it was much less remote.

However, these are only two pieces of an ancient and widespread tradition. Here is a small, selective survey:

German: *Die eilende Hündin wirft blinde Junge.* To this K. Wander adds, for example: "Die Letten: Geschwind geeilt, blind geboren. Die Kleinrussen: Wer rasch arbeitet, bringt blinde Junge zur Welt."[13]

English: More's *Utopia, The hasty bitch brings forth blind whelps.*[14] It is cited as a Latin proverb; cf. Erasmus, *Canis festinans caecos parit catulos.*[15]

Greek: in a scholion to a probably corrupt line of Aristophanes (*Peace* 1078), "according to the proverb, 'The bitch in her haste gives birth to the blind'" (*para tēn paroimian hē kyōn speudousa typhla tiktei*), which is repeated by the paroemiographus Makarios (fifteenth century A.D.) with the explanation, "regarding those who fail through haste" (*epi tōn dia spoudēn hamartanontōn*).[16] The hasty bitch also appears in a fable of Aesop. She boasts to the sow of the speed with which she produces her young, and this the sow concedes but also notes, "You give birth to the blind" (*typhla tikteis*).[17] Particularly noteworthy, because it pushes the Greek tradition back at least to the seventh century B.C., is the discovery of a new fragment of Archilochus (*aut Archilochus aut diabolus*, as one critic has said to the doubters).[18] There we read (ll. 26–27): "I am afraid lest, acting hastily out of eager-

[13] Karl Friedrich Wilhelm Wander, *Deutsches Sprichwörter-Lexikon* (Darmstadt, 1964) 2. 904, "Hündin."

[14] Cited from G. L. Apperson, *English Proverbs and Proverbial Phrases: An Historical Dictionary* (London, 1929) 289.

[15] As cited from the *Adagia* by Wesselski (see above, n. 12) and Apperson (see above, n. 14). Morris Palmer Tilley, *Elisabethan Proverb Lore in Lyly's 'Euphues' and in Pettie's 'Petite Palace'* (New York, 1926), 78, also quotes the *Similia: Uti canis properans in enitendo caecos parit catulos, ita praecipitata opera non possunt esse absoluta.*

[16] *Corpus Paroemiographorum Graecorum* (Göttingen, 1851) 2. 181, No. 32, and see note.

[17] A. Hausrath, *Corpus Fabularum Aesopicarum* (Teubner) I/2, No. 251 = B. E. Perry, *Aesopica* I (Urbana, 1952), No. 223.

[18] R. Merkelbach and M. L. West, "Ein Archilochus-Papyrus," *Zeitschrift für Papyrologie und Epigraphik* 14 (1974) 97–112. The text has been re-edited by D. Page, *Supplementum Lyricis Graecis . . .* (Oxford, 1974), No. 478. The literature on this fragment is already considerable; Professor John Van Sickle has kindly furnished me with an up-to-date bibliography [see his article in *The Classical Journal* 71 (1975), 1–15, and for the problem of authorship especially 15]. It seems that most classicists accept the attribution to Archilochus.

ness, I beget like the bitch in the proverb children blind and untimely" ([*de*]*doich' hopōs typhla kalitēmera* / [*sp*]*oudē epeigomenos tōs hōsper hē k*[*yōn tekō*]).[19]

The tradition in the west of the hasty bitch that cuts short her time of gestation and rushes into birth, thereby producing what is untimely and defective, of course proves nothing about the meaning of a word in Mesopotamian sources.[20] But it does confirm what common sense and the Mesopotamian evidence already argued: the blindness of puppies is a fact of nature so evident and so striking as to furnish the stuff of wisdom. And perhaps, as we shall see, the western tradition is even more relevant.

This understanding of *ḫuppudu* has certain implications that should be noted. Since this blindness is universal, then its cause must in some way be equally universal. If all puppies are born blind, then *ina šu-te-*B*u-ri-ša* must explain why; anything else would not be an expression of wisdom. This suggests two possibilities. The first is that reference is made to something constant and characteristic of bitches. This is the position of Bauer and *CAD*; bitches are notoriously promiscuous. It leads to the additional inference that we are dealing with proverb as anecdote, a not uncommon form, though rare in the statement of general truths of this type; on this view, the verb *ūlid* becomes a kind of "gnomic aorist" (Bauer, "wirft"; *CAD*, "gives (lit. gave) birth").[21]

[19] Or, less literally and in language more worthy of the text (Van Sickle):

I fear some dark and premature result
    if I should act in a rush (the saying's "hasty bitch, blind pups").

For a discussion of the problem of Archilochus' comparing himself and not the hated Neobule to the bitch, see Mekelbach-West, 108–9. In view of the opinion of Bauer and *CAD*, it may be noted that one scholar wishes to emend the text and introduce the promiscuous Neobule.

[20] A slight ambiguity is perhaps discernible in the bitch's haste. The latter may be the speed with which she goes through her period of gestation (most clearly in Aesop, with the moral that things an judged not by speed, but by perfection), but it is also the haste of the precipitate act, giving birth before due time [so Archilochus, and down through the ages; cf. Erasmus' *praecipitata opera*; "My first burden coming before his time must needs be a blind whelp," see Tilley, loc. cit. (see above, n. 15); Bishop Hockett's use of the proverb in the sense that there is a proper time for everything, as cited by V. S. Lean's *Collectanea* (Bristol, 1903) 3. 391].

[21] See Lambert, *Babylonian Wisdom Literature*, 236: 17–18; 237 iv 9–10; 240:22–5; 241: 50–3; 267: 1–9; 280 rev. iv 4–7, 11–12; especially 146: 52; 226 ii 4–6; 226 ii; 245: 14–17. Proverb as anecdote is characteristic of oriental wisdom; see A. Taylor, *The Proverb*, 157–8; B. E. Perry, *Studium Generale* 12/1 (1959) 19. Allusion to such a proverb may be the explana-

If, however, the connection between what is said of the bitch and the fate of her litter is purely casual, then the only universality one can think of is that of the primordial, with its implication of "and ever since all puppies. . . ." In other words, the narrative is not only a short-fable but also an etiology. For this, in the wisdom tradition as preserved, I do not believe there is a real parallel.[22] Restricted, however, as the scope of our sources is, the absence of parallels is not decisive.[23] Still, *ceteris paribus*. . . .

What did the bitch do, or what happened to her? As we have already noted, on this subject there is both considerable variety of opinion—each, we may add, with its own difficulties[24]—but general

---

tion of the preterite in "Just as the vagina of the bitch held fast (*iṣbatu*) the penis of the dog" (R. Biggs, *TCS* 2 33:10).

[22] In the fable of the eagle and the serpent an etiology of the former's ever renewed vigor may be embedded [see R. J. Williams, *The Phoenix* 10 (1956) 70–77], but the main thrust of the fable lies elsewhere.

[23] The association of wisdom and the folklore of etiologies is an easy one; cf. B. E. Perry, *Studium Generale* 12/1 (1959) 32, on Aesop as the teller of etiological myths, occasionally even those with no metaphorical meaning.

[24] Against Finet: the rarity of the Dt infinitive [in *AHw* and *CAD* only ten or eleven forms attested, only three or four in contexts: *butalluṭu, gutaššuru, kutunnu* (Dtn? Cf. *GAG*, paradigm 28), *putallusu*]; because in the nominalization of clauses the distinction between active and passive is regularly neutralized, the rarity in any conjugation of pass. forms of the inf.; the extreme rarity of inf. pass. with subject expressed (I know only *na'lud lilli, nenšê māti = nanšê māti? naḫbut bītīia, naptu ḫarrānim, naspuh nišīsu/mātisu/bīt awīli*; see also *nashuru*—a certainly incomplete list, but also certainly a representative one).

Driver: same difficulties with Št-pass; a rare conjugation in any form (I count twelve occurrences in OB period, according to dictionaries); the assumed West Semitism (Heb. *ʿibbar* is cited in support); a banality, once the meaning of *ḫuppudu* is established.

Against $Št_2$ as proposed: none conforms to the established categories of (reflexive) causative of Gt/N reciprocal, intr. inner passives, occasional replacive of Dt (see *GAG* and *Ergängzungsheft* § 94; D. O. Edzard, *AS* 16, 111–20); to Dt reciprocal add Dt reflexive; HSM 7494: 8, *ᵈŠamaš šu-te-bi-ib, "Šamaš,* cleanse yourself"; the dupl. AO 7032:8 [*RA* 38 (1941) 87, *šu-te-x*-[x], requires collation; cf. *mu-ti-si ᵈŠamaš qurād*[*um*]. "Wash yourself, valiant Šamaš" *JCS* 22 (1968) 26:21], and none, so far as I can see, has any clear support in other uses of the $Št_2$, however ill-defined these remain.

Against Bauer and *CAD*: as recognized by *CAD*, apart from its use in the terminology of extispicy (*CAD*, "to extend beyond," *ebēru* is said almost exclusively of crossing bodies of water, and when occasionally reference to the latter is not clear (add *TIM* 2 16: 4, 12 32), it should probably be understood. Nowhere is *ebēru* clearly used of simply moving to another place or traversing land. There is no support for the restoration [*i-bi*]-*ir-šum-ma* in *En. el.* V 79 [so J. V. Kinnier Wilson and B. Landsberger, *JNES* 20 (1961)

agreement that in citing the proverb Šamši-Adad implied his criticisms of what Yasmaḫ-Addu and his cohorts have been doing in their engagements with the enemy. They are thus understood to be accused of some folly that has placed them and their cause in jeopardy. The passage, which begins immediately after the formulaic greeting (1-3), reads as follows (4–16): "You, for your part, keep trying ruses and *twisting* him *about* in order to defeat the enemy, and the enemy in the same way keeps trying ruses on you and *twisting* you *about*. Like wrestlers, each keeps trying ruses on the other. Heaven forbid that, as in the ancient proverb, "The bitch by her . . . gave birth to the blind," you for your part now do the same thing. Heaven forbid that the enemy keep *twisting* you *about* in ambushes."[25]

At this point there is an unfortunate break, with only the ends of four lines preserved. Šamši-Adad goes on to tell them not to keep on worrying and not to move about very much.[26] He assures them that his departure (with reinforcements; cf. ll. 36–43) is imminent. In the meantime, they are to keep their own forces safe, an order which he repeats at the end of the letter with special emphasis, saying it should be their sole concern (44–45).

162]; read with Lambert [*i-ṭi*]*-ir-šum-ma*, "he embraced him." In *En. el.* IV 141, *šamê ībir*, "he crossed the heavens," we should see an allusion to the waters of Tiamat; cf. "her waters," in the previous line, yielding *mêša // šamê*. Cf. too *RAcc.* 134:240–1, (Marduk) *ēbir šamê šāpiku erṣeti // mādidi mê tâmti murriš mērištu*, "who crosses the heavens, piles up the earth, // who measures the waters of the sea, plants the plantation." (This clear allusion to *En. el.* IV 141 argues against emending the latter or reading *ibēr* "he tested," with M. Held, AOAT 25, 233 n.1) In brief, nothing suggests a basis for the development of a *šutēburu*, "to gad about, to pass here and them." No better grounded, in my opinion, is Bauer's appeal to context (see above, n. 7); see below.

[25] *Attunu ana dâk nakrim šibqī teštenê u tēteneggirāšu u nakrum qātamma ana kunūšim šibqī ištenî u īteneggirkunūtī kīma muštapṣī aḫum ana aḫim šibqī ištenî assurrī kīma tēltim ullītim ša ummāmi kalbatum ina šu-te-Bu-ri-ša ḫuppudūtim ūlid attunu inanna kī᾿am teppešā a*[*ssu*]*r*[*r*]*ī nakrum ina šubātim l*[*ā itene*]*ggirkunūti. šibqī šite᾿ û* and *etegguru* probably belong to the technical jargon of wrestling. If we are dealing with belt-wrestling, as stems likely [see Jack Sasson, *Or* 43 (1974), 407] then *etegguru* may refer to holding the kit and twisting; cf. the position of the wresters in *OIP* 60, Pl. 54. But this is only one possibility, as the variety of blocking and twisting positions shown at Bani Hasan makes evident; see C. H. Gordon, *HUCA* 23 (1950–1) 131ff. especially pls. IV–V. On *šubtu*, "ambush," see A. K. Grayson, *Studies Presented to L. Oppenheim* (Chicago, 1964) 90–4, and, most recently, B. Alster, *Dumuzi's Dream* (Mesopotamia 1; Copenhagen, 1972) 99, 103. Add perhaps *YOS* 10 17:12 and CT 20 26:7 (so *CAD* A/2, 237a).

[26] For a possible source of worry, see W. von Soden *Or* 21 (1952) 76.

Now, what suggest that Šamši-Adad considers the ruses and the twistings nothing but folly, a silly wasting of one's energies, etc.? It is obvious that he is worried, and he is afraid his son's forces will end up trapped. But expressions of fear are not necessarily criticisms, and to urge great caution and a purely defensive line of action until an apparently outnumbered army is reinforced is not to condemn the probings and stratagems attempted so far. After all, if this is folly, then the enemy is no less guilty.

But, in my opinion, what rules out the allegedly implied criticism is the simile of the wrestlers. If Šamši-Adad condemned his son's policy, is this the simile he would have chosen? Wrestlers feinting, twisting, dodging, but coiled within and ever ready to seize the advantage, are not an image of folly. They present a picture of the economy of forces, caution and utter concentration, amid ever mounting tension. If any value judgment is implied in these lines, it is a favorable one. *Homo ludens* is not a fool.

It is in the situation that has now developed that Šamši-Adad's fears begin ("Heaven forbid that . . . *now* you do the same thing"). The proverb is cited, not to condemn the past, but to warn against the possibilities of the future.

Of the latter one could be the danger of the lulling effect of protracted repetition and the consequent loss of concentration. For the *tēltu* with an appropriate lesson in these circumstances we may find some support in OB Lu, Rec. A 287 (*MSL* XII 166): lú-igi-bal = *e-et-*[*x*]-*ru*. In view of context and igi-bal = *ṣabāru*, "to wink," and lú-igi-bal = *ṣabru*, "winker," it is virtually certain that the entry in question refers to eyes, and specifically to some distinctive feature or abnormality in the movement or position of the eyes.[27] The writing indicates a root ’-$_3$-$_5$-x-*r* or *y*-x-*r*, and a formation of the *pitrās*- or *pitrus* type. For the former, the candidates are only two. Considerations of morphophonemics rule out many roots,[28] and those of meaning exclude others.[29]

[27] The context is two more entries apparently concerned with eyes: lú-igi-bal = *mu-*[*te-er i-nim*], lú-igi-nigín-na = *mu-te-e*[*r i-nim*]. If our restoration and remarks are pertinent, one might consider restoring the first entry as *mu-*[*uš-te-bi-rum*]. The problem of distinguishing the respective meanings of *ṣabāru* / *ṣabru* versus *ṣapāru* / *ṣapru* of no particular importance in the present discussion. A. Falkenstein, *SGL* I 36 proposed igi-bal, "(falschen) Augen verdrehen." Note also igi-bal = *ṣip-pa-tum* (Izi XV ii 10', *MSL* XIII 169; *AHw*, 1104, *ṣippatu* III).

[28] *esēru, eṣēru, ešēru, ezēru.*

[29] *edēru, emēru, epēru, eṭēru.*

Left are *ebēru*, "to cross," and *egēru*, "to lie/lay athwart (etc.)." Strongly favoring the former is bal = *ebēru* (cf. also bal-ri = *ebertān*, *ebertu*), whereas *egēru* and derivatives (including *itguru*) correspond to Sum. gil(-gil).

To cross, said of eyes, suggests reference to esotropia, and thus *e-et-*[*bu*]*-ru*, "mutually crossed," seems the most likely reading. From this one could derive *šutēburu*, a normal $\check{S}t_2$, causative of Gt, "to cross (the eyes), to squint." The *tēltu*: "The bitch by her squinting gave birth to the blind."

If this is right, Šamši-Adad cites a short, etiological fable, the background of which we can only guess at. For whatever reason, the bitch was led to squint as she gave birth to her litter, and ever since all puppies have been born, not squinting too, but blind. The moral would be that like does not always produce like, and actions can have effects with unforeseen and even painful pluses.

Recollection of this truth would not be out of place in Yasmaḫ-Addu's situation. With neither side at the moment gaining the advantage, the moves of one being met by the same or similar moves of the other, the *etegguru* and *šibqī šiteʾû* of both sides matching each other, like was producing like. A timely reminder would be that this is not always true, and that Yasmaḫ-Addu's *etegguru* may not simply provoke another, but one with a painful plus—*ina šubātim*, "in ambushes."

This is, I believe, a plausible interpretation, but no more than that. Then is of course the obvious difficulty that it begins with a restoration. It implies, too, an etiological fable, which we have already seen to be unparalleled in our sources. But most serious of all, I think, is that the fable becomes in its application a rather abstract lesson on causality and in the situation probably not the most urgently needed piece of advice.

What would fit the context perfectly? As should be obvious, I want to say that it would be the proverb of the western tradition. The one piece of advice that is in accord with both the image of the wrestlers and Šamši-Adad's own orders is a counsel of patience, a warning against precipitate action. As Yasmaḫ-Addu with his forces continues to probe and feint and defend, and all this goes on and on, he might clearly be tempted to end the increasingly intolerable tension and to commit himself and his men to some reckless course of action. An athlete understands the situation, and so does Šamši-Adad. He cites the wisdom of the proverb, "The bitch in her overeagerness gives birth to the blind." And then, to bolster his son's determination, he assures him that the period of waiting will be brief, for soon he will be at his side with the needed reinforcements and the enemy can be faced, in a decisive battle, without undue risk. No one, I think, will deny that a proverb with this lesson would fit the context, and would fit it perfectly.

In its support one might entertain the possibility that, related to *ebēru*, "to cross over," there existed a $\check{S}t_2$, *šutēburu*, "to cross too soon, to act precipitately." However, I think more pertinent is A V/1 180ff. (*AS* VII 44): $^{a\text{-}si\text{-}il\text{-}la}$ŠIM = *rīšātu e*-BI-*rù, qūlu,* $^{mu\text{-}ud}$ŠIM = (same meanings). To, the second noun both dictionaries (*e-bi-rù = ebiru, CAD; e-bé-rù = ebēru, AHw*) ascribe the meaning "joy," though *AHw* with a cautionary "uns(icher)," and associate it with *rīšātu*, "expressions of joy," rather than with *qūlu*, "silence."[30] The curious polarity in the meanings of the Sum. words (and of nì-me-gar) makes the definition of *e*-BI-*rù* particularly difficult. The range of possibilities is from jubilation to silence, from "a mixture of joy and silent admiration" (Civil) to the dumbness of awe and deep anxiety.[31] Perhaps one can do no better than "eine (freude) Erregung, die sich verschieden veräussern kann."[32] Within this broad spectrum, one possibility—and note that "(tense) anticipation" has been independently suggested for the Sum. equivalents[33]—is that *e*-BI-*rù* means "anxiety, eagerness, alacrity," with the added possibility of a corresponding *šutēburu*, "to be overanxious, overeager, too full of alacrity."[34]

Tenuous as the evidence, apart from the context of *ARM* I 5, may be for the presence of the hasty bitch in Mesopotamia, her example with

30 *AHw* compares Ar. *ḥabira*, "to rejoice."

31 M. Civil, *Studies Oppenheim* (see above, n. 25), 88-9; Alster, *Dumuzi's Dream*, 54:18, and commentary, 89 (the reference to Sjöberg is now *AfO* 24 34: 112).

32 Cl. Wilcke, *Das Lugalbandaepos* (Wiesbaden, 1969) 138.

33 Åke Sjöberg, *TCS* 3, 103–4.

34 Cf. Ar. *ġabira*, "to bear rancor," and in the IV-form, "to exert oneself zealously"; Heb. *ʿebrā*, "arrogance, insolence, wrath," and *hitʿabbēr* "to be infuriated." For the postulated relationship of *ebēru* and *šutēburu*, cf. *ašāšu*, "to worry," and *šutāšušu* "to become very worried" [*CAD* A/2, 424b; delete the references to *EA* 82:50 and 93:4, reading with J. A. Knudtzon *ú-ul ta-ša-aš* (subject: land of Amurru, glossed *ad sensum.* 3rd pl. *naqṣapû*), and [*a*]-*ta-ša-aš* (glossed *naqṣapti*). Verbs like *šutānuḫu, šutamruṣu, šutapšuqu* could also contribute to a *šutaprusu*-pattern of emotional and physical states *in malam partem.*

its warning against losing one's patience is so apposite to both the probing combatants and the wrestlers they are compared with, that I think we may pose the additional question: from Šamši-Adad to Archilochus?

Of course, it is possible that close observers of nature might independently associate two distinctive features of the bitch, her short period of gestation (nine weeks) and the affliction of her litter, and draw from them the same lesson. But proverbs also diffuse themselves, cross the boundaries of language and are translated. In the present instance, there is virtually a word-for-word correspondence between the Akkadian and the Greek:

kalbatum ina šutēburīša ḫuppudūtim ūlid
hē kyōn speudousa typhla tiktei.
(The bitch by her haste gave birth to the blind.)

The Gr. pred. adj. ("being in haste") expresses exactly the force of the Akk. *ina* + inf., and both agree in the terse "blind," with no explicit mention of the young. The difference is the minimal one, at the end, and that, simply one of tense. If the Gr. is not a translation, or a translation of a translation, it could certainly pass as one. In view of this and Greece's known debt to Mesopotamian wisdom, we should perhaps add this proverb to the ledger.[35]

ʿēt lāledet . . . ʿēt laḥᵃšôt.[36]

[35] See R. J. Williams (see above, n. 22); B. E. Perry, *Studium Generale* 12/1 (1959) 25; Lambert, *Babylonian Wisdom Literature,* 339 [but read *diq-diq-qu*, a bird, with R. Borger, *Or* 33 (1964) 462, and M. Stol, *RA* 65 (1971) 180; for the fable of the *diqdiq / duqduq*-bird, see *CT* 51, No. 93]; M. L. West, *Harvard Studies in Classical Philology* 73 (1969) 113–34.

[36] Addendum: It is gratifying to note that, thanks to W. von Soden (*ZA* 66 [1977] 292) the verb *šutēpuru*, "to act (too) hastily," has been recovered from an old misreading. However, still misinterpreting the context, and apparently unaware of the western tradition on the hasty bitch, he denies the relevance of his discovery for our understanding of the Mari proverb. In my opinion, we may now delete, or at least make a little smaller, the question mark in the title of this article.

CHAPTER 10

New Evidence from Mari on the History of Prophecy

multaque per terras vates oracula furenti pectore fundebant . . .
Cicero, *De divinatione* I xi 18

Of the many contributions the documents from Mari have made to Old Testament studies unquestionably one of the most important has been the light they have thrown on the historical background of the prophetic movement in Israel.[1] The appearance, therefore, of the tenth

[1] The texts in question are: G. Dossin, "Une révélation du dieu Dagan à Terqa," *RA* 42 (1948) 128-131; idem, *apud* A. Lods, "Une tablette inédité de Mari, intéressante pour l'histoire ancienne du prophétisme sémitique," in *Studies in Old Testament Prophecy Presented to T. H. Robinson* (Edinburgh, 1950) 103-104 (transliteration only); *ARM* II 90; *ARM* III 40 and 78; *ARMT* XIII 23, 112-114. For discussions and other translations (for the latter note especially the articles of Malamat and von Soden) see the following: F. M. Th. de Liagre Böhl, *Opera Minora* (Groningen, 1952) 63-80; J. Lindblom, *Prophecy in Ancient Israel* (Oxford, 1952) 30ff.; A. Malamat, "Prophecy in the Mari Documents" [Hebrew], *EI* 4 (1956) 74-84; idem, "History and Prophetic Vision in a Mari Letter" [Hebrew], *EI* 5 (1958) 67-73; idem, *EI* 8 (1967) 231-240; idem, "Prophetic Revelations in New Documents from Mari and the Bible" (VTSup 15; Leiden, 1966) 207-227; M. Noth, *Gesammelte Studien zum Alten Testament* (Munich, 1957) 230-247; H. Schult, *ZDPV* 82 (1966) 228-232; H. Schmökel, *TLZ* 76 (1951) 53-58; W. von Soden, *WO* 1/5 (1950) 397-403; C. Westermann, *Grundformen prophtischer Rede* (Munich, 1960) 82-91 [= *Basic Forms of Prophetic Speech*, trans. by H. C. White (Philadelphia, 1967) 115-128]; idem., *Forschung am Alten Testament* (Munich, 1964) 171-178; H. W. Wolff, *Gesammelte Studien zum*

volume of the *Archives royales de Mari*, the long awaited "correspondance féminine,"[2] must be considered an event of some moment for biblical scholarship. In this large and unique collection of one hundred seventy-nine letters there are fourteen which cite prophecies, dreams or other channels of revelation, not including many references to the findings of the haruspex. Instead therefore of the nine texts on which previous studies were based, we now have twenty-three. Not surprisingly, this great increase of evidence requires revision of some earlier discussions, solves some old problems and raises new ones. The investigation of prophecy and related religious phenomena at Mari thus enters a new stage, and it cannot fail to be of interest to students of the Old Testament.

The purpose of this article is to make these new texts, of which only the cuneiform copies and a selection in translation[3] have so far appeared, more generally accessible. We present them here in transliteration and translation, together with a brief general introduction and short commentaries. The task of tracing and elaborating their significance for biblical studies we leave to others.

I.

One of the most striking features of the new texts[4] when compared with those previously published is the sharp divergence in the contents

---

Alten Testament (Munich, 1964) 206-231; and (since this article was submitted) F. Ellermeier, *Prophetie in Mari und Israel* (Theologische und orientalische Arbeiten 1; Herzberg, 1968). [See now A. Malamat, *Mari and the Bible* (Leiden, 1998), 59-162; and the full published corpus in J.-M. Durand, *ARMT* XXVI/1: *Archives épistolaires de Mari I/1* (Paris, 1988), 377–452; idem, *Documents épistolaires du palais de Mari. Tome 3* (LAPO 18; Paris: Cerf, 2000), 74–91, 278–84, 314–29, 403–5. – Ed.]

[2] G. Dossin, *ARM* X: *La correspondance féminine* (Textes cunéiformes du Louvre 31; Paris, 1967). To this correspondence add *ARM* II 66, 112-117.

[3] G. Dossin, "Sur le prophétisme à Mari," *La divination en Mésopotamie ancienne et dans les régions voisines* (Paris, 1966) 77-86. It is to be hoped of course that the companion volume *ARMT* X will not be delayed much longer. However, Dossin's translations and interpretations in "Prophétisme," which we may assume will reappear by and large in *ARMT* X, frequently differ considerably from our own, and not always on trivial points. Hence we see no danger of simply duplicating his work, especially since the format of *ARMT* X precludes any but the briefest notes. [See G. Dossin and A. Finet, *ARMT* X: *La correspondance féminine* (Paris, 1978)—Ed.]

[4] These are *ARM* X 4 (No. 11 below), 6 (No. 5), 7 (No. 1), 8 (No. 2), 9 (No. 12), 10 (No. 10), 50 (No. 6), 51 (No. 7), 53 (No. 4), 80 (No. 13), 81 (No. 3), 94 (No. 8), 100 (No. 14), 117

of the revelations. The earlier ones—and to these we may add some still unpublished which Dossin has cited in translation[5]—are mostly concerned with the temples and their interests: *RA* 42, with Zimrī-Lim's failure to keep his messengers in regular attendance upon the god Dagan at Terqa; *ARM* III 40 and II 90, with the performance of mortuary-offerings and the date of their observance; "Lods" and A. 2925, with a land-grant to Adad of Kalassu; A. 455, with the water the Dagan of Tuttul is drinking; A. 4260, with gifts the king owes to various temples. Two others deal with the construction of a house (*ARM* III 112) and a gate (*ARM* III 78).[6] Only four look to the political situation.[7] *ARMT* XIII 113 is badly broken but seems to treat of military matters, and *ARMT* XIII 23 and 114 predict either victory over Babylon or at least deliverance from its threat. In *ARM* X, however, the picture is just the opposite. Here only four (*ARM* X 9, 94, 100, 117) have any manifest interest other than the person of the king, either his personal safety, the threat of insurrection, or—and this most frequently—his military successes. None urges, at least not openly, the cause of any sanctuary. The contrast is evident, and, since it emerges from a fairly large corpus of letters, it is hardly fortuitous.

An explanation, or at least the beginnings of one, seems to lie in the geographical distribution of the material. None of the revelations in the first group took place at Mari; they were experienced in Aleppo, Sippar, Terqa and Tuttul.[8] But in the texts of *ARM* X it is in Mari that

(No. 9). In the order of treatment below: No. 1 = *ARM* X 7; No. 2 = X 8; No. 3 = X 81; No. 4 = X 53; No. 5 = X 6; No. 6 = X 50; No. 7 = X 51; No. 8 = X 94; No. 9 = X 117; No. 10 = X 10; No. 11 = X 4; No. 12 = X 9; No. 13 = X 80; No. 14 = X 100.

[5] Dossin, "Prophétisme," 78ff. The texts are A. 455 (79-80), A. 2925 (78), A. 4260 (85-86). A. 2925 establishes Nūr-Adad, Zimrī-Lim's ambassador to Aleppo, as the writer of 'Lods' and repeats the god's request in the latter. A. 4260 shows the existence of an *āpilum* of Shamash at Sippar!

[6] Strictly speaking, *ARM* III 78 should not be included here; the prophet speaks simply in his own name, though his meddling may be authorized by a divine communication of which we have no record.

[7] The dream in *RA* 42 does bring up Zimrī-Lim's struggle with the Yaminites, and perhaps should be included here. However, the point of the dream is, as we have already said, to stimulate Zimrī-Lim's patronage of the temple. 'Lods' promises an extension of Zimrī-Lim's boundaries, but in vague, general terms, as a reward for acceding to the god's request; A. 4260, victory over Hammurapi of Kurda.

[8] At least they are reported there, and if experienced elsewhere, it could not have been far away. The problem of which Tuttul is involved need not detain us here; see A.

the dreams or visions are seen, the prophecies inspired, or in some other way the gods disclose the future. The only exceptions are *ARM* X 80, 94, 100 and 117, and in this list we find three of the four texts which we have already noted as exceptional in not sharing the dominant concern of the others with the person of the king. The pattern is clear: in the revelations at Mari the king appears as ruler and warrior, elsewhere, he is, above all, the patron and benefactor of the local sanctuaries.

The contrast is not surprising. In the provinces the king would be a rather unfamiliar figure, and only exceptionally would his fate be closely bound up with that of the members of the community; at places like Aleppo and Sippar, which were outside his political control, his significance would be even less. In the capital, however, he would loom large in the lives not only of his family but of the administrative and religious circles. Here, through affection, loyalty, or at least enlightened self-interest, they would share deeply in his major interests and concerns, which were political and military.[9] They would know all his comings and goings and the dangers they might involve. They would pick up rumors of sedition, which would be current in the capital as nowhere else. They would have an awareness impossible in the provinces of the larger political scene, with its shifts in the balance of power and threats to the ruling house. All this necessarily meant a different relationship and a different attitude towards the king. From a psychological viewpoint, these differences could not fail to be reflected in the prophecies and dreams.

Of course, the element of self-interest transcends geographical boundaries. We may point to some of its less subtle manifestations with the cautionary note that we do not mean thereby to impugn the honesty and sincerity of the persons involved; however questionable their motives at times may appear, at least with the evidence at hand we cannot distinguish the charlatan.[10] In the pattern of revelations

---

Malamat, "Prophetic Revelations," 216, n. 3. On Ugaritic *dgn ttlh*, see now M. Astour, *JNES* 27 (1968) 14.

[9] These dominate the investigations of the haruspex on behalf of the king. The most frequent topics are revolutions and wars of both aggression and defense. The convergence of these *signa impetrata* and the *signa impertita* we are studying should be noted.

[10] Cf. E. R. Dodds, *The Greeks and the Irrational* (Berkeley, 1951) 74: "We cannot see into the minds of the Delphic priesthood, but to ascribe such manipulations in general to conscious and cynical fraud is, I suspect, to oversimplify the picture. Anyone famil-

outside Mari self-interest is obvious. They have little to say to the king that does not promote in one way or another the local cult-centers. In the Mari revelations it will be seen that it is the goddess Annunitum who is most generous with inspirations of her temple personnel or other devotees in order to warn the king and promise him protection and victories.[11] This looks quite disinterested until we read that she is doing all this despite the king's rejection of her.[12] Clearly, for unknown reasons, the goddess and, therefore, her cult and staff had fallen under royal displeasure and it seems very likely that this situation goes far towards explaining the spate of prophecies. Similarly, in the dream of the priest of the god Itūr-Mer a goddess protests against the king's too frequent visits to the "family-house" as involving unnecessary risks to his person;[13] however, as we shall see below, these visits probably also included the observance of religious rites honoring a god other than Itūr-Mer. Seen in this light the dream looks like a clear case of "wish-fullfilment."

2.

Whatever the complexity of motives and other factors behind the prophecies and dreams may have been, the related problem of authenticity was certainly confronted. The practice of sending along with the report of the allegedly divine message a lock of hair and the fringe of the dreamer's or prophet's tunic is well known, and it is commonly agreed that its purpose was both to identify the person and to guarantee his veracity; these personal articles gave one, symbolically but quite really, legal control over their owner.[14]

This practice is now further documented in *ARM* X 7:23ff. (No. 1), 8:19ff. (No. 2), 50:29ff. (No. 6), 81:19ff. (No. 3), and A. 455. On the basis of this new evidence we can begin to see more clearly why it was fol-

iar with the history of modern spiritualism will realise what an amazing amount of virtual cheating can be done in perfectly good faith by convinced believers."

[11] Cf. *ARM* X 6 (No. 5), 7 (No. 1), 8 (No. 2), 50 (No. 6), 81 (? No. 3).

[12] *ARM* X 8: 9-11 (No. 2).

[13] *ARM* X 51 (No. 7); see commentary.

[14] See most recently A. Malamat, "Prophetic Revelations," 225-226. The article of A. Finet on the subject, which he promises in "La place du devin dans la société de Mari," *Divination en Mésopotamie*, 93, n. 1, is inaccessible to me.

lowed in some cases and not in others. The rule for dreams is the most difficult to establish, and here there must have been a large margin of personal judgment.[15] However, in other predictions of the future or warnings to the king, if they were communicated *privately*, be it by professional or layman, the legal symbols were never required, to judge from present evidence.[16] On the other hand, it seems they had to be handed over if the message was announced *publicly*, that is, in the temple and presumably in the presence of worshipers.[17]

To the last rule there seem to be three exceptions. One is found in *ARM* X 50:21ff. (No. 6) where it is reported that an "ecstatic" (*muḫḫūtum*) delivered her inspired message in the temple of Annunitum, and yet nothing is said about sending the hair and the fringe. However, in *ARM* VI 45 the governor of Mari writes to the king that he has received from a priest called Aḫum the hair and fringe of a *muḫḫūtum* and he is now dispatching them. This Aḫum we know to have been a priest in the temple of Annunītum,[18] and so in view of the standard procedure in other cases of public prophecy we may safely assume that *ARM* VI 45 and *ARM* X 50:21ff. deal with the same event.

The other possible exceptions are "Lods" and A. 2925, both reporting the request of Adad of Kalassu (Aleppo). Here the situation is quite

[15] The legal symbols actually accompany the report on a dream only in *ARMT* XIII 112 and *ARM* X 50 (No. 6), though in the case of *RA* 42, as the writer of the letter admits, they should ordinarily have been required. Elsewhere (*ARMT* XIII 113; X 51 [No. 7]; X 94 [No. 8], probably X 117 [No. 9] and possibly X 9 [No. 12—see commentary]) the dreams are simply passed on to the king. (The state of the text in *ARM* X 10 [No. 10], which recounts a vision, leaves this case doubtful). One distinction that seems to obtain in general is that in the latter instances the issues are much less important, and may therefore have more easily dispensed with the more solemn form of guarantee; contrast however, *ARMT* XIII 113 with 112.

[16] By a professional (*āpilum—āpiltum, muḫḫûm—muḫḫūttum, qamatum*?): *ARM* II 90; III 40; *ARM* X 80 (No. 13? see commentary); by a layman: *ARM* X 4 (No. 11), 100 (No. 14), and almost certainly 6 (No. 5). *ARM* XIII 114 is badly preserved and must remain questionable.

[17] By a professional: *ARM* X 81 (No.3, on the public character of this prophecy, see below, p. 108, n. 30), A. 455; by a layman: *ARM* X 7 (No. 1), 8 (No. 2). *ARMT* XIII 23 and *ARM* X 53 (No. 4) are broken at the end, where reference to the symbols is usually made.

[18] In *ARM* X 8: 20 (No. 2) it is Aḫum the priest who acts after a prophecy in the temple of Annunītum, and in *ARM* X 52 it is Aḫum the priest who is concerned for Annunītum's cult paraphernalia. This is the only priest of this name known at Mari.

complicated. As reported in 'Lods' the oracle speaks of Zimrī-Lim in the third person, which is not the style of public prophecies;[19] this is found rather in the oracle as recounted in A. 2925, where Zimrī-Lim is addressed directly in the second person. The former does not look like the original oracle, and the text speaks, it will be noted, of repeated appearances either of the god or of the prophets.[20] Hence, to judge from "Lods," the oracle may have been reported earlier and the hair and fringe sent on at that time. Certainly A. 2925 is not the first time the king is apprised of the god's request; not only does the god explicitly say he has already written to Zimrī-Lim, but the writer of the letter says he himself has written five or six times about the matter. So we do not expect a reference here to the legal symbols.

It is also possible, and we should say very probable, that the symbols not only were not, but could not be sent, precisely because of their legal implications. Aleppo was not under the jurisdiction of Zimrī-Lim; it belonged to his father-in-law Yarīm-Lim. Legally, therefore, the king of Mari had no control over the temple personnel there and could not demand the symbols of their persons in lieu of their actually appearing before him. Hence we should probably not expect that the question of the hair and fringe should even arise in "Lods," A. 2925, or any other report on oracles delivered outside the king's realm.

The distinction, therefore, between private and public prophecies seems well founded. It is also understandable. The former could be handled at the discretion of the king; he could do "what in accordance with his deliberation pleases him."[21] In the case of the latter, however, he could come under strong social pressure to comply with an oracle, and this in some circumstances could prove very difficult and at times even impossible. Requiring the legal symbols, with their implications of possible sanctions, seems calculated to keep both the professionals and the laity from airing their inspirations too casually and to make them strictly accountable for giving them public expression.

[19] See below, p. 109.

[20] Cf. lines 25-26 where, if we adhere to the text (*ina tērētim ittanazzaz*, "he keeps appearing in/at the omens"), the subject must be Adad; if we correct the text and read *ittanazzaz<zū>*, then the subject must be the prophets.

[21] So *ARM* II 90: 26-28 with regard to a prophet's words. Similarly, "let my lord do what pleases him" at the end of *ARM* III 40.

Once, however, the king was in possession of the legal symbols, what did he do? Were they alone considered sufficient guarantee? We may now point to some indications of further checks on the authenticity of the revelations. In *ARM* X 81:19ff. (No. 3) Zimrī-Lim's daughter cites the message of a prophetess and then goes on to say: "I now hereby send to the Star (Zimrī-Lim) the hair and the fringe. Let the Star have an omen taken so that the Star may act in accordance with his omens." The expression "to have an omen taken" *(tērtam šūpušum)* always refers to the exercise of the craft of the haruspex,[22] whose specialities were hepatoscopy and extispicy. In effect, therefore, the girl proposes that her father submit the message of the prophetess to the control of the technician. If his results confirm the message, then the king is to act "in accordance with his omens," that is, the message of the prophetess and the response of the haruspex.

Another instance of the same practice, though in this case there is no question of public revelation, is found in *ARM* X 94 (No. 8) where a dream is reported that demands action of the king. The writer's advice is, "Let my lord have the haruspex look into the matter, and if *this dream was seen*," the king should comply. Again the "natural" sign is checked against the "artificial" one in the liver or exta.

These are the only explicit references to such control, but we suspect that it was customary whenever the legal symbols were taken. This is suggested by *ARM* X 81 (No. 3), which we have just cited. In lines 15-18 the prophetess, right after she has acted as the mouthpiece of the goddess, says, "I hereby give you my hair and my fringe. Let them declare 'clean.'" This last request is unparalleled, but its meaning, we believe, is fairly clear. First of all, it is obvious that it does not refer to physical cleanliness, but should be understood in the common figurative meaning of clearing from (legal) claims;[23] such a request fits perfectly with her action of handing over the symbols of such claims. Secondly, if we may trust her Akkadian, the subject of the verb *lîzakkû* (precative 3 pl. masc.) is not the hair and the fringe, for if they were, the two nouns being both of feminine gender (*šārtum* and *sissiktum*), the verb would be *lîzakkê* (precative 3 pl. fem., Mari dialect for standard Old Baby-

[22] See *CAD* E, 222-223 (*tērta epēšu*), 232, 4b (*t. šūpušu*); also *ARM* XV, "Répertoire analytique," 272 (sub *têrtum*).

[23] See *CAD* Z, 30-31 (cf. 26-27).

lonian *lîzakkiā*). Hence she is not asking that the symbols in some way effect this declaration, as if they alone could confirm the authenticity of her message. Finally, note the parallelism between her request and that of the writer of the letter: the prophetess gives her hair and fringe and asks for a declaration of freedom from legal claims; the writer says she is sending the hair and the fringe and asks, "Let my lord have an omen taken." It is, therefore, the haruspex who "tries the case" and it is his response that will in effect declare the prophetess "clean."[24]

All of which, of course, does not prove that recourse to the haruspex was general practice.[25] However, it is clear that the prophetess knows of some such procedure, and it is hard to see what it could have been except the one actually attested. An oath could only establish her sincerity, but it would reveal nothing about the real source of her message.[26] To prove that revelation is really revelation one needs revelation, and to have a system of proof one needs a systematic source of revelation. Within the Mesopotamian framework this could only be found in the craft of the haruspex.

The implications of such a system of controls are far-reaching. It integrates the accepted sources of revelation within a hierarchy and gives primacy to the "science" of the technician. In this system dreams and prophecies can never demand unqualified acceptance or reveal absolute imperatives. They can merely "propose"—it is the haruspex who "disposes." However, precisely because the system is so dependent on him it cannot have obtained in general practice. His skills were too rare to be easily called upon.[27] The sophistication of the Mari

[24] Note that the response of the haruspex was thought of as revealing a divine "decision" (*dīnu*, see *CAD* D, 152). The legal metaphor we postulate is, therefore, not an isolated case. What the sanctions may have been in case of an unfavorable response is not clear.

[25] Gudea submits his dream to such a test (Cyl. A xii 16-17) and only when the response is favorable does he begin the construction of Eninnu. Cf. also the two Old Babylonian omens in A. Goetze, *Old Babylonian Omen Texts* (Yale Oriental Series X; New Haven, 1947) 51 iv 20-21 = 52 iv 21-22, which have as their apodoses "the dreams of the king will be trustworthy" (*šunāt šarri(m) kînā*), "his dreams will be false" (*šunātūšu sarrā*); see A. L. Oppenheim, *The Interpretation of Dreams in the Ancient Near East* (TAP 46/3; Philadelphia, 1956) 207 for this and other checks on dreams.

[26] As a guide to action, an oracle requires more than a sincere medium; it should be authentic.

[27] See *ARM* V 65 where Asqudum must take the omens in towns as important as

court, drawing perhaps on older and analogous practices in Babylonia,[28] was certainly not normal and would not have been confronted by the prophets except in the larger urban centers.[29]

3.

The new evidence of *ARM* X also permits us to define more exactly the typology of the reports on dreams and prophecies. One form that emerges concerns the introduction to the public prophecies. Note the following:

(a) *aplûm ša Dagan ša Tut*[*tul*] *itbēma kīʾam iqbi ummāmi,* "the 'prophet' of Dagan of Tuttul arose and spoke as follows, thus," + direct quotation (*ARM* XIII 23:6-8; cf. also lines 16ff.);

(b) [*āp*]*ilum ina bīt Ḫišamētim Iṣi-aḫu šumšu itbēma ummāmi,* "the prophet, Iṣi-aḫu by name, arose in the temple of Ḫišamētum and thus (spoke)," + direct quotation (*ARM* X 53:5-7, No. 4);

Sagarātum and Terqa, and if an outlying district is to have an haruspex, the king must send one (*ARM* II 15). We cannot agree with A. Finet ("Place du devin," 90-91) who maintains that as a rule such a diviner was to be found in the hinterland. Apparently he accepts Jean's restoration and translation in *ARM* II, 15. 26-27: [*pa-tu-um*] *ba-lum bārêm* [*ú-u*]*l ib-ba-aš-ši,* "[Un *patum*] sans devin [n]'existe pas." Whatever a *patum* may be, *ibbašši* does not mean "be, exist," which would *ibašši*, but rather "come into being" (N, always ingressive with *bašû*). *ARM* II 15 seems, therefore to be requesting the services of an haruspex temporarily for "the coming into being" of the *patum* (if correctly restored). We may also remark that furnishing a sheep would be an expense that not many could afford.

28 See above, n. 25.

29 Social factors may have contributed to the ascendancy of the haruspex. His position in society was a high one (A. Finet, "Place du devin," 91ff.), whereas the ranks of the prophets and ecstatics were probably drawn from the lower classes (see *ARM* X 53 [No. 4], and A. L. Oppenheim's remarks in *Ancient Mesopotamia* [Chicago, 1964] 221; note, however, E. Klengel-Brandt, *Or* 37 [1968] 82), as seems to have been true in Greece, too (see Dodds, *Greeks and the Irrational,* 72). Often, too, they must have been people with deep psychological disturbances and emotionally very unstable (see below, n. 47). In the enlightened and refined circles of the court, revulsion and contempt for these irrational and socially inferior figures may have been fairly common. In this regard it may be significant that Zimrī-Lim never makes the slightest reference to the prophets, though he is quite concerned with the reports of the haruspex. It may also be significant that no prophet or ecstatic is yet attested as belonging to, the gods who probably ranked highest in the official cultus—Dagan, Itūr-Mer, Bēlet-ekallim.

(c) *Innibana āpiltum itbēma kīʾam idbub ummāmi*, "Innibana the prophetess arose and spoke as follows, thus," + direct quotation (*ARM* X 81:4-6, No. 3);[30]

(d) *muḫḫūtum ina bīt Annunītim itbēma ummāmi,* "the ecstatic arose in the temple of Annunītum and thus (spoke)," + direct quotation (*ARM* X 50: 22-23, No. 6);

(e) "Et par devant Dagan, le 'prophéte extatique' s'est levé et il a parlé en ces termes," + direct quotation (A. 455);

(f) *ina bīt Annunītim šalšam ūmam Šēlebum immaḫūma umma Annunītumma*, "in the temple of Annunītum on the third day Šēlebum went into a trance and thus (spoke) Annunītum," + direct quotation (*ARM* X 7:5-7, No. 1);[31]

(g) *ina bīt Annunītim ša libbi ālim Aḫātum ṣuḫārti Dagan-mālik immaḫīma kīʾam iqbi ummāmi*, "in the temple of Annunītum in the city, Aḫātum, the servant of Dagan-mālik, went into a trance and spoke as follows, thus," + direct quotation (*ARM* X 8:5-8, No. 2).

With minor variations, the constant elements are: (1) designation of subject by profession (a, d, e), or name (f, g—both lay), or both (b, c); (2) the place of prophecy (exceptions: a, c);[32] (3) verb *itbe*, said of professionals, or *immaḫ*$^{i}/_{u}$ said of laity; (4) various formulae introducing direct quotations; (5) direct quotation.

(1) establishes identity; since the tendency is not to name the professionals, this probably means that a god customarily had in his temple only one prophet or ecstatic. (2) not only locates the sacred place but also implies the identity of the god who is to speak; it is an important element because the god would, otherwise remain unidentified, (f) in

[30] We include this passage under the public prophecies, though no temple is mentioned, because: (1) *itbe* is elsewhere used only against the temple-background; (2) *idbub* implies she addressed a group (cf. *iqbi* in a and g), for if she had spoken only to the writer of the letter, we should have *idbubam*, "she spoke to me." Either *ina bīt Annunītim* (? see commentary) was omitted by mistake, or Innibana was known to the king and it could be presumed he would know in which temple she had spoken.

[31] On the translation of *namḫû* by "to go into a trance," see below, p. 110. The transcription of UD$_3$.CAM is not certain.

[32] On c, see n. 30 above. As to a, in the lines prior to those cited it is stated that sacrifice had just been offered to Dagan before the prophet arose; hence, the mention of place could be dispensed with.

this respect being unparalleled.[33] (3) has the interesting distinction between the professional and the layman; since the activity of the former would be more likely to give rise to this generally formulaic description, *immaḫ* $^{i}/_{u}$ is probably a secondary modification. "He arose" implies that the professional was usually sitting, kneeling or crouching until inspiration seized him. (e) suggests that he was before the statue of the god. Here we may imagine him arise and, facing with the statue towards the worshipers, become *vox dei*. For the witnesses this must have been an impressive and at times even terrifying experience.

The god's message also exhibits some characteristic features. First of all, it is never introduced by the formula "god so-and-so sent me." The prophets use this elsewhere, but not in the setting of a temple.[34] Here the god is uniquely present, and so he does not send—he possesses. The speaker is not a messenger, he is the mouthpiece of the deity. The most striking expression of this is found in "Šēlebum went into a trance and thus (spoke) *Annunītum.*"

Typical, too, of the message is that it is addressed to an individual in the second person, and in five out of seven examples the first word is a vocative: "O Babylon" (a), "O Zimrī-Lim" (c, d, f, g). The form of direct address is maintained, it should be noted, even though in only one case (e) is the one addressed actually present. The exception is instructive, for (e) is also one of the two cases where the vocative is not employed. It would seem, then, that the function of the vocative is to make clear to the bystanders to whom the oracle is directed. The retention of direct address in a situation where it no longer applies is one more example of the rigidity of form.

[33] The fact that naming the place is equivalent to naming the deity who speaks shows the intimate between the numinous presence and the inspiration. In Annunītum's temple, for example, where her power is particularly concentrated, presumably she alone can take possession of another.

[34] See Malamat, "Prophetic Revelations," 221. The new material does not support, in our opinion, Malamat's view ("Prophetic Revelations," 209) that the sense of of mission is the primary feature of Mari prophecy. Rather, mission is secondary and even incidental. The prophets belong in the temple where they are the voice of a god; transmission of their message outside is usually carried out by others.

4.

In using the term "possession" we touch upon the difficult question of the psychic state of these prophets. Though the nature and the meagerness of the evidence urge extreme caution, one or two points may be made. First, to judge from the speeches, which we have no reason to suspect owe their present form to the mediation of anyone like the Delphic *prophetes*, the cases of possession do not belong to the extreme forms of mantic frenzy. The sobriety and coherence of the language cannot be reconciled with the tortured babblings of delirium.[35] This must be said despite the use of the verb *namḫû* which would seem to point to a kind of fury and madness.[36] We think of course of convulsions, hyper motor-excitement, and other extraordinary phenomena that often accompany possession. However, it is possible either that the verb came to be used conventionally of all prophetic outbursts by the laity, or that it actually had a broader meaning, either originally or secondarily, "to become beside oneself," which like Greek *ekstasis* could be applied to a wide range of psychic abnormalities. Thus, it could be used of a trance, and it is trance that seems to answer best to all the data.

In two instances, moreover, it seems that we can define the trance as being of the lucid rather than the somnambulistic type,[37] that is, a trance in which the medium retains consciousness of himself. This is what we seem to have in *ARM* X 81 (No. 3). Here, despite the break in lines 11-14, it is virtually certain that the prophetess abruptly shifts from her role as mouthpiece of the god and begins to speak in her own name ("I hereby give you my hair . . ."). Unless the report has been severely telescoped, the woman seems never to have lost awareness of her own identity. Similarly, in *ARM* X 80:6ff. we find someone who probably received her inspiration in Terqa, journeying to Mari, gaining access to the writer of the letter, and then launching into her speech *in persona dei*. Not only is a trance unlikely in these circumstances, but it seems

[35] Malamat, "Prophetic Revelations," 210-211.

[36] See *AHw*, 586.

[37] For the distinction see T. K. Oesterreich, *Possession, Demoniacal and Other among Primitive Races in Antiquity, the Middle Ages, and Modern Times* (New York, 1930) 26ff. Both types are also known from Greek sources; see Dodds, *Greeks and the Irrational*, 297.

excluded by the introductory *umma šīma*, "thus she (spoke)," which despite the "I" of the speech being Dagan, attributes the words to the *qamatum,* not to the god (contrast *umma Annunītumma* above in (f)). In this case we seem to have an example of memory of the oracle as it was originally delivered, which would again argue for consciousness of oneself while under inspiration.

Of course from these two cases we may not generalize and conclude that this type of trance was the rule. The prophets may often or even regularly have lost consciousness of themselves and become subjectively identified with the god within them. On the other hand, it is also true that we cannot exclude simulation or dramatic imitation.[38] At this point we are groping among a wide range of possibilities with no evidence to guide us. One thing seems clear, and it bears repetition: a prophet, professional or lay, in the proper environment of the temple, had to speak as one divinely possessed.

5.

To the dreams of *RA* 42, *ARMT* XIII 112 and 113, we may now add *ARM* X 50 (No. 6), 51 (No. 7), 94 (No. 8), 117 (No. 9); *ARM* X 10 (No. 10) recounts a vision. As in *RA* 32—*ARMT* XII 112, and 113 are broken at the place in question—the description of the dreams begins with *ina šuttiya*, "in my dream" (*ARM* X 50:8; 51:8; 117:10; cf. 94:5'); this looks like a convention.[39] Like *RA* 42, too, it dispenses with all details regarding the circumstances of the dream; only *ARM* X 50 departs slightly from this rule to add a notation on the time the dream was experienced. This is quite contrary to the normal Mesopotamian "pattern,"[40] and in this respect Mari and Terqa seem to have had their own literary tradition. In the content of the dream we do find the fact mentioned that so-and-so "stepped up (to me)" (*izzizzam*, *ARM* X 51:9; *izziz*, *ARM* X 94:6'), a feature, too, of many dreams in the Babylonian tradition, which may indicate some influence on Mari,[41] Unlike *RA* 42

[38] Cf. Mircea Eliade, *Shamanism: Archaic Techniques of Ecstasy* (New York, 1964) 24-25, 200, etc.

[39] For this feature some parallels exist in Mesopotamian sources; but there it is not consistent enough to be considered typical.

[40] Cf. Oppenheim, *Dreams*, 195.

[41] Ibid. 188-189.

and, probably, *ARMT* XIII 112, none of the dreams in *ARM* X is purely auditory, the visual element either dominates (*ARM* X 50, first dream), or at least is present (*ARM* X 50, second dream; 51 and 54; 117?); this is also true of the vision in *ARM* X 10. The content of the dreams in *ARM* X 50 and of the vision in *ARM* X 10 is "symbolic" and here again we have something new, this type of dream hitherto having appeared in Mesopotamia only in literary documents.[42] In *ARM* X 51 and, probably, in 94, there is a message for the king, but only indirectly and implicitly. At least in *ARM* X 51 it seems clear that the priest is supposed to report this dream with its (implied) warning to him. Its real meaning, therefore, depends on inference, and in this respect it shares to some extent in the indirection of the "symbolic dream." For this type of dream there do not seem to be any parallels in Mesopotamian sources.[43] In brief, the new material on dreams in *ARM* X exhibits many original features and is an important addition to our corpus of texts on this subject.

No. 1 (*ARM* X 7)[44]

1 *a-na be-lí-i[a]* 2 *qí-bí-ma* 3 *um-ma* ^{mí}*Ši-ib-tu* 4 GEMÉ-*ka-a-ma* É.GAL-*lum ša-lim* 5 *i-na* É *An-nu-ni-tim* UD 3.⌜KAM⌝ 6 ^{m}*Še-le-bu-um* 7 *im-ma-ḫu um-ma An-nu-ni-tum-m[a]* 8 ^{m}*Zi-im-ri-Li-im* 9 *i-na ba-ar-tim* 10 *i-la-at-ta-ku-ka* 11 *pa-ga-ar-ka ú-ṣú-ur* 12 ÌR.MEŠ *eb-bi-ka* 13 *ša ta-ra-am-mu* 14 *i-ta-ti-ka* 15 *šu-ku-un* 16 *šu-zi-is-sú-nu-ti-ma* 17 *li-iṣ-ṣú-ru-*⌜*ka*⌝ 18 *a-na ra-ma-ni-k[a]* 19 *la ta-at-ta-na-a[l-la-a]k* 20 *ù* LÚ.MEŠ *ša i-la-a[t-ta-ku-k]a* 21 *a-na qa-*⌜*t*⌝*i-ka* L[Ú.MEŠ *š*]*u-nu-ti* 22 *ú-ma-a[l-la]* 23 *i-na-an-na a-[nu-um-ma]* 24 *ša-*⌜*ar*⌝*-ta-[am ù sí-sí-ik-tam]* 25 *ša as-s[i-in-ni-im]* 26 *a-na ṣ[e-er be-lí-ia]* 27 *ú-ša-bi-[lam]*

1-4 Speak to m[y] lord: Thus Šibtu your maid-servant. The palace is safe and sound. 5-7 In the temple of Annunītum, on the third day (of

[42] Ibid. 207.

[43] *ARMT* XIII 112 is also of this type; cf. Malamat's remarks, "Prophetic Revelations," 221-222, where biblical parallels are adduced. In *RA* 42 the message to the king is explicit.

[44] Translated by Dossin, "Prophétisme," 78ff.—The text are grouped: Nos. 1-5 public and private prophecies; Nos. 6-10 dreams and visions; Nos. 11-14 miscellaneous.

the month)[45] Šēlebum went into a trance. Thus (spoke) Annunītum: [8-11] "O Zimrī-Lim, with a revolt they would put you to the test. Guard yourself. [12-19] Put at your side servants, your controllers[46] whom you love. Station them so they can guard you. Do not go ab[ou]t by yourself. [20-22] And as for the men who wo[uld p]ut you to the test, I shall deli[ver] these men into your hand." [23-27] I have now hereby dispatched to my lord the hair and the fringe of the cult-[player].[47]

Lines 1-4: Šibtu—occasionally Šibtum—was the daughter of Yarīm-Lim of Aleppo and the wife of Zimrī-Lim, to whom she here writes; see G. Dossin, "Šibtu, reine de Mari," *Actes du XXIe Congrès International des Orientalistes* (Paris, 1949) 142-143.

Line 5: Annunītum is of Akkadian origin and in the south was worshiped especially in Agade and Sippar (D. Edzard, *Wörterbuch der Mythologie* I [Stuttgart, 1965] 42; on the problem of the etymology of her name, see R. Borger, *Einleitung in die Assyrischen Königsinschriften* I [HO 5; Leiden, 1961] 59-60). Her cult at Mari is well attested and goes back at least to the Ur-III period (*ARMT* VII 169, 194). Dossin (*Studia Mariana* [Leiden, 1950] 47) suggests she is the goddess in the so-called investiture scene (cf. M.-T. Barrelet, *Studia Mariana* 9ff.; A. Parrot, *Le Palais* II [Mission archéologique de Mari 2; Paris, 1958] 53ff.); for our own opinion see below, No. 2.

Line 6: Šēlebum is also mentioned in No. 13. He probably belonged to the cult-personnel of Annunītum's temple, and it was perhaps in the course of the liturgy that he went into his trance.

Lines 8-22: Concern for the king's safety is often expressed (No. 2, 6, 13 and *ARM* X 11:12ff., 54:16ff., 107:7ff.; see also *ARM* III 18) and as here he is advised against moving about unescorted, even in Mari (No. 13). In No. 13 the conspirators seem to be sympathizers with Ešnunna; perhaps this applies here too. Note that Šēlebum is referred to in No 13. Since Zimrī-Lim's father was murdered in a palace revolution, he is likely to have been inclined to take such warnings quite seriously; see

[45] "For three days" is grammatically possible, but ruled out by the context.

[46] For *ebbum* (pl. *ebbū*) at Mari, see J. Bottéro, *ARMT* XIII p. 160 and A. Finet, *RA* 60 (1966) 21. New occurrences: *ARM* X 3:13'; 12:8.

[47] Following *CAD* A/2; Dossin, "eunuque"; *AHw*, 75, "Buhlknabe (im Kult)"; B. Landsberger, *WZKM* 56 (1960) 120, n. 31, "'Festpriester' (Päderast)." It is probably not just a coincidence that an *assinnu* is inspired; see also No. 5.

also n. 9, above. The men Zimrī-Lim "loves" are the objects not only of his affection but of the favors and benefactions which "love" implies; cf. the Esangila which Hammurapi "loves" (CH xxivb 93-94). Hence their loyalty could be counted on.

No. 2 (*ARM* X 8)[48]

[1] *a-na be-lí-ia* [2] *qí-bí-ma* [3] *um-ma* ^{mí}*Ši-ib-tu* [4] GEMÉ-*ka-a-ma* [5] *i-na* É *An-nu-ni-tim ša li-ib-bi a-lim* [6] $^{\text{m mí}}$*A-ḫa-tum* SAL.TUR ^{d}*Da-gan-ma-lik* [7] *im-ma-ḫi-ma ki-a-am iq-bi* [8] *um-ma-mi Zi-im-ri-Li-im* [9] *ù šum-ma at-ta mi-ša-ta-an-ni* [10] *a-na-ku e-li-ka* [11] *a-ḫa-ab-bu-ub* [12] *na-ak-ri-ka* [13] *a-na qa-ti-ka* [14] *ú-ma-al-la* [15] *ù* LÚ.MEŠ *Šar-ra-ki-ia* [16] *a-ṣa-ab-ba-at-ma* [17] *a-na ka-ra-aš* ^{d}NIN-É.GAL-*lim* [18] *a-ka-am-mi-is-sú-nu-ti* [19] *i-na ša-ni-i-im* u_4*-mi-im* [20] ^{m}*A-ḫu-um* ŠANGA *ṭe*$_4$*-ma-am* [21] *an-né-e-em šar-ta-am* [22] *ù sí-is-sí-ik-tam* [23] *ub-la-am-ma a-na be-lí-ia* [24] *aš-pu-ra-am šar-ta-am* [25] *ù sí-is-sí-ik-tam* [26] *ak-nu-ka-am-ma* [27] *a-na ṣe-er be-lí-ia* [28] *uš-ta-bi-lam*

[1-4] Speak to my lord: Thus Šibtu your maid-servant. [5-7] In the temple of Annunītum in the city, Aḫātum, the servant of Dagan-mālik, went into a trance and spoke as follows, [8-14] saying: "Zimrī-Lim, even though for your part you have spurned me,[49] for my part I (shall) *embrace*[50] you. Your enemies I shall deliver into your hand. [15-18] Moreover I shall seize the men of Šarrākīya[51] and gather them to the destruction of Bēlet-ekallim."[52] [19-28] The following day Aḫum the priest brought me this report (together with) the hair and the fringe,

[48] Dossin, "Prophétisme," 82.

[49] Dossin: "même si tu me negliges." The use of *šumma* to introduce a concessive clause is not Akkadian but reflects West Semitic influence; *u šumma* perhaps represents an effort to distinguish the concessive from the usual conditional meaning of *šumma*.

[50] *ḫabābu* remains difficult (see *CAD* Ḫ, 2-3, "to caress?"). Without excluding the connotations of dalliance, we choose "embrace" as also implying protection.

[51] Dossin, "En outre, mes voleurs, je (m'en) saiserai," reading *šar-ra-qí-ia*; however, see *ARM* X 81:7 (No. 3).

[52] Dossin: "et je les rassemblerai au camp de Bêlet-ekallim." The expression *ana karāši(m) kamāsu(m)*, "to gather to destruction," is attested elsewhere in Old Babylonian (*ša . . . nišī ikmisu ana karāši*, "(Enlil) who . . . gathered the people to destruction," *Cuneiform Texts in the British Museum* 46, pl. 16:53-54, pl. 18:42-43).

and I have written to my lord. I have sealed the hair and the fringe and have dispatched (them) to my lord.

Line 5: Annunītum seems to have had two temples at Mari. This one was in the "heart of the city," which may mean inside the city as opposed to outside the city walls in the countryside (*kīdum*, *ARM* VI 37:11'; *eqlum*, *ARMT* XIII 107:13), or perhaps "the inner city" within the inner wall (*dūrum*) as opposed to the area between the inner and outer wall (*šalḫūm*).

Line 6: Aḫātum is perhaps the "housekeeper" of this name mentioned in *ARM* VIII 88:2; if so, she was part of the palace staff.

Line 15: The place is also mentioned in No. 3, but is otherwise unknown. Cf. Āl-šarrākī, *urbs oblatorum* (so A. Goetze, *JCS* 17 [1963] 20, with reference to relevant literature). In neither passage, it will be noted, is it promised that Zimrī-Lim will himself conquer it. Rather, it seems that an enemy will be removed by an ally or someone whose interests here coincide with those of Mari.

Line 17: Bēlet-ekallim, "the mistress of the palace," is listed in the "Ur-III pantheon" (Dossin, *RA* 61 [1967] 99 and in the Old Babylonian period she belongs to both the official cult and popular piety (for Mari references see Bottéro, *ARMT*: VII 194; add *ARM* IX 14; X 4 [No. 11], 50 [No. 6], 78:7; 112:16; 115:9,22[?]; 141:24; note also the personal names *Bēlet-ekallim + ummī* [*ARMT* XIII 1:65, vii 64] or *nirī* [*ARMT* XIII 1 xi 1]). She is a Sumero-Akkadian divinity, and as "the eldest daughter of Sin" is to be identified with Inanna (see R. Frankena, *Tākultu: De Sakrale Maaltijd in het assyrische Rituel* [Leiden, 1954] 105-106). At Mari she seems to be the patroness of the dynasty: it is her absence from her temple that symbolizes the exile of the exile of the Yaḫdun-Lim dynasty and parallels the absence of Dagan, who gives kingship in the land (No. 6); she is the only goddess marching with the god as they escort Zimrī-Lim in his struggle with Išme-Dagan of Assyria (No. 11). Her unique position is also implied here; the goddess Annunītum effects a destruction which either allows a role for Bēlet-ekallim or is of the type she effects, that is, we suggest, one that protects the dynasty. She is, therefore, our candidate for the "investiture" scene (see above, p. 113); cf. already Bottéro *ARMT* VII 196 (sub *iltu*).

Line 20: On Aḫum, see above p. 103.

Line 26: Sealing (see also No. 6) is a precaution against substitution.

No. 3 (*ARM* X 81)

1 *a-na Ka-ak-ka-bi* 2 *qí-bí-ma* 3 *um-ma* $^{\mathrm{[m]í}}$*I-ni-ib-ši-na-ma* 4 ^{m} ^{mí}*In-ni-ba-na a-pí-il-tum* 5 *it-bé-ma ki-a-am id-bu-ub* 6 *um-ma-a-mi Zi-im-ri-Li-im* 7 *a-lam Ša-ar-ra-ki-ia*[53] 8 [*a-na*] *a-ia-bi-šu ù ša i-ta-ti-šu* 9 [*i*]-*sà-aḫ-ḫu-ru* 10 [a-na-ad-di-iš]-*šu* 11 [ ] 12 [ ] ri x 13 [ ]*ta-al-l*⸢*a-a*⸣*k* 14 [ ] *i-*⸢*š*⸣*a-am-ma*[54] 15 *la i-*⸢*ša*⸣*-ak-ka-an* 16 *a-nu-um-ma ša-ar-ti* 17 *ù sí-sí-ik-ti ad-di-na-ki-im* 18 *li-za-ak-ku-ú* 19 *i-na-an-na a-nu-um-ma* 20 *ša-ar-tam ù sí-sí-ik-tam* 21 *a-na Ka-ak-ka-bi ú-ša-bi-lam* 22 ⸢^{m}*Ka*⸣*-ak-ka-bi te-er-tam* 23 [*li-še*]-*pí-iš-ma a-na zi-im* 24 *te-re-ti-šu Ka-ak-ka-bi* 25 ⸢*l*⸣*i-pu-úš* ^{m}*Ka-ak-ka-*⸢*bi*⸣ 26 *pa-ga-ar-šu li-iṣ-ṣú-ur*

1-3 Speak to (my) Star: Thus Inibšina. 4-5 Innibana the prophetess arose and spoke as follows, 6-10 saying: "O Zimrī-Lim, the city Šarrākīya [*I shall giv*]*e* [to] its enemies and those who [en]circle it. 11-15 . . . he must not place, 16-18 I hereby give you my hair and my fringe. Let them declare (me) free." 19-21 I now hereby send the hair and the fringe to (my) Star. 22-26 Let (my) Star [have] an omen taken so that he may act in accordance with his omens. Let (my) Star guard himself.

Line 1: Zimrī-Lim is addressed as "the Star" or "my Star" in about twenty letters. The writers are Kirû(m), Erešti-Aya, Narāmtum, Inibšina and Šibatum. Since all except the last are called his "daughter" and most address him as "father," "Star" must be a sobriquet practically reserved to the family circle and was perhaps a term of affection.

Line: 3 Inibšina is also the author of No. 13 as well as *ARM* X 82 and 83. According to M. Birot, *RA* 50 (1956), 68 line 17, she was Zimrī-Lim's daughter and according to lines 4-5 a NIN·DINGIR·RA ^{d}IŠKUR, that is, either an *entu*-priestess or an *ugbabtu*-priestess of Adad; for the two

[53] *lam* is defectively written, but no other reading is possible. That Šarrākīya is a city is clear from the reference to its "environs" (*itātīšu*, and cf. *ARM* II 137: 28-29. *itāt ālim . . . isaḫḫur)*. Nor can there be question of "the city of my thieves" (see No. 2), which would be *āl šarrāqīya*.

[54] Though the copy favors *-ša-*, *išamma* (or *–i šamma*) yields no sense in context. Read *itâmma*? *itâm šakānum*, "to establish a limit"? [Addendum: perhaps [x-x *a*]-*i-*⸢*ša*⸣*-am-ma,* "he/it is not to place [x-x an]ywhere."—W.L.M.]

terms see J. Renger, *ZA* 58 (1967) 114-149, and on Inibšina's relationship to Zimrī-Lim, 148, n. 262.

Lines 4-5: This prophetess is otherwise unknown. In view of the similar oracle in No. 2, she probably was in the service of Annunītum. On the lack of reference to a temple, see above, n. 30.

Lines 7-9: As already noted (No. 2), this city is not to be handed over to Zimrī-Lim.

No. 4 (*ARM* X 53)

1 *[a-na] be-lí-ia* 2 *[qí]-bí-ma* 3 *[um]-ma* mí dIM-*du-ri-ma* 4 [GEM]É-*ka-a-ma* 5 *[a-p]í-lum i-na* É d*[Ḫ]i-ša-me-tim* 6 *I-ṣí-a-ḫu šu-um-šu* 7 *[i]t-bé-ma um-ma-mi* 8 [š]a *wa-ar-ki-ka-ma* 9 [kar-*k*]*a-i-ka-lu* 10 [ù k]a-*as-ka* 11 [i-ša-a]*t-tu-ú*[55] 12 [it-t]i-*ka la* x a y a im 13 [(x)]-*né-e-tim* 14 *[b]e-el a-wa-ti-ka* 15 [in-*n*]*é-ṣú-u*[56] 16 *[a-n]a-ku-ma ka-ab-sà-ak-šu-nu-ti* (break)

1-4 [Sp]eak [to] my lord: [Th]us Addu-dūrī your [maid]-servant. 5-7 [A pr]ophet, Iṣi-aḫu by name, [a]rose in the temple of [Ḫ]išamētum, and (spoke) thus: 8-11 "Only your [*f*]*ollowers* will eat your [*ram*] [and *dri*]*nk* your [*cu*]*p*. 12-16 . . . your [ad]versaries will be [*sl*]*it open*. I alone have trampled them down."

Lines 3-4: Addu-dūrī also writes No. 6-7 as well as *ARM* II 114 and X 52, 54-61 (all except the last to Zimrī-Lim), she receives No. 9 from a certain Timlû and *ARM* X 142-150 from the king. She resided at Mari and was clearly a woman of considerable importance. She is also mentioned in *ARM* VII 105, *ARMT* XI 68 (see p. 130, n. 10), and *ARMT* XIII 10.

Line 5: Ḫišamētum, "the one of Ḫišamta," derives her name from one of the most important towns in the district of Terqa (see Kupper, *Syria* 41 [1964] 105). She had a temple at Mari (*Studia Mariana* 44: 22), which is referred to here, and "the gate of Ḫ." is mentioned in *ARMT*

55 Restorations based on *ARM* VIII 13:11-14: *kāram īkulū kāsam ištû u šamnam iptaššū*, "they ate the ram, drank the cup, and anointed themselves with oil," which describes the meal concluding the negotiations of the contracting parties.

56 We can make nothing out of the copy on line 12. Line 13 *a*]*nnêtim?* Line 15, as if from *eṣû* (*inneṣṣû*), but a *pis aller*. A form of *šutēṣûm* (*uštēneṣṣû*) would make some sense, but the space does not allow us to restore [*uš-te-n*]*é-ṣú-ú*.

XIII 31:8. To judge from *ARM* X 128, the queen was quite devoted to her. The exact nature of the goddess eludes us.

Line 6: PN *šumšu,* lit. "PN his name" is used at Mari of slaves (*ARM* VIII 9:2-3; 10:1), as is also the practice in Babylonia. This is perhaps some indication of the prophet's origins and present social status.

No. 5 (*ARM* X 6)[57]

^{1} *a-na be-lí-ia* ^{2} *qí-[b]í-ma* ^{3} *um-ma* ^{mí}*Š[i-i]b-tu* GEMÉ-*ka-a-m[a]* ^{4} É-GAL-*l[um] ša-lim* ^{5} ^{m}*I-[lí-ḫa-a]s-na-a-ia* ^{lú}*a[s]-s[i-i]n-n[um]* ^{6} *ša* DINGIR [x]-x-*li-i[m]* ^{7} *i-na* T[U-]-X ^{8} [a-na É An-nu-ni-tim i-ru-*u]b-ma* ^{9} [DINGIR-lum aš-šum LÚ x-x-(x)]-x^{ki} ^{10} [a-na be-lí-ia *iš-t]a-ap-ra-šu* ^{11} [ki-a-am *i]q-bi* ^{12}[um-ma-mi a-na]-*ku* $^{rev.\ 1'}$ [ ]x A[N x-x-(x)] $^{2'}$ w-x-y-z *áš-ta-al-⌜ma⌝* $^{3'}$ LÚ *šu-ú ma-da-tim a-na ma-a-tim an-ni-tim* $^{4'}$ *ú-ša-am ú-ul i-ka-aš-ša-ad* $^{5'}$ *be-lí i-im-ma-ar ša* DINGIR-*lum* LÚ *ša-a-ti* $^{6'}$ *i-ip-pé-šu ta-ka-aš-ša-as-sú* $^{7'}$ *ù e-li-šu ta-az-za-az* $^{8'}$ *u*$_4$*-mu-šu qé-er-bu ú-ul i-ba-al-lu-uṭ* $^{9'}$ *be-lí an-ni-tam lu-ú i-de* $^{10'}$ *la-ma te*$_4$*-em Ì-li-ḫa-as-na-a-⌜ia⌝* $^{11'}$ *ša An-nu-ni-tum iš-pu-ra-aš-[š]u* $^{12'}$ [U]D.5.KAM *a-na-ku áš-ta-a-al-[m]a* $^{13'}$ [*ṭe*$_4$]*-mu-um ša An-nu-ni-[tum]* $^{14'}$ [*iš-p*]*u-ra-ak-kum* $^{15'}$ *ù ša a-ša-lu* $^{16'}$ *iš-ti-in-ma*

$^{1-4}$ Sp[ea]k to my lord: Thus Š[i]btu your maid-servant. The palace is safe and sound. $^{5-10}$ I[lī-ḫa]snāya, the c[ul]t-p[la]ye[r] of . . .,[58] in . . . [*enter*]*ed* [*the temple of Annunitum*] and [*the god(dess)* ha]s sent him here [*to my lord with regard to the man of* . . .] . . . $^{11-12}$ [*Thus she* sp]oke, [saying: "I] (Break). Rev. $^{1'-2'}$ [ ] . . . I inquired, and $^{3'-4'}$ this man is determining many things for the land. He will not succeed. $^{5'-9'}$ My lord will see what the god(dess) will do to this man. You will conquer him and over him you will stand. His days are short. He will not survive. My lord should know this. $^{10'-16'}$ Before the report of Ilī-ḫasnāya which Annunītum sent here, on the fifth [d]ay (of the month) I myself had made inquiry, and the [rep]ort which Annunītum sent here to you and that which I asked for agree perfectly.

[57] The reverse 3'ff. is translated by Dossin, "Prophétisme," 82-83.

[58] Dossin identifies Ilī-ḫasnāya as a eunuch of Annunītum. Unless this is on the basis of unpublished evidence, it must come from his reading of line 6. How the traces of X can be reconciled with *An-[nu-ni-ti]m* or what is then to be done with *li-i[m* + possibly a small sign] we do not see. On *assinnu*, "cult-player," see n. 47.

Lines 5-12: According to Dossin, Ilī-ḫasnāya, who appears only here, was the bearer of a prophecy on Hammurapi of Babylon. This identification of Zimrī-Lim's adversary, attractive as it may be, seems questionable since in the two places on which the identification could possibly be based, the copy does not support KÁ·DINGIR·RA^{ki}, either in line 9 ([KÁ. DINGIR· R]A^{ki}) or in line 1' ([K]Á·DIN[GIR· RA^{ki}).

Lines 1'-2': By the time the text resumes after the break (roughly 15 lines), in our opinion it is Šibtu herself who is here waxing optimistic. Dossin, who leaves lines 1'-2' untranslated, encloses lines 3'-9' within quotation marks, so that in his opinion either the goddess is still speaking or Ilī-ḫasnāya is commenting on his own. Neither seems likely. Certainly the goddess made no inquiries (*aštālma*, Line 2'), and the one inquiring in line 2' is speaking in lines 3'ff. Moreover, it would be unparalleled for the agent of the deity to add an exegesis of his message; he is either one with the deity or its messenger, but not its commentator. So the speaker must be Šibtu, and this fits perfectly with the fact that in lines 12' and 15' she reappears as the inquirer.

Lines 3'-8': The style is noteworthy. Note the careful balancing of long clause (*awīlum šû . . . ušām*), asyndetic short clause (*ul ikaššad*), long clause (*bēlī . . . ippešu*, one syllable shorter than the first long clause) asyndetic short clause (*takaššassu,* same length, same vocable as in parallel), expansion (*u elīšu tazzaz*); finally, two terse clauses, again with asyndesis. Here conciseness reflects the reality, the few days remaining to the enemy, just as in the opening sentences the stylistic contrast reflects the contrast between the "many things" planned and the sharp check of defeat. In a kind of *inclusio*, the fate of the enemy is summed up in (*ul ikaššad*) . . . *ul iballuṭ*. Intervening is the goddess, and the juxtaposition of her action (*ippešu*, "she will do") and the king's (*takaššassu*, "you will conquer him") gives expression to their essential unity in the reality of victory. In short, this seems to us a prose of an uncommonly high level for these letters. On possible influences see below.

Lines 10'-16': Dossin translates: "Avant la communication de Ili-haznâia que (la déesse) Annunîtum t'a envoyée,[59] moi-même je l'avais interrogé. La communication que (la déesse) Annunîtum t'a envoyée et ce sur quoi je l'ai interrogé sont tout à fait identiques." Thus, accord-

[59] "to you" is not in the Akkadian.

ing to him, before the revelation of Annunītum Šibtu had already been in contact with Ilī-ḫasnāya and had made inquiries from him about Zimrī-Lim's enemy. If true, this would be quite important; it would mean that this type of revelation could be sought and in a sense provoked; thus, a new psychological factor would be introduced to explain the origin of the revelations. However, we do not accept Dossin's interpretation of these lines for the following reasons: (1) it depends on a dubious reading in line 12' (*aštāl*[*š*]*u* instead of *aštāl*[*m*]*a*, our reading) and on reading in the suffix *–šu* ("him") in line 15' where the text simply has *ašālu* (not *ašālušu*); (2) though Šibtu obviously thinks there is something remarkable present, it is hard to see what is really remarkable about the communication of the goddess bearing on a matter of prior inquiry; (3) it is not likely that the queen would consult an *assinnu* instead of a professional like the *āpilu*, to say nothing of the haruspex;[60] (4) Dossin's translation obscures or misses the fact that there are two reports involved, the one the goddess sent and the one Šibtu asked for,[61] which only makes sense if she had consulted someone else besides Ilī-ḫasnāya; it also makes her argument very clear: two independent reports yielding the same results, assurance of the king's victory, mutually confirm one another. Of course, the most likely source of one report is the haruspex, and this is borne out by the language, which is strongly reminiscent of the apodoses of the omen literature.[62] In view, too, of what we have already seen above about

[60] For another type of consultation, see No. 11.

[61] This is the most natural reading of 13'-15', *ṭēmum ša . . . u ša*. Moreover, *ṭēmam šâlum* (*ARM* I 103:12; for the restoration, see von Soden, 21 [1952] 82) or *šitūlum* (*ARM* II 29:11, 45:8; 96:14; 141:8; VI 27:15; 59:6; 60:5'; 62:9) is well attested; cf. also No. 11:3-6 (*aššum ṭēm . . . aštālma*). Finally, note *ṭēmum šû ul ištēn*, "the information (in two different reports) is inconsistent" (*ARM* VI 44:10), and *wurti bēliya . . . u wurti RN . . . ištêt*, "the order of my lord . . . and the order of Hammurapi . . . agree" (*ARM* II 24:11'-12'). Šibtu's report is found in lines 3'-8'; for the sequence of *aštāl* + *ma* + report, cf. below No. 11:6ff. (*aštālma igerrûm . . .*).

[62] *eli x izuzzum*, "to step up and stand over someone" ("qui traduit l'attitude 'sculpturale' du vainqueur," J. Nougayrol, *RA* 44, 93): *RA* 44, 9:5; *YOS* X 35:7-8, 39 rev. 9; 45:49; 47:78 = 48:17; 48:35 = 49:7; 49:36 = 49:8; 56: i 29-30, iii 28-29 (all Old Babylonian). *ūmūšū qerbū*: cf. *ūmātūšu qerbā* (Old Bab. omen; Oppenheim, *AfO* 18/l [1957] 63: 18). *ul iballuṭ*: see passages cited *CAD* B, 54 (without the negative, which has a closer parallel in the Esnunna laws: see p. 57 3' b); and cf. J. Nougayrol, *Or* 32 (1963) 382:1-2; 384:35. *Kašādu* of course is too common to need citation.

the control of prophecy by the haruspex, under this hypothesis the full force of Šibtu's argument becomes apparent: the consoling message brought by Ilī-ḫasnāya has been already submitted in a sense to the haruspex, and therefore it can be taken as a basis of action.

No. 6 (*ARM* X 50)[63]

^{1} *a-na be-lí-ia qí-bí-ma* ^{2} *um-ma* $^{mí\,d}$IM-*du-ri* GEMÉ-*ka-a-ma* ^{3} *iš-tu šu-lu-um* É *a-bi-ka* ^{4} *ma-ti-ma šu-<ut>-tam an-ni-tam* ^{5} *ú-ul a-mu-ur it-ta-tu-ia* ^{6} *ša pa-na-nu-um* ^{7} [*an*]*-ni-it-ta-an* ^{8} *i-na šu-ut-ti-ia a-na* É ^{d}NIN-É.GAL-*lim* ^{9} ⌜*e*⌝*-ru-ub-ma* ^{d}NIN-É.GAL-*lim* ^{10} *ú-ul wa-aš-ba-at* ù ALAM.ḪI.A ^{11} *ša ma-aḫ-ri-ša ú-ul i-ba-šu-ú* ^{12} *ù a-mu-ur-ma ar-ṭú-ub ba-ka-a-am* ^{13} *šu-ut-ti an-ni-tum ša ba-ra-ar-tim*[64] ^{14} *a-tu-ur-ma Da-da* ^{lú}ŠANGA ^{15} [*š*]*a Eš$_{4}$-tár-pí-iš$_{7}$-ra* ^{16} *i-na* KÁ ^{d}NIN-É.GAL-*lim* ^{17} *iz-za-az-ma pí-ú na-ak-rum* ^{18} [*ki*]*-a-am iš-ta-na-ás-si* ^{19} *um-ma-mi* ⌜*tu*⌝*-r*[*a*] ^{d}*D*[*a-ga*]*n* ^{20} *tu-ra* ^{d}*Da-gan ki-a-am* ^{21} *iš-ta-na-ás-si ša-ni-tam* ^{22} ^{mí}*mu-uḫ-ḫu-tum i-na* É *An-nu-ni-tim* ^{23} *it-bé-e-ma um-ma-mi Zi-im-ri-Li-im* ^{24} *a-na* KASKAL.A *la ta-al-la-ak* ^{25} *i-na Ma-ri*^{ki} *ši-ib-ma* ^{26} *ù a-na-ku-ma a-ta-na-ap-pa-al* ^{27} *be-lí a-aḫ-šu la i-na-ad-di* ^{28} *a-na pa-ag-ri-šu na-ṣa-ri-im* ^{29} *a-nu-um-ma ša-ar-ti* ^{30} *ù sí-sí-ik-ti* ^{31} ⌜*a*⌝-[*na-ku*][65] *ak-nu-ka-am-ma* ^{32} *a-na ṣe-er be-lí-ia* ^{33} *ú-ša-bi-lam*

$^{1\text{-}2}$ Speak to my lord: Thus Addu-dūrī your maid-servant. $^{3\text{-}7}$ Since the peace of your father's house I have never had this dream. These were my signs before.[66] $^{8\text{-}11}$ In my dream I entered the temple of Bēlet-ekallim, and Bēlet-ekallim was not in residence nor the statues before her present.[67] $^{12\text{-}13}$ And I saw (this) and then went on weeping. This

[63] Translated by Dossin, "Prophétisme," 84.

[64] Dossin's translation ("Ce songe que j'ai eu est [un présage de] révolte") is a slip, reading *bārtum* for *barartum*.

[65] Hardly space for two signs, but no other restoration seems possible.

[66] Dossin: "Les signes que j'ai eus auparavant étaient (tout) autres." *annittān* = "(tout) autres"? Dossin perhaps reads [*sa*]*-ni-it-ta-an,* as suggested to us by J. Finkelstein, but such a form—both the allophone *-itt* for *it*, and the *an* ending—seems to us improbable.

[67] On the problem of the nature of Bēlet-ekallim's presence, see Agnes Spycket, *Les statues de culte dans les textes mésopotamiens des origines à la Ier Dynastie de Babylone* (Paris, 1968) 97-98; she correctly identifies the other statues as those of kings of the dynasty and other worshipers.

dream of mine was in the evening-watch. [14-21] Again (I dreamt) and Dāda, the priest of Ištar-pišrā, was on duty in the gate of Bēlet-ekallim, and an eerie voice kept crying this over and over, saying: "'Come back, O Dagan. Come back, O Dagan.'"[68] This it kept crying over and over. [22-23] Moreover, the ecstatic arose in the temple of Annunītum and thus (spoke), saying: "Zimrī-Lim, [24-26] "do not go on an (the?) expedition. Stay in Mari, and then I alone will take responsibility." [27-28] My lord must not be negligent in guarding himself. [29-33] I my[self] hereby seal my hair and fringe and send (them) to my lord.

Lines 3-7: A dream from which Addu-dūrī has not suffered since the restoration of the dynasty, she has now seen again.[69] This she finds ominous, the more so in that an ecstatic has recently warned the king to stay in the city (21-26). This only deepens her uneasiness, and so she writes Zimrī-Lim. As a measure of her concern and sincerity, and possibly, too, as a means of forcing Zimrī-Lim to submit the matter to the haruspex, she sends the legal symbols of her own accord (27-33, and note the emphatic *anāku* in line 31). What are the "signs"? There are several ways of explaining the plural, but we think the most likely is that in her earlier dream, which in its recurrence seems to have been interrupted (line 13), she both saw the empty temple and heard the eerie voice. As to what makes them signs, it must be noted that, though in the present situation they could well be considered portents, this could not have been true earlier, because neither the temple nor the voice gave any hint of the future. On the contrary! We submit that they were signs because they were indications of another reality—the absence of the dynasty.[70] This would explain why Addu-dūrī finds their reappearance so very troubling.

[68] Dossin: "Tura-Dagan! Tura-Dagan!" But what is a personal name doing here? A Tūra-Dagan was governor of Mari in the Ur-III period (F. Thureau-Dangin, *RA* 34 [1937] 172ff.; E. Nassouhi, *AfO* 3 [1926] 109ff.; G. Dossin *apud* A. Parrot, *Le palais de Mari*, II/3, 251) but it is hard to see why he should be singled out to be called upon.

[69] The fact of the recent recurrence was pointed out to me by Professor Thorkild Jacobsen.

[70] For a recent discussion of "sign" in Akkadian, including the one previous occurrence at Mari (Dossin, *Syria* 19 [1938] 126), see B. Landsberger, *WO* 3 (1964) 71ff., especially 73, n. 97, C. Other occurrences at Mari are now *ARM* X 4 (No. 11), where the meaning is "portent," X 117 (No. 9), and X 141:25, in both passages *lū ittum*, "let this be a sign." The poorly preserved state of the former makes it difficult to analyze the term

Lines 8-11: On Bēlet-ekallim, see above, No. 2, and on "In my dream" see above, p. 111.

Line 13: We think it more likely that this remark applies only to the recent recurrence of the dream. Unquestionably the time is mentioned as a detail of some significance. The general context suggests that it only added to the ominousness, but there is no outside evidence to corroborate this.[71]

Line 14: The significance of a priest of another goddess at the gate of Bēlet-ekallim may be that this alien presence reflects the latter's absence, her clergy having departed with her. Ištar-pišrā(n) is known only at Mari (see Bottéro, *ARMT* VII, p. 343); she is associated with Šamaš in Mišlān, a town between Mari and Terqa.[72] Her priest is otherwise unknown, unless he is the Dāda who is so frequently associated with Šamaš as a creditor in temple-loans.[73]

Lines 17-21.: Since the cry is one of lamentation, at once a mourning for the departure of the god and a plea for his merciful return, the voice cannot be hostile, and nothing suggests that it was "foreign." Hence it must be strange, eerie.[74] Dagan was "the king of the land," and to this ancient lord of the Mari region its rulers owed their power and authority.[75] For the dynasty of Yaḫdun-Lim whom he made king,[76] the absence of the god could only mean the end of its rule.

Lines 22-26: The "quietism" of the oracle (see also below, No. 11), which would keep the king within the protecting walls of the capital and reserve all real action to divine intervention, anticipates by centuries the similar advice of the Ištar of Arbela to Assurbanipal (*ANET* 451). Of course it also recalls the silent, passive ranks of Exodus 14 and the extreme position of Isa 30:15. On the connection between this passage and *ARM* VI 45, see above, p. 103.

---

in context. In the latter, the meaning is clearly "signal": *lū ittum inūma šamû iznunū ḫussinnīma* . . . , "let this be the signal: when the skies rain, remember me . . ."

[71] Oppenheim, *Dreams*, 187, 240-241.

[72] On Mišlān, see J. Kupper, *Syria* 41 (1964) 105-106.

[73] See *ARM* VIII 27ff.

[74] Cf. *nukkur*, "(x) ist sehr fremdartig" (*AHw*, 720).

[75] For Dagan in the Mari documents, see Dossin, *Syria* 21 (1940) 165-168.

[76] *Dagan šarrūtī ibbi*, "Dagan pronounced my kingship" (inscription of Yaḫdun-Lim, F. Thureau-Dangin, *RA* 33 [1936] 51:9-10).

No. 7 (*ARM* X 51)[77]

1 *a-na be-lí-ia* 2 *qí-bí-ma* 3 *um-ma* $^{\text{mí d}}$IM-*du-ri* 4 ^{m}*I-din-ì-lí* ^{lú}ŠAN-GA 5 *ša* ^{d}*I-túr-me-er* 6 *šu-ut-tam iṭ-ṭú-ul* 7 *um-ma šu-ú-ma* 8 *i-na šu-ut-ti-ia* 9 ^{d}NIN-*bi-ri iz-zi-iz-za-am-ma* 10 *ki-a-am iq-bé-em* 11 *um-ma ši-i-ma* 12 *di-ru-*⸢*t*⸣*um na-*a[m-l]a-a[k-t]a-[šu] 13 *ù pa-lu-um du-ur-šu* 14 *a-na* É *ki-im-tim* 15 *a-na mi-ni-im i-te*$_{9}$*-né-el-li* 16 *pa-ga-ar-šu* [*li-iṣ-ṣ*]*ú-ur* 17 *i-na-an-na be-lí a-na na-ṣa-ar* 18 *pa-ag-ri-šu* 19 *la i-ig-ge*

1-3 Speak to my lord: Thus Addu-dūrī. 4-7 Iddin-ilī, the priest of Itūr-Mer, saw a dream. Thus he (spoke): 8-11 "In my dream Bēlet-biri stepped up to me and spoke as follows. Thus she (spoke): 12-16 ". . .[78] is [*his*] *k*[*in*]*gs*[*hi*]*p* and the rule is his permanent possession.[79] Why does he keep going up again and again to the 'family-house?'[80] [Let him] guard himself." 17-19 Now my lord must not be negligent in guarding himself.

Lines 4-5: Itūr(Yatūr)-Mer was the patron god of Mari; in *ARM* X 63:16 he is called "the king of Mari," and his cult there goes back to at least the Ur-III period, though at that time he does not seem to have enjoyed such prominence.[81] He is an "Erscheinungsform" of Mer (Old Akkadian)-Wer (Ur III and later).[82] On his priest we have no further information unless he is to be identified with the man of the same name who in the time of Šamšī-Adad is designated a *kumrum* (a type of priest) in *ARM* VIII i:37 (cf. also *ARMT* XIII 74:4?).

Line 9: The Mesopotamian goddess Bēlet-biri, apart from a month

[77] Translated by Dossin, "Prophétisme," 84.

[78] Dossin: "grandeur (?)."

[79] Dossin: "sa condition(?)." For *dūru(m)*, "permanent status or property," see *CAD* D, 198; *AHw*, 178; as something belonging to the family and inherited, see T. Jacobsen, *ZA* 51 (1957) 120-121, n. 63.

[80] Dossin: "Pourquoi s'adresse-t-il continuellement aux présages?" He must read *(g)is-ki-im-tim*, but the only form attested is masc. *giskimmu*; see *CAD* G, 98; *AHw*, 291. [Addendum: Father Richard Caplice reads ^{gis}*di-im-tim,* "(siege-) tower," which makes excellent sense, is probably correct, and hence renders dubious our remarks based on the reading *bīt kimtim*.—W.L.M.]

[81] See Dossin, *Syria* 21 (1940) 154-159; see also the Ur-III "pantheon" text, Dossin, *RA* 61 (1967) 100.

[82] See I. Gelb, *Glossary of Old Akkadian* (2d ed.; Chicago, 1957) 180.

named after her, is mentioned only here in the Mari documents. The month name implies a festival for her at that time, but no sanctuary of hers is known and her popularity does not seem to have been great, to judge from her absence in personal names. The significance of her presence here escapes us.

Lines 12-16: The interpretation of these lines depends largely on the meaning of the expression "family-house." The goddess seems to argue that, since Zimrī-Lim's kingship is hereditary and permanent, his frequent trips to the "family-house" are unnecessary. This implies that the motive behind the trips was in some sense to render his rule secure, as if he now doubted its permanence. The "family-house" is mentioned elsewhere only three times,[83] and only one occurrence gives any clear indication of its purpose. This is an inscription of Sennacherib, in which *bīt kimti* is used of his grave.[84] A second occurrence[85] which is found in a copy of the time of Assurbanipal, but which could well go back to the Old Babylonian period, heads a list of "houses" that might be visited by a man in a dream; nothing points to its being a grave, but on the other hand nothing is opposed to such a meaning. Finally, a Hittite king asks the king of Babylon for an engraver or sculptor who can make images to be placed in the "family-house" (written logographically, É IM.RI.A).[86] Here it can hardly mean grave, which is called the "stone-house" in Hittite sources, but it might be some sort of mortuary-chapel which at least in the case of the royal family we know in one instance to have been decorated with a statue and wall-reliefs.[87]

Family grave or mortuary-chapel would certainly fit the context of

[83] See *AHw*, 479.

[84] *Keilschrifttexte aus Assur historischen Inhalts* (WVDOG 16; Leipzig, 1911) 42: 3 (É *kim-ti šuršudu*, "firmly built *b.k.*). E. Weidner, *AfO* 13 (1939) 215, n. 72, deduces that members of Sennacherib's family were also buried with him at Assur. F. Delitzsch, *Das Land ohne Heimkehr* (Stuttgart, 1911) 13, is reminded of OT "being gathered to one's fathers."

[85] Oppenheim, *Dreams*, 312 rev. 10 (following *AHw*'s reading *ki-im-ti-šu* instead of *ki-sit-ti-šu*).

[86] *Keilschrifttexte aus Boghazköi* I (WVDOG 30; Leipzig, 1930) 10 rev. 58; text is cited in *CAD* E, 350 sub *ēṣiru*.

[87] On the existence of such a chapel at Yazilikaya, see H. G. Güterbock, *MDOG* 86 (1953) 65-76, especially 74-76. If "family-house" should prove inapplicable to such a structure in Hittite sources, this would not be an insuperable difficulty for the meaning we postulate in Mesopotamia proper.

bīt kimtim in our passage. At such a place filial reverence would be shown to the ancestors of the dynasty, and here too would special cultus be given to Dagan, who was both "the king of the land" and "the lord of mortuary-offerings."[88] It is obvious how such observances could be thought of as especially suited to make fast a throne that had begun to appear insecure.[89] In a time of severe crisis, behind which we should probably see the threat of Hammurapi, this extraordinary zeal for the *manes* of former rulers and sheikhs and especially for the god on whom all kingship in the area ultimately depended, makes perfect sense.

Under this hypothesis, too, some of the psychological factors behind the dream are perhaps also hinted at. A priest of Itūr-Mer, "the king of Mari," could well be perturbed if the king's devotion to Dagan had in his eyes become excessive. His resentment might find release in a dream which, in perhaps censored form, he could pass on to the king.

No. 8 (*ARM* X 94)

[1] *a-na be-lí-ia* [*Kak-ka-bi-im qí-bí-ma*][90] [2] *um-ma* [mí]*Ši-ba-t*[*um* GEMÉ-*ka-a-ma*][91] [3] *iš-tu* u_4*-mi-im ša iš*-[x-x-x-x-x] [4] *ma-di-iš al-ta*-[su-um] [5] *ù a-la-ni ka-la-šu-nu a*-[ta-ma-ar] [6] *ša ki-ma šu-ba-at be-lí-ia*] [x-x-x-x] [7] *ù ša ki-ma be-lí-ia i*-[x-x-x-x] [8] *i-na-an-na šum-ma be-lí a-n*[*a* x-x-x-(x)] [9] *a-na a-la-ki-im pa-nu-šu ša*-[*ak-nu*] [10] [x-x-x] *li*-x-y-z[x-x-x-(x)] (Break) Rev. [1'] [x-x-x-(x)] *a-na pa-an* [*be-lí-ia*] [2'] [x-(x)]-x *ú-ṣa-ab-ba*-[*at*-(ma)] [3'] *ù pa-an be-lí-ia* [lu-mu-ur] [(x-x-x)] [4'] *ù aš-šum i*-x

[88] *bēl pagrê* (*ARM* X 63:15). For the latter term, see *ARM* XV, *Repertoire analytique* 238, and cf. Ugaritic, *pgr*, "mortuary-offering" (W. F. Albright, *Archaeology and the Religion of Israel* [Baltimore, 1946] 106). How *pagrû* differed from *kispū*, the ordinary Akk. term for mortuary-offerings, is not clear; we suspect the former is a West Semitic synonym. Properly speaking, the offerings to Dagan would be made in the é-ki-si-ga (Akk. *bīt kispī*); such a sanctuary Šamšī-Adad built for Dagan at Terqa (E. Ebeling - B. Meissener - E. Weidner, *Die Inschriften der altassyrische Könige* [Leipzig, 1926] 26, no. 5).

[89] The word *palûm* (line 13) suggests of itself only a "turn" at ruling; for the various nuances of the term, with references to earlier literature, see J. Finkelstein, *JCS* 20 (1966) 105-106.

[90] Restoration based on *ARM* X 95:1.

[91] Or perhaps Šimatum (so Dossin in index of *ARM* X).

[x-x]-*ar* x-[x-x-(x)] 5' *i-na šu-ut-ti*[92] *um-ma* LÚ *mi*-[x-x-x-x] 6' *iz-zi-iz-ma um-ma šu-ma* 7' SAL.TUR.DUMU.MUNUS ᵐᶦx-*pa-hi-im* x-[x-(x)] 8' ᵐ ᵐᶦ*Ta-gi-id-na-ti-e li-i*[*š-ša-si*] 9' *an-ni-tam iq-bé-e*-[*e*]*m i-na-an-na* 10' *be-lí wa-ar-ka-tam* DUMU.MÁ[Š.ŠU].GÍD.GÍD 11' *li-ša-ap-ri-is-ma šum-ma* [*š*]*u*-⸢*u*⸣*t-tum š*[*i-i*] 12' *n*[*a-a*]*ṭ*-⸢*la*⸣*-at be-lí* SAL.TUR *ša-a-ti* 13' *qí-im-*[*m*]*a li-iš-ša-si* 14' *ù šu-lum be-lí-ia lu-ú* x-y-z-[(x)]

1-2 [Speak] to my lord [the Star]: Thus Šibat[um your maidservant]. 3-7 From the day that [. . .], I have [*run about*] a good deal and *ha*[*ve seen*] all the cities which like the dwelling(s?) of my lord [. . .], and which like my lord [. . .]. 8-10 If my lord is determined to go t[o . . .], [. . .] let him . . . [. . .] (Break) Rev. 1'-4' *I shall set out* [. . .] to (*meet*) my lord and the face of my lord I *would see*. And with regard to . . . 5'-8' In the dream (it went) thus: A man of [. . .] stepped forward and thus he (spoke): "Let the girl, the daughter of X-pahim . . ., Tagidnatê, be sum[moned]." 9'-14' This he said to me. Now let my lord have the ha[rus]pex look into the matter, and if this [dr]eam was s[e]en, my lord, have confidence in this girl[93] and let her be summoned. And may the *health* of my lord . . .[94]

Line 2: Šibatum is also the writer of *ARM* II 115 and *ARM* X 95; she is referred to in *ARM* X 32:20'; 33:6, 33. In the latter passages she is residing with Kirûm, a daughter of Zimrī-Lim, in the house of a certain Ḫalisumu, probably the ruler of Ilanṣūra. It is perhaps from there that she goes about inspecting the cities, possibly in view of a visit of

[92] Or *šu-ut-ti-*<*ia*>, "in <my> dream"? See above, p. 123.

[93] We assume *qīpma* > *qīmma* (see *GAG* § 27 c). Also possible is *kīnma* > *kīmma*, but no meaning of *kunnum* yields any sense, except perhaps "to check on, verify," and even this is objectionable, since after the favorable response of the haruspex one does not expect any further action on the king's part except to summon her. In any case, in view of the oblique *šâti*, we are dealing with a verb form; there is room at the end of line 13' for one or two signs, but not enough for a verb. The imperative is not expected; mistake for <*li*>-KI-*im-ma*? (Is there also an omission in line 3: *ištu ūmim ša* <*bēlī*> *iš*[*puram*], "from the day my lord wrote me . . ."?)

[94] The illegible traces are not those of *ka-ia-(a)-an* or *sa-di-ir*, both of which are so frequently used as predicates of *šulum bēliya*, "the greeting of my lord." Besides, the prep. phrase *ana ṣēriya* (or the like) is missing. Hence we prefer taking *šulum* as "health," with the possible implication that the girl in question has some healing powers.

the king (? lines 3-10). On the implications of her addressing him as "Star," see No. 3.

Lines 5'-8': Lacking context, we cannot see the full import of the dream.

Lines 10'-12': On the significance of this request, see above, p. 105.

No. 9 (*ARM* X 117)

^{1} *a-na* $^{mí\ d}$IM-*du-ri be-el-ti-ia* ^{2} *qí-bí-ma* ^{3} *um-ma* ^{mí}*Ti-im-lu-ú* GEMÉ-*k*[*a-a-ma*] ^{4} *lu-ú it-tum-ma ša i-nu-ma* DIŠ-x-[x] ^{5} *i-na li-ib-bi Ka-sa-pa-a*^{ki} ^{6} [^{m}]*Ia-ar-ib-*^{d}*Ab-ba ú-še-ṣe-i*[*n-ni*] ^{7} [*ù a-n*]*a*[95] *ṣe-ri-ki al-li-ka-a*[*m-ma*] ^{8} [*ki-a-am*] *aq-bi-ki-im um-ma* ⸢*a*⸣-[*na-ku-ma*] ^{9} [*šu-ut-t*]*a-am a-mu-ra-ki-i*[*m-ma*] ^{10} [*i-na šu-u*]*t-ti-ia An-nu-um-ti-*[*il-la-ti*] ^{11} [x-x-x-x-x *iš-p*]*u-ra-an-ni* [(x-x)] (Break)

$^{1-3}$ Speak to Addu-dūrī my mistress: Thus Timlû yo[ur] maidservant. $^{4-8}$ Let it be a sign[96] that at the time of . . . Iarʾib-Abba expelled me from Kasapâ, I came to you and said this to you, saying: $^{9-11}$ "I had a [dre]am concerning you and [in] my [dre]am Annumti[*llatī*][97] [. . . *she* s]ent me (Break).[98]

Line 3: Nothing more is known about Timlû. If on being expelled from Kasapâ, a town somewhere to the north of Mari, she came to the capital, then she may be mentioned in *ARMT* XIII 1 viii 73.

Line 10: Annu(m) is well documented in personal names, especially those of women; the identity of this god is a problem that need not detain us here. Whether Annum appeared, or a person with a name bearing this theophorous element (so our restoration), cannot be decided.

[95] Space requires the restoration of *ù*; if *inūma* is a conjunction, then on the construction, see A. Finet, *L'accadien des lettres de Mari* (Mémoires Academie Royale de Belgique, Classe des lettres et des sciences morales et politiques 51; Brussels, 1956) § 85f.

[96] On *ittum* here, see above, n. 70.

[97] Cf. the personal name Annu-tillatī, *ARMT* XIII 1 x 2.

[98] We omit the reverse, which is badly broken. What is legible has no apparent connection with the obverse.

No. 10 (*ARM* X 10)[99]

^{1} *[a-na be-lí-ia qí-bí]-m[a]* ^{2} *[um]-ma* ^{mí}*Ši-ib-tu* GEMÉ-*ka-a-m[a]* ^{3} É DINGIR.MEŠ DINGIR.MEŠ É.GAL-*lum* ^{4} *ù ne-pa-ra-tum ša-al-ma* ^{5} *ša-ni-tam* ^{mí}*Ka-ak-ka-li-di* ^{6} *i-na* É ^{d}*I-túr-Me-er i-mu-ur* ^{7} *um-ma-a-mi* 2 ^{giš}*má-ma-al-lu-ú* ^{8} *ra-ab-bu-tum na-ra-am pa-ar-ku-ma* ^{9} LÚGAL *ù* $^{\text{lú.meš}}$*re-du-um* ^{10} ŠÀ-*ba ra-ki-ib ša i-mi-it-tim* ^{11} ⸢*ù*⸣ *šu-mi-lim* ^{12} *[i]-ša-as-su-ú* ^{13} *[u]m-ma šu-nu-ma šar-ru-tum* ^{14} *[ḫa-a]ṭ-ṭú-um [ù]* ^{giš}⸢GU⸣.ZA ^{15} ⸢n⸣a-*ma*-⸢ad⸣-d⸢u⸣-*tum e-li-tum* ^{16} *ù*⸢*ša*⸣-*ap-li-tum* ^{17} *a-na Zi-im-ri-li-im* ^{18} *na-ad-na-at ù* $^{\text{lú.meš}}$*re-du-ú-um* ^{19} *ka-lu*-⸢*šu i*⸣-*ip-pa-al* ^{20} *a-na Z[i]-im-ri-Li-im-ma* ^{21} *na-ad*-⸢*na*⸣-*at* ^{22} ^{giš}*má-m[a-a]l-lu-ú šu-nu* ^{23} ⸢*a-na ba*⸣-*ab* É.GAL-*lim* ^{24} [x-x-x]-*ma* ^{25} [ ]-*šu* (Break)

$^{1\text{-}4}$ [Speak to my lord]: Thus Šibtu your maid-servant. The temples, the gods, the palace, and the workshops are safe and sound. $^{5\text{-}7}$ Moreover, Kakkalidi had the following vision in the temple of Itūr-Mer: Two huge *mamallû*-boats[100] $^{8\text{-}13}$ were blocking the river, and the king with the soldiers were on board in the center. Those on the right and the left were [sh]outing. Thus (they spoke): "Kingship, $^{14\text{-}18}$ [sce]pter and throne, the upper and the lower *region*,[101] have been given to Zimrī-Lim." And the soldiers $^{19\text{-}21}$ to a man were answering: "To Zimrī-Lim alone have they been given." $^{22\text{-}25}$ These *mamallû*-ships to the gate of the palace . . .

Lines 5-7: The visionary is otherwise unknown. That this is a vision and not a dream seems certain; if it were a dream, the text would say so.

Lines 8-13: "Those at the right and the left" are not the soldiers (so Dossin), for the latter answer. They are either people on both sides of the river, or, as seems to us more likely, the crews along the sides of the ships who flank the king and his soldiers in the center (*libba*).

[99] Translated by Dossin, "Prophétisme," 83.

[100] Dossin: "deux bateaux *mallû*." Our own opinion: *mamallû* < *malallû* (*AHw*, 594, "Lastschiff") by regressive assimilation. Note the use of the *mamallû*-ship elsewhere to transport king (2×) and divine statues (1×). [Addendum: In view of Sum. ^{giš}má.lá, Dossin's reading is preferable.—W.L.M.]

[101] Dossin: "région," but with no question mark. *namaddūtum—si vera lectio*—is otherwise unattested; it looks like an abstract of *namaddum*, which is well known but in a meaning (measuring-vessel, *AHw*, 725) not apposite here.

No. 11 (*ARM* X 4)

1 *a-na be-lí-ia qí-bí-ma* 2 *um-ma* ^{mí}*Ši-ib-tu* GEMÉ-*ka-a-ma* 3 *aš-šum ṭe*$_4$*-em ge-er-ri-im* 4 *ša belí i-la-ku it-ta-tim* 5 *zi-ka-ra-am ù sí-in-ni-iš-tam* 6 x-y[102] *áš-ta-al-ma i-ge-er-ru-ú-um* 7 *a-na be-lí-ia ma-di-iš da-mi-iq* 8 *a-na Iš-me-*^{d}*Da-gan qa-tam-ma* 9 *zi-ka-ra-am ù* ⸢*sí*⸣*-in-ni-iš-tam* 10 *áš-ta-al-ma i-ge-er-ru-šu* 11 *ú-ul da-mi-iq* 12 *ù ṭe*$_4$*-em-šu ša-pa-al še-ep be-lí-ia* 13 *ša-ki-in um-ma šu-nu-ma be-lí ḫu-ma-ša-am* 14 *a-na Iš-me-*^{d}*Da-gan «ḫu-ma-ša-am» iš-ši-ma* 15 *um-ma-<mi> i-na ḫu-ma-ši-im e-le-i-ka* 16 *ši-it-pu-ṣú-um ši-it-pa-aṣ-ma* 17 *i-na ši-it-pu-ṣú e-le-i-ka* 18 *um-ma a-na-ku-ma be-lí a-na ka-ak-ki* 19 *i-ṭe*$_4$*-eḫ-ḫe-e um-ma šu-nu-ma* 20 *ka-ak-ku* 21 *ú-ul in-né-pé-šu* 22 *ki-ma ka-ša-di-im-ma* 23 *ti-il-la-tu-šu* 24 *is-sà-ap-pa-[ḫ]a* 25 *ù qa-qa-[ad Iš-me]-*^{d}*Da-gan i-na-ki-sú-ma* 26 *ša-pa-al še-ep [b]e-lí-ia* 27 *i-ša-ak-ka-nu um-ma-a-mi* 28 *ṣa-bu-um ša Iš-me-*^{d}*Da-gan* 29 *ma-ad ù šum-ma* ⸢*a*⸣*-[ka-aš-š]a-ad* 30 *til-la-tu-šu is-sà-a[p-pa]-ḫa-šu* 31 *til-la-ti-<im>*[103] *i-ia-at-tu es-ra* ^{d}*Da-gan* 32 ^{d}IM ^{d}*I-túr-Me-er ù* ^{d}NIN-É.GAL-*lim* 33 *ù* ^{d}IM-*ma be-el pu-ru-us-sé-e-em* 34 *ša i-na i-di be-lí-ia i-l[a-ku]* 35 *as-sú-ur-ri be-lí ke*[104]*-em i-[qa-ab-bi]* 36 *um-ma-a-mi i-na til-la-ni* ⸢*ú*⸣-[sa-aḫ-ḫa-ap-š]*u-nu-ti* 37 *mi-im-ma ú-ul* ⸢*ú-ša*⸣*-ad-ba-[ab-šu-nu-ti]* 38 *šu-nu-ma i-da-ab-bu-bu šu-nu-[ma]* 39 *im-ta-ḫa-[ru]* 40 *um-ma šu-nu-ma til-la-at Iš-me-*⸢^{d}⸣*[Da-gan]* 41 ^{lú}*a-sí-ru i-na sà-ra-tim* 42 ⸢*ù*⸣ *de-ṣa-*⸢*tim*⸣ *it-ti-šu it-ta-na-šu* 43 [x-x]-*sû*! *ú-ul i-le-qú-ú* 44 *[a-n]a pa-ni be-lí-ia ṣa-bu-šu* 45 *[is]-sà-ap-pa-aḫ*

1-2 Speak to my lord: Thus Šibtu your maid-servant. 3-7 For a report on the campaign which my lord is on, I asked a man and a woman . . . for the signs, and the word is very favorable to my lord. 8-11 Similarly, with regard to Išme-Dagan I asked the man and the woman, and the word on him is not favorable. 12-17 And as to the report on him, he has been placed under the foot of my lord. Thus they (spoke): "My lord

[102] BAR.KI?

[103] If the subject were *tillatī* (fem. sg. + pron. suff.), the verb would be *esret*. Besides, *tillātum* (fem. pl.) is the regular form. Therefore, we must assume an error, *iāttu(n)* for *iātti(n)*.

[104] Copy: *di*. Restoration *i[qabbi]* certain on basis of many parallels: F. Thureau-Dangin, *RA* 38 (1941) 41:10; *ARM(T)* III 1:20-21; 3:9-11; V 52:8-9; V 67:21; VI 23:10; XIII 9:22-23, etc.

lifted the *ḫumāšum*[105] to Išme-Dagan, and (spoke) thus: 'With the *ḫumāšum* I will beat you. Just wrestle and I will beat you in wrestling.'" [18-31] Thus I (spoke): "My lord is drawing near to battle?" Thus they (spoke): "A battle will not be fought. Right on arriving his (Išme-Dagan's) auxiliary troops will be scattered; furthermore, they will cut off the head of Išme-Dagan and put (it) under the foot of my lord. Thus (my lord will say): 'The army of Išme-Dagan is large, and if I *a*[*rriv*]*e*, will his auxiliary troops be scattered from him?[106] They have hemmed in my auxiliary troops.' It is Dagan, [32-34] Adad, Itūr-Mer, and Bēlet-ekallim—and Adad indeed is the lord of decision!—who ma[rch] at my lord's side. [35-36] Heaven forbid that my lord should s[ay] this, saying: 'By means of arms[107] I (must) [*lay*] them [*low*].'" [37-39] I am not making [them] spe[ak]. On their own they speak, on their [own] they agre[e]. [40-45] Thus they (say): "The auxiliary troops of Išme-[Dagan] are (made up of) prisoners. With acts of treachery *and deception*[108] they . . .[109] *with* him. They do not accept[110] *his* [. . .]. B[e]fore my lord his army will be scattered."

Lines 3-13: The war with Išme-Dagan has already started (see 31) and Zimrī-Lim is in the field, though so far the opposing forces have not clashed. In this situation the queen wants "signs," evidence from the

[105] *(ḫ)umāšu* as object of the verb *našû*, "to lift," must be the concrete object rather than "strength"; for a survey of occurrences, see W. von Soden, *ZA* 51 (1955) 142. J. van Dijk, *La sagesse suméro-akkadienne* (Leiden, 1953) 116, has proposed "maillon." On *ša umāši*, "athlete," see B. Landsberger, *WZKM* 56 (1960) 115-117; on the object *(ḫ)umāšu*, 116, n. 26. According to T. Jacobsen, *ZA* 51 (1957) 130-131, n. 90, the athlete in question is to be identified as a "bruiser, boxer."

[106] If this is an interrogative clause, as we interpret it, one would expect either *is-sà-ap-pa-ḫa-šu-ú* or *a-ka-aš-ša-a-ad*.

[107] Cf. *AHw*, 120 *bēlu* II. The pl. *tillānū* is not surprising at Mari, where this plural-morpheme is found also with *šipru*, etc.

[108] We assume a variant of *dāṣātum*, which is explained by *sarrātu* (see *CAD* D, 118); on *dâṣu*, "to cheat, dupe," see B. Landsberger, *WO* 3 (1964) 51, n. 27.

[109] If the verb is *našû* (*ittanaššû*, Gtn or Ntn pres.; but *-šu-ú* expected), "to break camp, leave," occurs as a possibility, but if desertion were meant, one would expect *ipaṭṭarū* (*iptanaṭṭarū*). The masc. ending suggests *<ša>* after *asīrū*. [Addendum: J. Finkelstein reads *it-ta-na-<la>-ku*, "they comport themselves." This seems convincing.—W.L.M.]

[110] Or read *i-li-ku-û*, "did they not go . . .?"

gods, on the outcome, and she asks a man and a woman. Our inability to read the first two signs in line 6 is particularly unfortunate, for they might help to understand better these somewhat enigmatic figures, who appeal to no authority—they are neither sent nor possessed by a god—and employ, so far as we can tell, no other mantic devices. They simply speak, make "utterances," which are an interesting blend of piety (31-34) and reasoning based apparently on some knowledge of the military situation (40-45). A crucial term here is *igerrûm* (6, 10), "utterance," which is still only imperfectly understood.[111] Oppenheim has shown that in some cases it is like the Greek *kledon*, a chance utterance with oracular significance.[112] But this does not fit here; the speeches of the man and woman are solicited by the queen. Perhaps they are considered oracular because of their independent agreement, or perhaps the essential point is that they are spontaneous and unprompted except for some general question like, "What do you know about my lord?" This would bring the *igerrûm* as used here fairly close to the chance utterance.

Lines 13-17: Did Zimrī-Lim actually make such a challenge? Is this a survival of the combat of champions?

Lines 25-27: Beheading an enemy of the king and sending the trophy to him are also mentioned in *ARM* II 33:5'-6' (cf. II 48:16; VI 37:7'ff.). It is to this prediction that Šibtu seems to refer in lines 12-13. Note there the use of the stative (*šakin*), which reminds one of the "prophetic perfect." Once the word of lines 25-26 was spoken, Išme-Dagan has been, and is (in the state of), placed under the foot of Zimrī-Lim.

Lines 27-31: Though a new speaker is not introduced, the content of these lines demands that they be ascribed to the king; for a similar abrupt transition see *ARM* II 33:8'. Peculiar to this passage is the fact that the king did not actually make this objection, which is rather foreseen by the speakers.

Lines 31-36: The objection from the size of Išme-Dagan's army and the parlous situation of Zimrī-Lim's own auxiliary forces is denied any validity on the grounds that divine assistance will more than compensate for lack of numbers. It is also hoped that the king will not be so lacking in faith as to suggest that wars are won with weapons. These

[111] See *CAD* E, 44, 3.b. "unidentified oracular utterance."

[112] *AfO* 17 (1954-55) 49ff.

lines will evoke in the minds of Old Testament scholars many a biblical passage. The gods who are at the king's side are, with the possible exception of Adad, just the ones we expect: Dagan, "the king of the land," Itūr-Mer, "the king of Mari," and Bēlet-ekallim, in our opinion the protectress of the dynasty. Adad is given a high rank, right after Dagan, and this is explained—he is "the lord of decision" (that is, through oracles he renders judgment?).

Line 37: The queen's insistence that she is not responsible for these favorable "utterances" indicates a cautious scepticism on the part of the king; see also above on line 36.

Lines 40-45: Despite some obscurities, the point of this speech is clear: the auxiliaries of Išme-Dagan are unwilling and disloyal conscripts, and hence no real threat to Zimrī-Lim.

No. 12 (*ARM* X 9)

^{1} *a-na be-lí-ia* ^{2} *qí-bí-ma* ^{3} *um-ma* ^{mí}*Ši-ib-tu* ^{4} GEMÉ-*ka-a-ma* É.GAL-*lum ša-lim* ^{5} ^{m}*Qí-iš-ti-*^{d}*Di-ri-tim* ^{6} *a-pí-lu-um ša* ^{d}*Di-ri-tim* ^{7} UD 2.KAM *a-na ba-ab* É.GAL-*l*[*im il-li-kam-ma*] ^{8} [*k*]*i-a-am iš-pu-ra-am* [*um-ma šu-ma*] ^{9} *a-na pa-ni* ^{giš}G[U].⌜ZA⌝ *Ma*-[ri^{ki}] ^{10} *ma-am-ma-an ú-ul i-q*[*a*-ab-bi] ^{11} *a-na Zi-im-r*[*i-li-im*] ^{12} *a-la-i-tum na-a*[*d*-na-at] ^{13} ^{gis}ŠUKUR LÚ *e*-[x-x-x-x-(x)] ^{14} *an-ni-tam* [iš-pu-ra-am] *ša-n*[*i-tam* . . .] (Break) Rev. $^{1'}$ *um-ma*[ ] $^{2'}$ *ki-im*-x-[ ] $^{3'}$ *ni-i*[*š* DINGIR-*lim* . . .] $^{4'}$ *a-šar* m[u-ú i-ba-aš-šu-ú] $^{5'}$ *ni-iš* DINGIR-*lim ni-n*[*u* ni-za-ak-ka-ar] $^{6'}$ ^{d}*A-šu-me-zu* ⌜mu⌝-*um*[ ] $^{7'}$ ^{d}*A-su-mu-um* ar-[ ] $^{8'}$ *a-wa-tam a-na* ^{d}*É*-[*a* iq-bi] $^{9'}$ *ša* ^{d}*A-sú-mu-um* [a-na ^{d}É-a iq-bu-ú] $^{10'}$ *ú-ul eš-me it*-[bé-ma ki-a-am] $^{11'}$ *iq-bi um-ma-mi* [la-ma *ni-iš* DINGIR-*lim*] $^{12'}$ *ni-za-ak-ka-ru ru*-[*ša-am*] $^{13'}$ *ù sí-ip-pa-am ša ba-ab* [*Ma-ri*^{ki} (x)]-x $^{14'}$ *li-il-qú-nim-ma ni-iš* DINGIR-*lim* [i ni-iz-ku-ur] $^{15'}$ *ru-ša-am ù sí-ip-pa-am ša ba*-[*ab*] *Ma-ri*^{ki} $^{16'}$ *il-qú-ni-im-ma i-na me-e im-ḫu*-⌜*ḫu*⌝-*ma*[113] $^{17'}$ DINGIR.MEŠ *ù i-la-tum iš-te-e* $^{18'}$ *um-ma* ^{d}*É-a-ma a-na* DINGIR.MEŠ $^{19'}$ *ti-ma-a ša a-na li-bi-it-ti* $^{20'}$ ⌜*Ma-ri*⌝^{ki} *ù ra-bi-iṣ* $^{21'}$ [<Ma-ri^{ki}> la-a tu]-*ga-al-la-lu* $^{22'}$ [DINGIR.ME]Š *ù i-la-t*[*um it-ma-a*] $^{23'}$ [*um-m*]*a-mi a-na li-bi-it-ti* $^{24'}$ [*Ma*]-*ri*^{ki} *ù ra-bi-iṣ* $^{25'}$ *Ma-ri*^{ki} $^{26'}$ *ú-ul nu-ga-al-la-a*[*l*]

113 The second -*ḫu* is a bit dubious, but no other reading seems possible. Of course "to dissolve" applies properly only to the "dirt," by zeugma to the "jamb" (*sippu* also includes the base of the door-frame).

[1-4] Speak to my lord: Thus Šibtu your maid-servant. The palace is safe and sound. [5-8] Qišti-Dirītim, the prophet of Dirītim, on the second day (of the month) [came] to the gate of the palac[e] [and] sent [t]his message to me. [Thus he (spoke). [9-15] "Before the throne of *Ma*[*ri*] no one *s*[*peaks*] (saying?), "To Zimrī-Lim the *alaītum* has been *g*[*iven*].' The lance of the . . . [. . .]. This is the message [he *sent me*]. An[other matter . . .] (Break) Rev. [1'] 'Saying [". . .] [2'] . . . [3'] an o[ath . . .] [4'] where [*there is*] *wa*[*ter*], [5'] we ourselves [*shall pronounce*] an oath. [6'] Ašume-zumum [. . .] [7'] Asumum [. . .] [8'] a word to E[a *he spoke*] [9'] What Asumum [*said to Ea*] [10'] I did not hear. *He a*[*rose and thus*] [11'-14'] he spoke, saying: "[*Before*] we pronounce [the oath], let them take the dirt and jamb of the gate of [Mari] . . . , and then [*let us pronounce*] the oath." [15'-17'] "The dirt and the jamb of the gate of Mari they took and dissolved in water, and then the gods and goddesses drank. [18'-21'] Thus (spoke) Ea: "Swear to the gods that [*you*] will [*not*] harm the brick-work of Mari or *a commissioner*[114] of Mari."[115] [22'-26'] [The god]s and goddess[es swore,[116] sa]ying, "We shall not har[m] the brickwork of [Ma]ri or the *commissioner* of Mari."

Lines 5-6: Dirītum had a temple at Mari and another at Zurubban, a town between Mari and Terqa; she is also well attested in personal names.[117] "The one of Dir (Der)," she may be named after Der in the

[114] No stable office of "commissioner" comparable to that of the "commissioners" in the Amarna and Ugaritic documents (see most recently, A. F. Rainey, *Or* 35 [1966] 426-28) is known at Mari. Hence the position is likely a temporary one, and in view of the role the gate plays we may suggest that the commission was the interrogation of the opposing parties in legal disputes, apparently on behalf of the city (cf. Old Assyrian *rābiṣ ālim,* and see B. Landsberger—K. Balkan, *Belleten* 14 [1950] 266).

[115] If we restore [*Ma-ri*[ki]] in 21' there is room for only one more sign, and *tu/ú-gallalu* yields no sense in the context. Hence our assumption of <*Ma-ri*[ki]>—haplography—and restoration *la-a tu*]-. The construction *timâ ša* . . . is unknown to the writer in Akkadian; West Semitic influence (cf. Gen 24:3: *wĕʾašbîʿăkā . . . ʾăšer lōʾ tiqqaḥ . . .*)? [Addendum: The proposed restoration, especially the 2 sg. *tugallalu,* has little to recommend it.—W.L.M.]

[116] The difficulty with *itmâ* is that the direct quotation does not exhibit any attested oath-construction. We would expect *lā nugallalu*. A restoration [*iq-bé-e*] would remove this difficulty, but create another—a contrast between Ea's command and the execution.

[117] The evidence on Dirītum at Mari is assembled by M. Birot, *Syria* 41 (1964) 55. Add *ARM* X 142:30; 160:10; 171:10.

east Tigris area, or possibly after the town of the same name near Mari; cf. Ḫišamētum above (No. 4).

Lines 9-15: Its very poor state of preservation makes this text extremely obscure. Of the obverse we can say little except that the prophet does not seem to have a message from his goddess, but only a personal protest against something or other; cf. *ARM* III 78.

Lines 1'ff.: The reverse is no clearer. It may or may not be connected with the issue of the obverse. Someone (the prophet of Dirītum?) seems to witness (10' "I did not hear")—in a dream? in a vision?—a meeting of the assembly of the gods of the Ea-circle.[118] The background, which is probably lost in the break and would identify the subject of "let them take" and "they took," is completely obscure. The point of putting the jamb of the gate and dissolving some of its dirt in water (of a river? 4'?) is perhaps to put the "essence" of the brickwork of Mari in a form that can be imbibed by the gods, who by their swearing about it interiorize, so to speak, the oath itself and put its power within themselves.

No. 13 (*ARM* X 80)[119]

[1] *a-na Ka-ak-ka-bi* [2] *qí-bí-ma* [3] *um-ma* [mí]*I-ni-ib-ši-na-ma* [4] *i-na pa-ni-tim Še-le-bu-um as-sí-in-nu* [5] *te-er-tam id-di-*[*na*]*m-ma aš-pu-ra-kum* [6] *i-na-an-na* [m mí]*qa-ma-tum* [7] *ša* [d]*Da-*[*gan*] *ša Ter-qa*[ki] [8] [*i*]*l-li-ka-am-ma* [9] *ki-a-am iq-bé-e-em* [10] *um-ma ši-i-ma* [11] *sa-li-ma-tum ša* LÚ *Èš-nun-na*[ki] [12] *da-aṣ-tum-ma* [13] *ša-pa-al* IN.NU.DA *mu-ú* [14] *i-il-la-ku ù a-na še-tim* [15] *ša ú-qa-aṣ-ṣa-ru a-ka-am-mi-is-sú* [16] *a-al-šu ú-ḫa-al-la-aq* [17] *ù ma-ak-ku-ur-šu* [18] *ša iš-tu aq-da-mi* [19] [*l*]*a šu-ul-pu-ut ú-ša-al-p*[*a-a*]*t* [20] *an-ni-tam iq-bé-e-em* [21] *i-na-an-na pa-ga-ar-ka* [22] *ú-ṣú-ur ba-lum te-er-tim* [23] *a-na li-ib-bi a-lim*[[ki]] [24] *la te-er-ru-u*[*b*] [25] *ki-a-am eš-me um-ma-a-mi* [26] *a-na ra-ma-ni-šu iš-ta-na-ar-r*[*a*]*-a*[*r*] [27] *a-na ra-ma-ni-ka la ta-áš-t*[*a*]*-na-ar-ra-a*[*r*]

[118] In 18'-19' they swear "to the gods," so those discussing and eventually swearing must be a smaller group. Ea of course is mentioned, and, if the water imbibed is river-water, this would best fit with Ea and his entourage. The gods Ašumezumum (?) and Asumum are otherwise unknown. (Asumum = Us(u)mu, the Janus-figure and vizier of Ea?)

[119] Translated by Dossin, "Prophétisme," 83.

[1-3] Speak to the Star: Thus Inibšina. [4-9] Earlier Šēlebum, the cult-player, gave me an oracle and I wrote to you. Now the *qamatum* of Dagan of Terqa came and said this to me, [10-12] thus she (spoke): "The peace-moves of the man of Ešnunna are sheer deception. [13-19] Beneath the straw the waters course,[120] but I shall gather him into a net which holds fast.[121] I shall put an end to his city, and his property, which from ancient times has not been destroyed, I shall destroy."[122] [20-24] This is what she said to me. Now guard yourself. Without an omen do not enter the city. [25-27] Here is what I hear, thus (it is said): "He keeps moving about by himself." You are not to keep moving out by yourself.[123]

Lines 1-3: See above, No. 3.

Lines 4-5: Whether there is any connection between this oracle and Šēlebum's experience reported in No. 1, is not certain. However, both letters are concerned with the king's safety, the first because of sedition, this one because the peace-moves of the king of Ešnunna are not to be trusted. Some connection seems probable.

Line 6: [m mí]*qa-ma-tum* looks like a personal name because of the first determinative, but this is virtually excluded by the following phrase, "of Dagan." So *qa-ma-tum* must be a common noun. Dossin trans-

[120] Dossin: "elles [= les marques d'amitié = *salimātum*] sont de l'eau qui coule sous la paille." The Akkadian does not permit such a rendering, which should reflect something like *mû (ša) šapal tibnim illakū šinā(ma)*. Besides, such a translation misses the point (see commentary).

[121] Dossin: "mais avec le blé que je moissonnerai." He obviously reads *še-im* for the *še-tim* of the copy, and then interprets *qaṣāru* in the light of West Semitic (cf. Hebr. *qāṣîr*). The undissimilated form, instead of *ukaṣṣaru*, is West Semitic, but if the copy is accurate (*še-tim*), then it has nothing to do with harvesting. Instead of "which holds fast," perhaps "which I shall draw tight."

[122] Dossin: "Et, quant à son trésor, qui (existe) depuis des temps anciens, je le saccagerai aussi de fond en comble." This seems to ignore the first sign in line 19, and to be based on *šu-ul-pu-tam ušalpat*. At Mari, however, we should have *šulputum(ma) ušalpat*. We assume an error, *šulput* for *šulputu* (cf. *ARM* II 48:19; III 5:20; V 46:6). A reading *šulputam* would obviate this difficulty, but we see no reason for a ventive.

[123] Dossin: "'Il a continuellement peur (?) pour sa personne.' Pour ta personne, n'aie aucune peur (?)" After the warning 21-24, this hardly fits the context. For our own translation: (a) *šarāru* = *alāku* (commentary on Šurpu II 78; see E. Reiner, *AfO* Beiheft 11 [Graz, 1958] 51: 31); (b) No. 1, line 18, *ana ramānika lā tattanallak*. Cf. W. von Soden, *GAG* §101g, "*šarāru* etwa 'hin und her schwanken.'"

lates "prophétesse extatique," but without comment; he perhaps thinks of West Semitic *qûm*, "to rise." Or is the right reading *qa-ba-tum* and the form *qabbātum* (*parrāst* formation), "a (professional) speaker" (Akk. *qabûm*)? [Addendum: In view of PN *u* PN *ša bēliya* (*ARM* II 107:10) and PN *ša šipirtim (ARM* II 46:5) *qa-ma-tum* may be taken as a personal name.—W.L.M.]

Lines 11-19: Despite the introductory *umma šīma*, "thus she (spoke)," the "I" of lines 11-19 must be Dagan; the woman could hardly promise she would destroy Ešnunna, etc. On the "ecstatic style" here, see above p. 110f. To illustrate his charge against Ešnunna, the god adds to our collection of proverbs: "Under the straw the waters course." This clearly means that one should not trust appearances. Beneath the flotsam which seems to lie so quietly on the surface of the water, there is the dangerous movement of the current. The relative frequency in these prophecies of the metaphor of the net should also be noted (see *RA* 42 and *ARMT* XIII 23).

No. 14 (*ARM* X 100)[124]

[1] *a-na be-⌜lí⌝-i[a]* [2] *qí-bí-ma* [3] *um-ma* ^{mí}x-*na-na* GEMÉ-*ka-a-ma* [4] *i-nu-ma i-na ⌜Ga⌝-ni-ba-ti-im*^{ki}[125] *úš-bu* [5] ^{mí}*Ku-uk-ki-im-ḫi-ia a-na Ru-ub-be-en aš-pu-ur-ma* [6] *i-na a-la-ki-ša it-ba-lu-ši* [7] *ù* $^{\text{[d]}}$*Da-gan be-el-ka ú-ṣa-al-li-la-am-ma* [8] *ma-am-ma-an ú-ul il-pu-ta-an-ni* [9] ^{d}*Da-gan ki-a-am iq-bé-em um-ma šu-ma* [10] *pa-nu-ki e-li-iš ša-a[p-li]-iš* [11] *um-ma a-na-ku-ma ša-ap-li-i[š]-ma* [12] *al-li-ka-am-ma* [13] SAL.TUR-*ti ú-ul a-mu-ur* [14] *i-nu-ma a-na An-da-ri-iq*^{ki} [15] *be-lí il-li-ku* [16] *zi-im zi-mu ša* SAL.TUR-*ti-ia* [17] *it-ti Sa-am-me-e-tar* [18] *i-le-em-ma* [19] *al-li-ik-šu-um-ma a-an-na-am i-pu-la-a[n-ni]* [20] *i-tu-úr-ma ib-ba-al-ki-ta-an-ni-ma* [21] SAL.TUR-*ti ú-ul id-di-na-am* [22] ^{d}*Da-gan ki-a-am iq-bé-em um-ma šu-ma* [23] *a-di it-ti Zi-im-ri-Li-im* SAL.TUR-*ta-ki* [24] *la ú-še-ṣé-em ma-am-ma-an* [25] *ú-ul ú-wa-aš-ša-ra-[k]i-iš-<ši>* [26] *i-na-an-na ki* ŠÀ.DI.IB *ša* ^{d}*Da-gan* [27] SAL.TUR-*ti be-lí la i-ka-al-la*

1-3 Speak to my lord: Thus x-nana your maid-servant. 4-8 When I lived in Ganibātum, I sent Kukkimḫija (with a message) to Rubben,

[124] Translated by Dossin, "Prophétisme," 84-85.

[125] Dossin: *Qar-ni-ba-ti-im*^{ki}.

and on her way they made off with her, but Dagan, your lord, protected me[126] and so no one touched me. [9-10] Dagan said this to me. Thus he (spoke): "Did you head up (or) down?" [11-13] Thus I (replied): "Down, and I came here and did not find my girl. [14-18] When my lord went to Andariq, the very image of my girl appeared here with Sammêtar, and [19-21] I went to him and he ga[ve me] his consent. Again he broke faith with me[127] and so did not give me my girl," [22-25] Dagan said this to me. Thus he (spoke): "Until the time Zimrī-Lim frees your girl,[128] no one will release <her> to you." [26-27] Now, in accordance with the wrath of Dagan,[129] my lord must not detain my girl.

Line 4: Ganibātum was located on the Middle Euphrates between Terqa and Emar; for further identification, see M. Burke, *RA* 55 (1961) 147-151; W. W. Hallo, *JCS* 18 (1964) 73.

Line 5: The girl and the place (?) are otherwise unknown.

Lines 7-8: Dagan is also called Zimrī-Lim's lord in *ARM* X 62:14-15, a letter written from Terqa. This may suggest the provenience of our

[126] Dossin: "Ensuite, (le dieu) Dagan, ton seigneur, m'a fait coucher." It is on the basis of this understanding of *uṣallilam* that he suggests there is question here of incubation. But if there were a D-stem of *ṣalālu* which meant "to make (someone) lie down/sleep," the personal object would surely be in the acc., and here we would have *uṣallilanni*. Hence, despite the accompanying difficulties of interpretation, we take *ṣullulu* as a denominative of *ṣillu*, "shade, protection," distinguishing the transitive meaning "to roof" and the intransitive "to afford protection" (cf. the similar distinction in *dummuqu* and *gullulu* [on the transitive use of *gullulu* see Landsberger, *WZKM* 57, 11, n. 47]). This also clarifies the otherwise obscure "no one touched me." Perhaps the protection was that of sanctuary.

[127] Perhaps *itūr* does not have auxiliary force ("again"), but is to be taken literally, "he went back" (to where he came from). Dossin: "il revint (sur sa parole)." Does *târu* ever have this meaning? Our translation implies a somewhat loose use of *nabalkutu*, as if in being party in some way to the kidnaping, Sammêtar had already broken faith with her.

[128] Dossin: "Aussi longtemps qu'il ne fera pas sortir ta filette sur l'ordre de Zimrī-Lim." We take *adi itti* as the subordinating conjunction; cf. *itti* in *ARM* I 31: 30; and *AHw*, 405 "während."

[129] Dossin: "sur l'ordre de Dagan" (reading *ki-ma qí-ib?*). ŠÀ.DI.IB seems clear in the copy, and this we take as a syllabic spelling of ŠÀ.DIB = *zenû* "to be angry," etc. *kī* as a preposition would be new at Mari; read *ki-<ma>?* Dagan's wrath, it is true, is not apparent, but the writer may have thought this threat evident, given Dagan's interest in her case.

letter. Terqa fits well, too, with the accessibility of Dagan we find here.[130] In lines 5-6 there is nothing to suggest that the writer accompanied the girl. The protection, therefore, ascribed to Dagan, which came down to the kidnapers not coming into Ganibātum and making off with her too, seems a pious exaggeration (see, however, n. 126).

Lines 9ff.: There are two problems. The first is whether 9-25 constitute one dialogue, or Dagan speaks on two different occasions. Favoring the latter is the fact that one has the impression the god speaks fairly soon after the kidnapping, and by the time he speaks again a considerable period of search and negotiation has intervened. However, under this alternative, on the first occasion the god speaks he would simply ask a question and give no advice whatever. This seems implausible, and so we follow Dossin and take 9-25 as one dialogue. A more serious problem is how the god and the woman communicate. As it stands, the passage reads like an old epic. The intervention of the god is quite abrupt, without a hint of the circumstances.[131] Perhaps the answer to the problem lies in the identity of the writer. This is another unresolved question.

[130] Though Dagan was certainly worshiped at Mari, so far his "revelatory" activities have been confined to Terqa and Tuttul.

[131] Cf. the identical problem in the text W. 19900, 1 published by J. van Dijk, *XVIII vorläufiger Bericht über . . . die Ausgrabungen in Uruk-Warka* (Berlin, 1962), Tafel 28; cf. his remarks, pp. 61-62.

CHAPTER 11

An Ancient Prophetic Oracle

In the preface to *Morgenröte*, Nietzsche left us a memorable statement on the nature of the philological enterprise:

> Philologie nämlich ist jene ehrwürdige Kunst, welche von ihrem Verehrer vor allem eins heischt, beiseite gehen, sich Zeit lassen, still werden, langsam werden—als eine Goldschmiedekunst—und kennerschaft des *Wortes*, die lauter seine vorsichtige Arbeit abzutun hat und nichts erreicht, wenn sie es nicht *lento* erreicht . . . sie lehrt *gut* lesen, das heisst langsam, tief, rück- und vorsichtig, mit Hintergedanken mit offengelassenen Türen, mit zarten Fingern und Augen lesen.[1]

In offering Norbert Lohfink a brief Babylonian interlude, this passage comes to mind, for I cannot fail to recall, well and fondly, the many times, many years ago, when we sat together and discussed a text. On those occasions I had the pleasure of watching at his task of love—slow and patient, with doors left open, with second thoughts, with looks ahead and looks behind, with sensitive eyes and touch—one of philology's true votaries. I learned much from this experience, and this seems a good place to acknowledge my debt and to record my gratitude.

I wish here to look briefly at an Old Babylonian document that is not without interest to the biblical scholar. Found at Ishchali, probably

[1] F. Nietzsche, *Morgenröte: Gedanken über die moralischen Vorurteile* (Insel Taschenbuch 678; Frankfurt am Main, 1983) 15.

ancient Nerebtum, a site east of Baghdad in the Diyala River basin, it belonged in the archives of the chief administrator (sangum) of the temple of the goddess Kititum, and it records a message of this goddess to Ibal-pi-el, king of nearby Eshnunna and the surrounding area, and a contemporary of Hammurabi of Babylon. It has been copied and edited, with extensive commentary, by Maria deJong Ellis.[2] The text, normalized and in sense lines, is as follows:[3]

A 1 *šarrum Ibal-pī-el*
2 *umma Kitītumma*
B 3 *niṣrētum ša ilī maḫrīya šaknā*
4 *aššum zikrum ša šumīya ina pīka kayyānu niṣrēt ilī aptanatti-akkum*
C 5 *ina milki ša ilī ina šipṭi ša Anim mātum ana bêlim nadnatkum*
6 *šēn mātim elītim u šaplītim tapaṭṭar*
7 *makkūr mātim elītim u šaplītim tabedde*
8 *maḫīrka ul imaṭṭi*
9 *ēm mātim qātka ikšudu . . . tanēḫtim . . .*
10 *išdī kussêka anāku Kitītium udannan*
11 *lamassam nāṣirtam aštaknakkum*
D 12 *uzukka libbašīam*

A 1 King Ibal-pi-el.
2 Thus Kititum:
B 3 The secrets of the gods lie before me.
4 Because the invocation of my name is ever in your mouth, I shall reveal to you, one by one, the secrets of the gods.
C 5 At the advice of the gods, by the decision of Anum, the country is given to you to rule.

[2] Ellis, "The Goddess Kititum Speaks to King Ibal-pi-el: Oracle Texts from Ishchali," *MARI* 5 (1987) 235-266. In this article Ellis also publishes a copy of another text, very badly damaged but of the same format.—I wish to acknowledge that before publication Dr. Ellis very kind sent me her copy of the text and has very generously acknowledged my own small contribution. If I use this occasion to register my occasional disagreements with her interpretation, it is only to make clear my own understanding and in no way to minimize either her contribution or my debt to her.

[3] For a transliteration, see Ellis, "Goddess Kititum," 258.

6 The sandals of the Upper Country and the Lower Country you will loosen.
7 The treasures of the Upper Country and the Lower Country you will have at your disposal.
8 Your trade will not slow down.
9 Wherever in a country your hand has reached, . . . peace . . .
10 The foundations of your throne I, Kititum, shall make firm.
11 With a protective spirit I have provided you.
D 12 Let your attention be mine.

Notes to Text and Translation

1: Despite the fact that it lacks the proper format, Ellis calls our document a letter, and in this she has been followed by D. Charpin and A. Malamat.[4] Consistent with this view, she translates: "O Ibal-pi-el, thus Kititum." But who is speaking? She does not say, nor does she offer any explanation why the proprieties of communication by letter were not observed.

Rather, then, than assume a breach of form and an unidentified speaker (writer), I take "King Ibal-pi-El" as an archival gloss to identify the "you" of the oracle that follows and probably, too, to serve for filing purposes.

The phrasing of the gloss should be noted. Normal word-order would put the personal name first, followed by title. In departing from the normal, the title is stressed and it deftly anticipates the content of the oracle, concerned as it is with themes of central importance to kingship. It is precisely as king that Ibal-pi-el is addressed by the goddess. The gloss is perhaps also a shorthand notation indicating the temporal context of the oracle, namely, the accession of the king or some time early in his reign.

2: The speaker is identified, but who serves as *vox deae*? The contemporary religious scene argues strongly in favor of a prophetic figure like the *āpilum* (*āpiltum*), so familiar from the Mari archives and now

[4] Ellis, "Goddess Kititum," 237; D. Charpin, "Le contexte historique et géographique des prophéties dans les textes retrouvés à Mari," *Bulletin of the Canadian Society for Mesopotamian Studies* 23 (1992), 30 n. 9; A. Malamat, *Mari and the Early Israelite Experience* (Oxford, 1989) 87, n. 64.

known to have exercised his profession as far south as Babylon.[5] Whether we should imagine him (her) as present at the installation ceremonies or as addressing the king, in the temple of Kititum, during a royal visit early in the new reign, are questions that at present can only be raised, not answered.

4: I restrict the promise of revelations to what immediately follows rather than seeing here either a general statement ("I reveal to you again and again") or a promise for the indefinite future ("I shall reveal . . ."). The use of the iterative verb-form is motivated, in my opinion, by the series of secrets now to be revealed.[6]

6: *šēnam paṭārum*, "to loosen a sandal," is a rare expression and elsewhere apparently without the legal significance it must have here; for the literature, see Ellis, "Goddess Kititum," 262-3. Ruth 4:8, in which a sandal is handed over as a gesture symbolic of the conveyance of the ownership of land, is perhaps relevant.

7: The meaning of *bedûm*, a rarely attested verb but belonging to the language of letters, is not certain, but "verfügen über" seems at least approximately correct.[7] Ellis, ibid., opts for *padum/pedûm*, "to ransom, redeem," but the latter base (*pedûm*) is a later, post-Old Babylonian development. Besides, dignity of the king would require, it would seem, that he simply appropriate and take control of another's treasures, rather than redeem them.

9: The broken text reads: *a-ka-*x (x-y?) *ta-né-eḫ-tim i-*x-y-z (w-x-y-z?). With considerable hesitation, Ellis reads *a-ka-al . . . i-ka*?-[*ni* (*-šum/kum*)], "the 'food of peace' will be secure [for it/for you]," or "it will enjoy" (reading *i-ka*?-[*al*]). The proposed readings are extremely dubious, some of them ungrammatical. Grammar requires: *ikânšim* or

[5] See Charpin, "Contexte historique," 28, 31, n. 35. Ellis, "Goddess Kititum," 254, followed by Malamat, *Mari*, insists that there is no evidence that the message passed through any cultic intermediary such as an *āpilum*; "the goddess is speaking directly." However, as must be evident, unless we are to believe in the existence of Kititum and assume a theophany, some human agency is required to explain the human language. The term *āpilum*, I might add, usually rendered by "answerer, "though he never answers, I would render by "interpreter," as in the Ebla dialect; see M. Krebernik, "Zu Syllabar und Orthographie der lexikalischen Texte aus Ebla. Teil 2 (Glossar)," *ZA* 73 (1983) 7; and G. Conti, *Il Sillabario della quarta fonte della lista lessicale bilingue eblaita* (Miscellanea Eblaitica 3; Firenze, 1990) 94 (this reference I owe to Piotr Steinkeller).

[6] This use of the iterative I shall discuss in detail elsewhere.

[7] See *AHw*, 1547.

ikunnaššim (feminine pronominal suffix, antecedent feminine *mātum*, "country"); *ikânkum* or *ikunnakkum*. Unfortunately, I can suggest nothing more convincing.

12: Literally, "let your ear become available to me."

Language and Style

One general feature common to both language and style is simplicity. For the most part, the sentences are short. The first (3) has four stresses. Then, lending a certain solemnity to the introduction of the revelations and to the first of the secrets revealed, the text expands into sentences of seven or eight stresses (4) followed by one of seven stresses (5). In 6-7, the initial rhythm of four stresses returns and then in 8 diminishes to two or three. In 9, a swelling to five or six stresses, and then a gradual diminution to four, then three, then two. The overall pattern: crescendo-diminuendo.

Increasing the impression of simplicity is the consistent use of clause asyndeton throughout the text. Clause follows clause without a single coordinating conjunction. There is a certain staccato effect; units are kept discrete and end abruptly, with full stops. This makes for more dramatic delivery and is more representative of natural speech.[8]

Of a piece with asyndeton is the rule of parataxis, with only two short exceptions in 4 and 9.

The diction is also of the utmost simplicity. Most words are extremely common, and only *tanēḫtum* seems to belong in a higher register.

Coherence is achieved by a number of devices. Most striking, in a sense, is what is not present: anaphora. Where it would be expected and seem quite natural it does not occur. Thus, in 4, after "the secrets of the gods" just before in 3, instead of "their secrets" (*niṣrētīšunu*), we have again, in a slightly variant form, "the secrets of the gods." Similarly, in 7, after "the Upper Country and the Lower Country" just before in 6, instead of "their treasures" (*makkūršina*), the long noun phrase is repeated.[9] One effect of such repetitions is maximal clarity and minimal demands on memory.

[8] D. A. Russell, *Criticism in Antiquity* (Berkeley, 1981) 38.

[9] Theoretically a candidate, but probably because of its length an unlikely form, is *aptanattiakkuššināti*, "I shall reveal them (the secrets) to you."

Coherence also results from many forms of recurrence, both full and partial. Lexical: "secrets of the gods" (3-4); "country" (4), "Upper and Lower Country" (6-7), "in whatever country" (9), with gradual expansion of perspective; the frame of 3/11, with partial recurrence of *nṣr* and *škn*. Phonological: *makkūr* (7) // *maḫīrka* (8); *tabeddi* (7) // *imaṭṭi* (8). Pronominal morpheme referents: first person singular (7x), "before *me*" (3), "*my* name" (4), "*I* shall reveal" (4), "*I*" (emphatic, 10), "*I* shall make firm" (10), "*I* have provided" (11), "*mine*" (lit., "*to me*," 12); second person singular masculine (10x), "*your* mouth" (4), "I shall reveal *to you*" (4), ". . . is given *to you*" (5), "*you* will loosen" (6), "*you* will have . . ." (7), "*your* trade" (8), "*your* hand" (9), "*your* throne" (10), "I have provided *you*" (lit., "I have placed *to/for you*," 11), "*your* attention" (lit., "*your* ear," 12). "I" and "you" are the main threads in the warp and woof of this text. Syntactical (besides lexical): object-genitive-2nd sg. present verb (5-6). Thematic: secrets (34); authority and power (5-6); wealth and prosperity (7-8); peace and security (9-11); relationship of goddess and king (4 // 9-12), with special reference to the former as revealing speaker and to the latter as dutiful listener (4 // 12).

Finally, it should be noted that the secrets number seven. Signifying as it so often does totality or completeness, the number is probably a compositional principle, conferring additional unity on 5-11.[10]

In brief, the text is closely woven and the unity tight.

The language and style of the oracle puts its prose somewhere between the quotidian and more loosely structured language of letters and the greater complexities and more intricate unities of most royal inscriptions. They are most reminiscent of what is known in classical rhetoric as the plain style.[11] There too, sentences are usually short and simple, with little or no use of hypotaxis. There, too, simple, ordinary words are the rule. The plain style seeks clarity –clarity of narration, clarity of proof—and therefore speaks to the mind rather than to the

[10] In "UET 6, 402: Persuasion in the Plain Style" (*JANES* 22 [1993] 113-20), I try to show the pervasive presence of seven as a compositional principle in a prayer to the moon god.

[11] For various descriptions in antiquity of the plain style, see D. A. Russell and M. Winterbottom, eds., *Ancient Literary Criticism: The Principal Texts in New Translations* (Oxford, 1972; reprint, 1988), index, 605. See also Russell, *Criticism*, "Theories of Style," 129-47, and the introduction to his *Anthology of Latin Prose* (Oxford, 1990), with his remarks on the *genus tenue*.

heart. But if it is plain, at its best it is also graceful, artful, with its own peculiar charm.[12]

These are all qualities that in their own way are present in Kititum's oracle. The context of communication from on high is certainly a potentially very emotional one, but here it is never exploited. The goddess does not overwhelm the king with epithets stressing her majesty and power. He is neither abased before her nor his own power greatly elaborated. All is measured. Sobriety is the rule. There is a certain matter-of-factness, a word-for-the-thing and a thing-for-the-word quality. The language is almost colorless. The metonym of 10 is a commonplace, and the legal metaphor of 6, if not deader than the evidence suggests, is a brief exception to the absence of tropes.

The oracle states facts, reassuring facts of deepest concern to the king. It makes these facts eminently clear. This is its evident and dominant purpose, and this it achieves surely and with a certain austere grace.

All of this adds up to another feature of the text: orality. In his discussion of the performance of ancient Greek poetry, Bruno Gentili has written:

> We are dealing with a technique of communication whose psychological and linguistic profile can be detected in the poetry of other oral cultures and also, we might add, in the stylistic structures—already studied by contemporary linguistics—of texts composed for radio broadcast or delivery in public: brief sentences and parataxis rather than hypotaxis, absence of expressions of an "intellectual" character, avoidance of any idiosyncratic—hence exhibitionist and indiscreet—use of the first person, absence of syntactic hyperbaton, and, in general, clear, concrete language used for the exposition of ideas and attitudes that are immediately comprehensible to an audience and that encourage it to listen. These are unbreachable norms, to be observed in any piece of oral communication.[13]

[12] Cf. Cicero's famous description of the style of Caesar's Commentaries: *nudi enim sunt, recti et venusti, omni ornatu orationis tamquam veste detracta* (Brutus, 262)—bald, stark (*nudi*), direct, straightforward (*recti)* unfigured, unadorned (*omni ornatu* . . .), but still not without a certain grace and beauty (*venusti*). Elsewhere (*Orator*, 78), he speaks of the careful carelessness (*negligentia diligens*) of the plain style and compares some women's not using makeup, the result in both cases being *quiddam in utroque quo sit venustius*.

[13] B. Gentili, *Poetry and Its Public in Ancient Greece: From Homer to the Fifth Century* (trans. A.T. Cole; Baltimore, 1990) 39.

And this, I submit, might serve as a fairly accurate description of the text of the Kititum oracle. In this oracle, as so often in the ancient world, verbal art is oral art.[14]

[14] Ellis, "Goddess Kititum," comes to a quite different conclusion. For her, the oracle as we have it is a literary (understand: written) composition, though probably based on "an actual oracular communication" (256). Noting some of the features I have described above, and finding the content scholarly and erudite, she makes the implicit inference that we must be dealing with a written work (see especially, "Literary Considerations," 241-2). On the basis of this inference, she then looks for orthographic ambiguities and possible double meanings (242-4), an exercise with results that, even if I thought the text was intended primarily as a written communication, I would find quite unconvincing. The Mari oracles she finds couched in a language compatible with composition *ad lib* (256), and when an *ad lib* performance at Aleppo (B. Lafont, "Le roi de Mari et les prophetes du dieu Adad," *RA* 78 (1984) 9, lines 14-28) produces a beautifully structured text and one in some ways more complicated than the Kititum oracle, with a language she herself calls "more finished [than the Mari oracles] and rather high-flown," this merits the dismissive observation that "the poetic formulation of the oracular message seems almost incidental. This contrasts strongly with the tightly structured Kititum oracle" (256). From beginning to end, Ellis seems unaware of the reality of oral literature and its possible sophistication and range of expression. One *caveat*: oral literature need not necessarily imply on-the-spot complete improvisation, nor does improvisation imply pure creativity, without dependence on training, memorization and tradition. See Gentili's illuminating discussion of "Orality and Archaic Culture," *Poetry and Its Public*, 3-23, and the astonishing reports on the performances of oral poets in the late eighteenth and early nineteenth centuries, especially in Italy.

CHAPTER 12

The End of the Unholy War and the Anti-Exodus

In his study of Deut 1:6–3:29, N. Lohfink has shown on the basis of G. von Rad's monograph on the Holy War[1] that in the description of the rebellion in the first chapter the Deuteronomist, while employing many of the motifs of the Holy War, has profoundly transformed them.[2] In context they are "inverted": they have lost their original meaning, they serve to describe the very opposite—an Anti-Holy-War.[3] But there is more involved than a Holy War. Through a series of allusions to Exodus 13–14, the ancient traditions on the Holy War *par excellence* are inverted, and the events of Kadesh-Barnea are portrayed as an Anti-Exodus.[4]

One passage, however, which we believe confirms this interpretation, if confirmation were needed, escaped Lohfink's attention. It is

[1] G. von Rad, *Der heilige Krieg im alten Israel* (ATANT 20; Zürich, 1951).

[2] N. Lohfink, "Darstellungskunst und Theologie in Dtn 1,6–3,29," *Bib* 41 (1960) 105–134, especially 110–114, 119–120.

[3] At the suggestion of L. Alonso Schökel, to whom I am grateful for a number of criticisms, I use the term "invert" or "inversion" rather than "pervert" or "perversion" with Lohfink, since the former is not so closely associated with morality.

[4] In the inversion of Holy War motifs the Deuteronomist is probably indebted to the prophets; cf. J. A. Soggin, *VT* 10 (1960) 79–83; also H. Reventlow, *ZAW* 71 (1959) 37, n. 18. For the role of the prophets in the history of the institution, see Robert Bach, *Die Aufforderung zur Flucht und zum Kampf im alttestmentlichen Prophetenspruch* (WMANT 9; Neukirchen, 1962). On the broader question of the inversion of images, see Luis Alonso Schökel, *Estudios de poética hebrea* (Barcelona, 1963) 305–6.

Deut 2:14–16. In these verses we have the real conclusion to the history of the first chapter, for they are concerned with the death of the rebellious generation. And here too, we submit, we have however briefly the same inversion of motifs which characterizes the earlier narrative. To the Anti-Holy-War—the Unholy War—and the Anti-Exodus, 2:14–16 provide the fitting, almost necessary, conclusion.

The Unholy War

At 2:14–16 the onward movement of the narrative is suddenly halted, the "rhythm" of command-execution which began in 2:2ff. is broken.[5] The style becomes particularly solemn. The first sentence (v. 14) is long with a slow and deliberate movement: "And the time that we marched from Kadesh-Barnea until we crossed the Wadi Zered was thirty-eight years, until had perished the entire generation, the men of war, from the camp, as Yahweh had sworn to them." Then in a short sentence marked by assonance (*wĕgam—bām—lĕhummām—tummām*, rhythm 4:4) and the repetition in chiastic order of words and phrases of the previous sentence (*ʿad tōm—miqqereb hammaḥăneh—YHWH // YHWH—miqqereb hammaḥăneh—ʿad tummām*), one agent of destruction is identified: "And even the hand of Yahweh was upon them to rout them in panic from the camp until they had perished." But this is not all. Once more 2:16 repeats (*ʾanšê hammilḥāmâ, tmm, miqqereb*): "And when all the men of war had perished in death from among the people"—then, and only then, follows the oracle of 2:17ff., and we hear the command, to which all others have pointed, to cross the Arnon and invade Sihon's territory in a Holy War (2:24f.).

The importance the author attaches to these verses is evident, and they are clearly intended as a solemn introduction to 2:17ff.[6] In effect, the author juxtaposes two wars, the Unholy and the Holy. Through allusion we are made in vv. 14–16 to recall the former, especially the oath of 1:35, the complete fulfillment of which is so strongly stressed. Somewhere beyond the Zered this war came to a close, and only because it did—this is clearly the author's mind—could the new and holy one begin. The contrast is unmistakable.

[5] On the "rhythm" of 2:2–9, 13, see Lohfink's remarks, "Darstellungskunst," 128–129.

[6] Cf. M. Noth, *Überlieferungsgeschichtliche Studien* (Halle, 1943) 35.

The contrast, however, is achieved by more than allusion. 2:14–16 has often provoked comment, especially the expressions *ʾanšê hammilḥāmâ* (14b.16) and *miqqereb hammaḥăneh* (14b.15a). So distinctive in fact is the vocabulary that it has been proposed that these verses are secondary,[7] and if this proposal has been commonly rejected, a problem still remains. In 1:35 where the oath against the rebellious generation is cited, the author adheres in essentials to his source (Num 14:22–23); nothing is said of "the men of war." In 2:14b, therefore, the restrictive apposition, "the entire generation, that is, the men of war," even though it does not contradict the earlier passage,[8] is nevertheless unexpected.[9] Moreover, though the topic of war is so frequent in Deut 1–3, the expression *ʾanšê hammilḥāmâ* is confined to these verses. In fact, the military character of Israel is rather assumed in these chapters or only alluded to in terms like *ʿam*;[10] the explicit references to weapons in 1:41 and later to warriors in 3:18[11] are quite exceptional. Why then the evident stress in 2:14–16 on the doomed generation precisely as warriors?

In *miqqereb hammaḥăneh* the same problem reappears, for, as Steuernagel has rightly observed,[12] reference to the camp belongs with the designation of those who died as "the men of war." Again however the same absence of parallels obtains; Israel's camp is never mentioned in Deuteronomy 1–3.[13] The expression *miqqereb hammaḥăneh*, it is

[7] So A. Dillmann, *Die Bücher Numeri, Deuteronomium, und Josua* (2d ed; Kurzgefasstes exegetisches Handbuch zum Alten Testament 3; Leipzig, 1886) 244.

[8] On the inner consistency of the author's thought see the remarks of E. König, *Das Deuteronomium* (KAT 3; Lepzig, 1917) 75; and H. Junker, *Das Buch Deuteronomium* (Bonner Bibel; Bonn, 1933) 30. This is even more apparent when Deut 1 is seen as the offer and rejection of a Holy War. Underlying the restriction in P (Num 14:29) of those punished to men twenty years old and up is probably the practice of military service beginning at that age; cf. the remarks of G. E. Mendenhall, *JBL* 77 (1958) 60, and J. A. Wilson in *ANET*, 415, n. 13.

[9] Those who perished in the desert are similarly identified in the Deuteronomic additions Josh 5:4,6 (cf. M. Noth, *Das Buch Josua* [2d ed.; HAT 7; Tübingen, 1953] 39); Num 32:13 substitutes "which did evil in the eyes of Yahweh"; on the secondary character of Num 32:6–15, see Noth, *Überlieferungsgeschichtliche Studien*, 198–99.

[10] Cf. L. Rost, *Festschrift Otto Procksch* (Leipzig, 1943), 145.

[11] *ḥălûṣîm* and *bĕnê ḥāyil* (cf. R. de Vaux, *Les institutions de l'Ancien Testament* (2 vols.; Paris, 1958–60] 1. 110; 2. 13).

[12] C. Steuernagel, *Deuteronomium und Josua* (HKAT I/3; Göttingen, 1900) 9.

[13] Elsewhere in Deuteronomy only in one law (23:10,11,12,15) and 29:10; within

true, is found in Num 14:44, and besides Deuteronomy 2 here alone in the Old Testament; since this verse belongs to the source used by the author in chapter one, dependence on the older tradition is here quite probable.[14] Dependence, however, does not explain its use; rather, it only makes the problem more acute. Why did the author fail to use the phrase in the first chapter, where in a sense it belongs, only to employ it here, unless there is reason for a decided emphasis at this point on Israel as an army?

The questions raised by the vocabulary of these verses find their answer, we believe, in the use of *lĕhummām* in 15a. For *hmm* also belongs to the vocabulary of war; it refers to the divinely inspired panic which is a characteristic feature of the Holy War.[15] In this sense it is found both in Deuteronomy and in the Deuteronomic History.[16] And that it should be so understood here is beyond doubt, for, as the author is at pains to make clear, its victims are members of an army, "the men of war" in "the camp." In other words, we have in 2:15 a motif of the Holy War, but one which apart from context is not free from ambiguity; *hmm* is not a panic confined to troops. This ambiguity the author removes.

In solving the problem of the vocabulary of 2:14–16 we have of course uncovered another inversion of a Holy War motif: Yahweh inspires panic, not in the enemies' ranks, as in the Holy War, but in Israel's.[17] The author has found for the inversion of the Holy War the obviously right conclusion, for the sin the proper punishment. It was in language taken from the Holy War that the rebels had accused Yahweh of leading them out of Egypt "to give us into the hand of the

Deuteronomy 1–3 tents are mentioned in 1:27. On the "camp-tradition" in Deuteronomy cf. A. Kuschke, *ZAW* 63 (1951) 78.

14 On Num 14:44b as part of the original J tradition, see R. de Vaux, *À la recontre de Dieu,* Mémorial Albert Gelin (Paris, 1961) 58–59.

15 Cf. von Rad, *Heilige Krieg*, 12. Ehrlich's proposal, *Randglossen zur hebräischen Bibel, II* (Leipzig 1909) 254, to read *lahămîtām* overlooks the numerous examples of pregnant constructions with *min* (cf. BDB, 578a), of which *mût miqqereb* in the following verse is one; *hmm* is construed with *min* in Jer 51:34; Esth 9:24; Eccles 21:48.

16 Deut 7:23; Josh 10:10; Judg 4:15 (on the last two texts cf. M. Noth, *Überlieferungsgeschichtliche Studien*, 56, n. 2). In general, when Yahweh is the subject of *hmm* (Exod 14:24; 23:27; Josh 10:1; Judg 4:15; 1 Sam 7:10; Ps 18:15 = 2 Sam 22:15; Ps 144:6; 2 Chr 15:6), it refers to war; Isa 28:28 is the only exception.

17 The inversion of the panic motif appears already in Amos 2:14–16; cf. von Rad, *Heilige Krieg*, 63.

Amorites, to destroy us utterly."[18] And so they were destroyed, but for some at least the hand was another and more terrible.

It may also seem not too implausible to suggest that this underlying law of talion is an additional reason for the author's borrowing *miqqereb hammaḥăneh* for the description of the punishment. In Num 14:44 it is recorded that Moses and the Ark remained in the camp when the Israelites insisted on fighting the Amorites. Despite being warned, they chose to abandon the camp and sinned a second time, leaving Moses and the Ark behind. In doing so they also chose—this we suggest is hinted at by the Deuteronomist—their final punishment: they were to be driven from this camp in terror and to their death.

The remaining expressions are compatible with a context of war. *dôr* causes no difficulty, *ʿam* we have already noted above, and *tmm* is quite in place, as *ʿad tummām* in Joshua (8:24; 10:20) to describe the final rout and slaughter of the enemy shows. Only "the hand of Yahweh" may raise some doubts, for though the hand and the arm of Yahweh as a god of war are frequently mentioned,[19] there is reason to believe that the author has in mind primarily death by pestilence.[20] This is suggested by a number of considerations: (1) this is a well-attested meaning of the expression;[21] (2) in Num 14:12, which belongs to the author's source, it is pestilence (*deber*) which Yahweh first proposes in his plan of total destruction, and when afterwards upon the intercession of Moses he relents and restricts the punishment to one generation, though it is not said how it will die, the passage is open to

[18] On *nātan bĕyād*, cf. von Rad, *Heilige Krieg*, 7ff., and Lohfink, "Darstellungskunst," 125f. The corresponding Akkadian expression, *ina qāti nadānu*, is used of a god granting victory over enemies as early as the Old Akkadian period; cf. H. Hirsch, *AfO* 20 (1963) 75 obv. III 2–6.

[19] Cf. H. Fredriksson, *Jahwe als Krieger* (Lund, 1949) 101–105.

[20] Judg 2:15; 1 Sam 12:15; 7:13 allow for a more general application of "the hand of Yahweh to be on (*bĕ*) someone," but for the reasons which follow the more particular meaning imposes itself.

[21] Cf. Exod 9:3, 15; 1 Sam 5:6, 7, 9, 11; 6:3, 5, 9; 2 Sam 24:16, 17; 1 Chr 21:15, 17; as a more general term for sickness, Ps 32:4; 38:3; 39:11. In Ugaritic texts (C. H. Gordon, *Ugaritic Manual* [AnOr 35; Rome, 1955], Text 54) we also find *yd ilm* as pestilence (*mtm*), and in Akkadian *qāt* DN ("hand of such and such a god") is used for various diseases (cf. R. Labat, *Traité akkadien de diagnostics et pronostics médicaux*, I [Paris-Leiden, 1955] xxiff., but on the problem of etymology discussed on xxi, n. 4, see A. Goetze, *JCS* 2 [1948] 269f.).

the interpretation that pestilence is to be understood as remaining the principal, if not only, instrument of punishment;[22] (3) in 1 Sam 4–6, incorporated by the Deuteronomist in his history, God's hand and panic are associated, and the former is to be understood of a deadly epidemic.[23]

However, if "the hand of Yahweh" in Deut 2:15 does refer to pestilence, as seems probable, this is less a difficulty than additional support for our interpretation, for pestilence fits perfectly in the context of war. To mention only a few examples, it is Pestilence which escorts the Warrior-God (Hab 3:5).[24] Pestilence is "the sword of Yahweh" (1 Chr 21:12).[25] In another inversion of Holy War motifs, it is with pestilence that Yahweh first smites man and beast in Jerusalem, and indeed "with outstretched hand and strong arm" (Jer 21:5–6). And as for 1 Sam 4–6, other motifs of the Holy War appear in this history of the Ark, and it is in their light that the hand of Yahweh and the divine panic are to be understood.[26]

An unresolved question is whether *wĕgam* in v. 15 implies that the hand of Yahweh was only one of several causes of death, or whether it stresses that the cause of death was none other than the hand of Yahweh. Recent translations and the remarks of commentators testify to the ambiguity of the Hebrew.[27] However, in view of the traditions

[22] In Num 14:37 (P) it is by plague (*maggēpâ*) that the scouts die; cf. also Num 17:13f.; 25:8f.

[23] *mĕhûmâ* occurs in 5:9,11; in 5:6 we should perhaps read *wayĕhummēm* for MT *wayĕšimmēm*. On the hand of Yahweh see n. 20. The exact nature of the Philistine affliction remains somewhat obscure, but that *ʿōpel* was mortal and reached epidemic proportions seems clear; see H. Hertzberg, *Die Samuelbücher* (ATD 10; Göttingen, 1960) 40–41.

[24] Cf. A. Caquot, *Semitica* 6 (1956) 57f.

[25] Pestilence and the sword are frequently associated (Lev 26:25f.; Jer 24:10; 29:17; 32:36; 34:17; Ezek 5:17; 7:15; 28:23; 38:21–22; Am 4:10, etc.). Cf. too the angel in 2 Kgs 19:35. The parallelism of "arrows" and "hand" in Ps 38:3 is also to be noted; see the remarks of H.-J. Kraus, *Psalmen* (BKAT 15/1; Neukirchen, 1961) 295.

[26] Von Rad, *Heilige Krieg*, 12, includes 1 Sam 5:11 among the examples of a Holy War panic. Another Holy War motif is that of Yahweh who fights for Israel (1 Sam 4:3,8), as is that of the *tĕrûʿâ* (1 Sam 4:5–6) and of course the entire story revolves around the Ark, Israel's palladium.

[27] Cf. the different options in the commentaries of Bertholet, Driver, Junker, König and Steuernagel, and in the translations of the RSV, Confraternity of Christian Doctrine, Bible de Jérusalem; Dhorme (Pléiade) deftly retains the ambiguity of the Hebrew.

which know of other causes of death and were certainly known to the Deuteronomist,[28] it seems more probable that in 2:15 he singled out the type of death which could be used in an inversion of a Holy War motif.

The Anti-Exodus

Deut 2:14–16 is also the end of the Anti-Exodus. Admittedly, the evidence in these verses alone is meager. It must however be considered in the light of the previous allusions to Exod 13–14, and then Exod 14:24 assumes special significance: "In the night watch just before dawn the Lord cast through the column of the fiery cloud upon the Egyptian force (*maḥăneh*) a glance that threw it into a panic (*wayyāhom*)." Certainly the similarity of vocabulary is striking, and since Exodus 14 was demonstrably one of the author's sources, the probability of its being drawn upon in 2:15 seems very high.[29] Besides, since the Unholy War theme of chapter one reappears in 2:14–16, consistency would demand that the Anti-Exodus theme be worked into the conclusion.

If we do have another case of inversion in 2:15, then "the hand of Yahweh" must probably also be included. Not only is the hand of Yahweh intimately associated with the Exodus, particularly in Deuteronomy,[30] but the author's source, Exod 14:31, which concludes the prose account and by way of summary underscores the significance of the events, tells of the people having seen "the great hand" (exploit) done by Yahweh which led them to fear and trust. Earlier in Deut 1:32 the author alluded to this verse of Exodus 14 when he contrasted the lack of trust shown by the people at Kadesh-Barnea. In describing the

Ehrlich, *Randglossen*, 253–254, takes *wĕgam* as concessive: the wandering lasted thirty-eight years, even though . . . (otherwise it would have been longer).

[28] Cf. Num 16:31f.; 21:6; 25:3–5.

[29] Exod 14:24 suggests that *maḥăneh* in Deut 2:14–15 be understood as the army itself rather than a place; the parallel expression *miqqereb hāʿām* in 2:16 also favors this sense.

[30] *yād ḥăzāqâ*: Exod 3:19; 6:1; 13:9; 32:11; Deut 4:34; 5:15; 6:21; 7:8,19; 9:26; 11:2; 26:8; 34:12; 1 Kgs 8:42; Jer 32:21; Ps 136:12; Dan 9:15; Neh 1:10; *ḥōzeq yād*: Exod 13:3,14,16; *yād* alone: 3:20; 7:5; 9:3,15; Ps 78:42. After the renovation of the Exodus miracle at the Jordan (cf. H. Wildberger, *Jahwes Eigentumsvolk* [ATANT 37; Zürich, 1960], 59–62), in Josh 4:24 all the peoples of the earth are to acknowledge "that the hand of Yahweh mighty" (*ʾet yad YHWH kî ḥăzāqâ hîʾ*). On the "hand"-motif in the later tradition, see P. W. Skehan, *CBQ* 25 (1963) 94–110.

punishment of this sin, Exod 14:31 may therefore have been of some influence.

It is however in Exodus 15 that the hand of Yahweh enjoys special prominence; to his right hand belongs the victory at the Sea of Reeds (Exod 15:6,12). The possible significance however of this for the interpretation of Deut 2:15 can only be appreciated when one realizes the profound influence of Exodus 15 on the composition of Deuteronomy 2–3. Since this has not been recognized, we present the evidence.

1. In Deuteronomy 2 the lack of resistance by the Edomites and Moabites, and the fear of the former (Deut 2:4), find their only support among the older traditions in Exod 15:14.[31]

2. Deut 2:25b unmistakably alludes to Exod 15:14:[32]

Deut: "This day I shall begin to put the dread and fear of you on the peoples (*ʿammîm*) under all heaven, who hearing (*yišmĕʿûn*) the report of you will tremble (*wĕrāgĕzû*) and writhe (*wĕḥālû*) before you."

Exod: "The peoples (*ʿammîm*) hear (*šāmĕʿû*) with trembling (*yirgāzûn*), Writhing (*ḥîl*) seizes the rulers of Philistia."[33]

In both passages we have the identical sequence of *šmʿ—rgz—ḥyl* to describe the effect of Israel on other peoples. Not only is this sequence unparalleled elsewhere in the Old Testament, but Deut 2:15 provides besides 1 Sam 31:3 the only other occurrence of the verb *ḥāl* in prose.

3. In Deut 2 the *Leitwort* is the verb *ʿbr*, occurring twelve times in this one chapter (vv. 4,8,8,13,13,14,18,24,27,28,29,30). In Exodus 15 the one and only action predicated of the people is precisely that of *ʿbr*,

[31] Lohfink, "Darstellungskunst," 130, n. 4, has already suggested the possibility of this connection. On the problem of whether the author's attitude to the peoples of Transjordan is to be explained by this dependence on sources or by contemporary political relations, see O. Bächli, *Israel und die Völker* (ATANT 41; Zürich, 1962) 40, n. 57 and the literature cited there; see also R. Bach's remarks, *Aufforderung*, 50.

[32] M. Noth, *Überlieferungsgeschichtliche Studien,* 34 n. 4, considers Deut 2:24a^{b}.b–25 as secondary because they anticipate 2:32ff. and employ the 2 sg. The oracle however in 2:24 is expected in the context of a Holy War, and for the shift in number cf. Jud 20:28b, another Holy War oracle. As to 2:25, it fits too well with the rest of the evidence for the use of Exodus 15 in these chapters to be secondary. See also Lohfink's observations, "Darstellungskunst," 129–130 on 2:24–31 as an imitation of the structure of chapter one.

[33] For the translation of *yôšĕbê* by "rulers," see F. M. Cross, Jr. and D. N. Freedman, "The Song of Miriam," *JNES* 14 (1955) 248f.

repeated twice (15:16b), and in the same context as in Deut 2, namely, the passing by other peoples towards and into the Promised Land.

4. In Deut 3:1–3, as Lohfink has acutely noted,[34] the scheme command-execution, which has been consistently used up to this point, is not carried through. The people is told neither to cross Og's territory (contrast 2:4,18) nor to cross the Jabbok (contrast 2:13,24). The avoidance of the verb *ʿbr* must be deliberate, especially is resumed in 3:18,21,25,28 about crossing the Jordan. Its avoidance is explained by the author's dependence on Exodus 15, where *ʿbr* is used of the movement of the Israelites to the Promised Land. This the attack on Og is not, but the crossing of the Jordan is, so whereas *ʿbr* is avoided in the first case, in the second it is added (2:29) to the account of the sources (cf. Num 20:14–21; 21:21–26).

5. As has been previously recognized,[35] Deut 3:24b is strongly reminiscent of Exod 15:11. Compare too Deut 3:24a, 25 with Exod 15:16–17:

Deut: "My lord, Yahweh, you have begun to show
your servant your majesty (*godlĕkā*) and
your strong hand . . .
Please let me cross over (*ʾeʿbĕrâ*) and
And see the good land across the Jordan—
this good mountain (*hāhār*) and Lebanon."

Exod: "Terror and dread falls upon them,
By the majesty (*gōdel*)[36] of your arm
they are made like stone,
Until your people, O Yahweh, crosses (*yaʿăbōr*)
Until the people you created crosses (*yaʿăbōr*),
And you bring them in and plant them
on the mountain (*har*) of your inheritance."

The similarity is evident and striking: first the majesty of God (*gōdel*), then the theme of crossing (*ʿbr*), and finally the very distinctive designation, for which there are very few parallels, of the Promised Land as

[34] Lohfink, "Darstellungskunst," 130.

[35] Dillmann, Driver.

[36] MT *gĕdol*, but read *gōdel* with G. Beer, *Exodus* (HAT 3, Tübingen 1939), 82, and Cross—Freedman, "Song of Miriam," 249.

a mountain(-range).[37] It is also in the light of Exodus 15 that we can understand why Moses speaks of only beginning to be shown God's majesty, for there it is said that this majesty terrorizes both sides of the Jordan, whereas Moses so far has seen its effects only in Transjordan (cf. Deut 2:25).

In brief, the points of contact between Deuteronomy 2–3 and Exodus 15 are too many and too specific to be explained except by the conscious and close dependence of the Deuteronomist on the ancient poem.[38]

Embedded therefore as Deut 2:15 is in a context in which constant reference is being made to Exodus 15, it is hard to see how "the hand of Yahweh" is not an echo—and an inversion—of the saving right hand so prominent in the author's source. The fact that in Deut 3:24, where the source (Exod 15:16) speaks of Yahweh's arm, the author substitutes "your strong hand," would seem to provide additional support for this view: in the author's mind it is the saving hand of the Exodus which is about to operate against Sihon and Og,[39] the hand therefore that destroys in preparing for this operation can hardly be another.

In Deut 2:15 therefore we propose the inversion of two elements of the Exodus tradition: the panic of the Egyptians inspired by Yahweh, the saving hand.

This, we submit, was the end of the Unholy War and the Anti-Exodus.

[37] The parallel passages are Deut 1:7; 32:13; Ps 78:54; see the writer's, "Some Remarks on the Song of Moses," *Bib* 43 (1962) 327.

[38] Cf. the additions in Josh 2:9b,10b,11b (Noth, *Josua,* 29–30), 10b refers to the conquest of Sihon and Og, and is attributed by Noth to the Deuteronomist. 9b is a virtual citation of Exod 15b–16a, interpreting the conquest in the light of the ancient poem; in view of Deuteronomy 2–3, Josh 2:9b should in our opinion also be attributed to the Deuteronomist.

[39] Cf. his argument from the victories in Transjordan with Deut 7:19b. As the references in n. 30 show, *yād ḥăzāqâ* was a formula traditionally referred to the Exodus; the implications therefore of its use in Deut 3:24 are that the conquest is an extension of the Exodus (cf. Josh 4:24!). Cf. Deut 1:29ff.; 7:17ff.; 20:1, which ground confidence in Yahweh's assistance during the conquest on the experience of the Exodus.

CHAPTER 13

The Repose of Rahab's Israelite Guests

The critical study of Josh 2:1–24 has been concerned almost exclusively with the problems which Israel's early historical traditions always pose: the question of literary sources,[1] form and tradition-history,[2] parallels in the ancient world to illustrate the social, legal, eco-

[1] Even the strongest champions of source-criticism and a Hexateuch have defended the unity of Joshua 2: for example, J. Wellhausen, *Die Composition des Hexateuchs und der historischen Bücher des AT* (3rd ed.; Berlin, 1899) 117; cf. also C. Steuernagel, *Deuteronomium und Josua* (HKAT I/3; Göttingen, 1900) 156. This is the view which today claims the most adherents; cf. the comments of D. Baldi, *Giosuè* (Sacra Bibbia; Torino, 1952); M. Noth *Das Buch Josua* (HAT 7; Tübingen, 1953), J. Bright, "The Book of Joshua" (IB 2; New York, 1953); et al. Only O. Eissfeldt, (*Einleitung in das AT* [3rd ed.; Tübingen, 1964] 336 = *The Old Testament, An Introduction* [trans. P. R. Ackroyd; Oxford, 1965] 252), adhering to his earlier view in *Hexateuch-Synopse* (Leipzig, 1922) 203ff., and C. A. Simpson, *The Early Traditions of Israel* (Oxford, 1948) 279ff., still argue for the presence of two Pentateuchal sources. H. Hertzberg, *Die Bücher Josua, Richter, Ruth* (ATD 9; Göttingen, 1964) defends a middle position; he favors the presence of two traditions in Joshua 2, but doubts they had taken a fixed form allowing for the distinction of "sources" in the chapter. Other early proponents of two sources were Gressmann, Holzinger, Oettli, Procksch, Smend, with Dillmann remaining on the fence. The best answer to their arguments remains W. Rudolph, *Der "Elohist" von Exodus bis Josua* (Berlin, 1938) 165ff.

[2] Cf. especially H. Gressmann, "Josua," in *Die Schriften des AT in Auswahl* 1/2 (2nd ed.; Göttingen, 1922) 134ff.; H. Windisch, "Zur Rahabgeschichte," *ZAW* 37 (1917–18) 188ff.; G. Hölscher, "Zum Ursprung der Rahabsage," *ZAW* 38 (1919–20) 54ff.; F.M. Abel, "L'anatheme de Jericho et la maison de Rahab," *RB* 57 (1950) 321ff.; M. Noth, *Josua*, 21ff.; K. Möhlenbrinck, "Die Landnahmesagen des Buches Josua," *ZAW* 56 (1938) 258ff.

nomic, political or religious background.[3] It has been practically only in the discussion of these problems that any consideration has been given to the specific individuality of the Rahab-tradition, that is, to the form given it by the craftsmanship of the narrator. Thus, the difficulty of forming a coherent picture of the sequence of events in the chapter, which might be taken a evidence of the combination of two sources,[4] has prompted some remarks on the peculiarities of Hebrew narrative style and the impossibility of applying to it or judging it by our own conventions.[5] Similarly, in countering the arguments for doublets,

[3] Besides the articles of Windisch, Hölscher and Abel just referred to, see J. A. Soggin, "Giosuè 2 alla luce di un testo di Mari," *RSO* 39 (1964) 7ff. Unfortunately, for the interpretation of the Mari text in question (ARM III 16) Soggin follows Noth *(Die Ursprünge des alten Israel im Lichte neuer Quellen*, Köln-Opladen 1961, 17f.) in accepting M. Du Buit's exposition of the letter; see "Quelques contacts bibliques dans les textes de Mari," *RB* 66 (1959) 577ff.; correctly understood, the text offers little or no support for the speculations of Du Buit on the Levitical cities, of Noth on early marriage institutions, or of Soggin on Rahab's relations with the Israelites. The correct translation of the crucial lines (*ARM* III 16:5–9) is not Soggin's (= Du Buit's): "nelle città dei Beniaminiti dei dintorni di Terqa, le donne del nemico, le quali, essendo i loro mariti in (troppo) scarso numero, dimorano col nemico, sono numerose a trovarsi nel mio distretto." It is A. Finet's (*L'accadien des lettres de Mari* [Mémoires Academie Royale de Belgique, Classe des Lettres et des sciences morales et politiques 51; Bruxelles, 1956] §84 k): "[dans les villes des Benjaminites des environs de Terqa] les femmes, épouses de l'ennemi, à savoir toutes celles dont les époux demeurent dans le Haut-Pays avec l'ennemi sont nombreuses et il y en a dans mon district." Finet's translation is based partly on W. von Soden's reading *[e-l]-e!-num* in line 7 for the *[im-ṭ]ú-nim* of the editio princeps (*Or* 21 [1952] 84); von Soden noted the difficulty of making any real sense out of *imṭûnim* (whence "in [troppo] scarso numeo"). But the translation is also based on sound grammar; apart from any doubtful readings, in no interpretation of the text can those who live with the enemy be the women mentioned, for the verb in question is *wašbū*, not *wašbā* (cf. *mādā* which follows hard upon *wašbū* and refers to the women). The situation therefore described in this letter is simply this: in the small villages or encampments of the Yaminites around Terqa a number of the men have joined the enemy in the Upper Country, leaving their wives behind. Frequently, however, they slip back at nights in groups of five or six and learn from their wives what is taking place in and around Terqa. It may also he noted, since the matter enters into the emulations of the above named scholars, that Du Buit's doubts (art. cit., 579) on the correctness of Kupper's view that *ālu*, "city," may also be used with reference to the very mobile settlements of the seminomads, are groundless; it is also found in this sense in the Old Babylonian Shemshara Tablets and later in a Hittite treaty (for references see *CAD* A 386, 3.c and 387, 3.f; on the Hittite text see Nougayrol's comments in *Iraq* 25 [1963] 114).

[4] Cf. the authors cited in n. 1.

[5] Hertzberg, *Josua*, 20.

Rudolph has noted in passing how the narrative is enlivened in vv. 6–8 by the retrospect and the rapidly shifting scenes.[6] We may also point to Noth's observations on the overall structure of the chapter,[7] and most recently to Weiss' comments on the irony of v. 7a.[8] We believe, however, that more may still be said about the author's technique, and the following remarks are offered as one illustration. They are also offered in the hope that they will be for the esteemed sexagenarian[9] an occasion of pleasant memories recalling school days long ago when he learned of Rahab as one shining in heaven "come raggio di sole in acqua mera."

We begin with what may be called the problem of the repose of Rahab's Israelite guests. According to v. 1 the spies entered Rahab's house . . . *wayyiškĕbû šāmmâ*; however, in v. 8, after all the excitement of vv. 2–7, to our surprise we find Rahab's ascent to the roof introduced by the chronological notation *wĕhēmmâ ṭerem yiškābûn*. In other words, it seems according to v. 8 that the spies had not yet "*šākab*-ed," whereas according to v. 1 they apparently did so immediately. Where this problem has been at least implicitly acknowledged, even though not always explicitly discussed, we find six solutions:

(1) the contradiction is evidence of the joining of two sources;[10]

(2) v. 8 should be understood in context simply in the sense of "before bed-time;"[11]

(3) in v. 8 the verb retains its usual meaning of "lie down (and/or go to sleep)," but in v. 1 it means "lodge;"[12]

(4) the *wayyiqtōl*-form in v. 1 has the modal nuance of wishing or intending;[13]

[6] "*Elohist*," 167.

[7] *Josua*, 29.

[8] M. Weiss, "Einiges über die Bauformen des Erzählens in der Bibel," *VT* 13 (1963) 462–63.

[9] P. Giovanni Rinaldi—Ed.

[10] H. Gressmann, *Diè Anfänge Israels* (Die Schriften des AT, 2/1; Göttingen, 1914) 129.

[11] C. Steuernagel, *Deuteronomium und Josua*, ad loc.

[12] LXX (v. 1 κατέλυσαν, v. 8 κοιμηθῆναι, *Syr* (v. 1 *bātw*, "pass the night," v. 8 *škēbw*); the RV, RSV, CCD translations; Baldi, *Giosuè* (v. 1 prendere alloggio, v. 8 coricarsi), Dillmann, Hertzberg, Holzinger (with the additional suggestion that in v. 1 the verb may have referred in an earlier version more directly to Rahab's profession); the lexicon of BDB.

[13] F. Nötscher, *Josua* (EchtB; Würzburg, 1950) where v. 1 is turned "Dort wollten sie sich zur Ruhe legen."

(5) in v. 1 it means "lie down, rest," but in v. 8 "go to sleep;"[14]
(6) the spies lay down (v. 1), but aroused by the events of vv. 2–7, they had not had the time to do so again before Rahab came up to see them on the roof (v. 8).[15]

The common denominator of all these solutions, except the first, is the assumption that *šākab* in vv. 1 and 8 must refer to different stages in the course of the spies' adventures in Jericho. And in our opinion none of them carries conviction. The first has against it the lack of evidence for two sources in the chapter as a whole;[16] besides, even the exponents of two sources have not in general appealed to this argument in support of their position. The second seems quite gratuitous and completely *ad hoc*; it has enlisted no followers.

The third solution we also reject, despite its support from the ancient versions. It may be remarked, first of all, that of the almost two hundred occurrences of *šākab* in the Qal, only in Josh 2:1 does the LXX render it by καταλύω. Moreover, among the modern lexicographers Brown-Driver-Briggs are alone in distinguishing a meaning "to lodge," and this in only four passages: Josh 2:1; Lev 14:47; 2 Kgs 4:11; 9:16. The evidence of these last three is in fact nil. In Lev 14:47 *haššōkēb* is paralleled by *habbā᾽* (v. 46) and *hā᾽ōkēl*, all three of whom are said to contract impurity in a house affected with "leprosy." The parallelism speaks for itself, and there is not the slightest reason for giving to *haššōkēb* a sense any less specific than that of the other two participles; in other words, "one who lies down (and sleeps)."[17] In 2 Kgs 9:16 (*šōkēb šāmmâ,* i.e. in Jezreel),[18] after the previous verse telling of Joram's return to Jezreel to recover from his wounds, the king is obviously not lodged there, but rather lying on his sick-bed; even BDB add to this reference the cautionary "yet perhaps *lie ill.*" There remains

[14] Vulg (v. 1 *quieverunt,* v. 8 *obdormierant*); F. Hummelauer, *Commentarius in Librum Josue* (CSS; Paris 1903) 110 (v. 1 *decumbere*, v. 8 *dormire*); and with some hesitation, A. Fernandez, *Comm. Lib. Josue* (CSS; Paris, 1938) ad loc.

[15] Rudolph, "*Elohist,*" 168, n. 1.

[16] We may refer simply to authors cited in n. 1, especially Rudolph.

[17] Cf. M. Noth, *Leviticus* (ATD 6; Göttingen, 1962) 87: "Wer aber in dem Hause geschlafen hat."

[18] This is the only passage appealed to by Hertzberg, *Josua*, 19, for support of "Schlafquartier machen, zum Schlafen hingehen."

only 2 Kgs 4:11, where we read of Elisha's taking advantage of the hospitality offered him by the pious Shunammite: *wayhî hayyôm wayyābōʾ šāmmâ wayyāsar ʾel-hāʿăliyyâ wayyiškab-šāmmâ*. Why "he lodged there?" Even the RSV, which opts for "lodge" in Josh 2:1 in this case translates "he rested there." Compare, too, the sequence of verbs here, namely, *bōʾ—sūr—šākab*, with that in Gen 19:36f., where Lot's mysterious guests arrive and accept his hospitality: *sūr—bōʾ—ʾākal—šākab*; also, *bōʾ—šākab – ʾākal* in Lev 14:46f. (see above), and *bōʾ—lūn—šākab* in 2 Sam 12:16. Within such a series *šākab* clearly retains its usual sense. And therefore, in brief, for the meaning "lodge" in Josh 2:1 there is no outside support in Old Testament usage, nor, it may he added, in related Northwest Semitic languages and dialects.[19]

Solutions (4)-(6), we must admit, are not as easily disproved. The modal usage of *wayyiqtōl* is possible in itself[20] and there is no denying either that *šākab* frequently has the added implication of sleeping, or that the spies might have been disturbed and then, as things settled down again, been contemplating a few winks more. Nevertheless, on closer examination these solutions are found to labor under serious difficulties and to be really no more satisfactory than their rivals.

For solutions (5)-(6) to be acceptable we must suppose that in v. 1 the narrator predicates an action of the spies, using the verb *šākab*, and then in v. 8, to fix the point in time at which Rahab goes up to them, he uses the same verb, but—*ex hypothesi*—has no intention of referring his reader (or hearer) to its previous occurrence, even though in the intervening narrative he has predicated no other action of the spies.[21] To say the least, this confronts us with an intolerable and, in a writer of demonstrable skill, incredible ambiguity. The situation is hardly saved by assuming that the same verb, within a few lines, suddenly takes on a new implication (sleeping) which somehow the reader should know is absent in its first occurrence.

[19] In the Mari letters ***maškabātum***, "beds" appears as a West Semitism *(ARM* III 16: 24). *škb* and ***mškb(t)*** are well attested in Ugaritic; cf. C. H. Gordon, *Ugaritic Textbook* (AnOr 38; Rome, 1965) 19.2411. In text 1029:16 (= *PRU* II 29:16) Gordon says *škb* is tantamount to "to reside, dwell (in a house);" this seems true in the context, but the notational character of the text does not justify a lexical distinction, nor does Gordon make it. In Phoenician and Aramaic *škb* means "to lie (down)."

[20] GK §111 n; see also P. P. Saydon, "The Conative Imperfect in Hebrew," *VT* 12 (1962) 124–126.

[21] Of course, the other solutions just reviewed are also to this objection.

Against solution (4), we may first note that it seems quite gratuitous to postulate a modal sense where nothing in the immediate context suggests it and when it is clearly excluded in all of the actions just predicated of the spies. Moreover, since v. 8 clearly refers the reader back to v. 1, a modal sense of *šākab* in the latter case would require that in v. 8 we translate "before they wanted to lie down." Obviously, this makes little sense.

So what is the answer to the problem? The bluntest way of putting it would be simply to deny that there is any problem at all; the discussion has proceeded on too narrow a basis, and therefore has created a pseudo-problem. For the explanation of *šākab* in v. 1 is to be found, in our opinion, not in the area of grammar or lexicon, but through the consideration of a factor which has been ignored. This factor in style, which in the case at hand means specifically the use of prolepsis. In other words, *wayyiškĕbû šāmmā* in v. 1 is not in its proper place from the viewpoint of chronology, but is anticipatory.[22]

However, before analyzing its use in Josh 2:1, a word about prolepsis in the Old Testament. It has been investigated, notably by König,[23] though a fresh inquiry is certainly a desideratum. Clear cases are not numerous, and some may be classified under a different heading. There is, for example, the fairly frequent initial compendious statement on an event or series of events, which is then followed up by a more detailed account (e.g., Exod 7:6); König prefers here to speak of "eine formelle Ankündigung."[24] Analogous are the relatively numerous instances, where, to quote S. R. Driver, "a new account commences, amplifying the preceding narrative regarded as a *whole*, and not meant merely to be the continuation, chronologically, of its concluding stage."[25] We may also mention the technique of resumption ("Wiederaufnahme"), which implies, if nothing else, that anticipatory statements were quite acceptable within the canons of Hebrew narrative.[26] Then there are examples like Deut 31:22, where Moses is said to

22 It should be remarked that Targ^J and a number of translations perhaps imply this interpretation; at least they translate *šākab* in the same way in both vv. 1 and 8. Cf. An American Translation, Bible de Jérusalem, Noth's translation, etc.

23 E. König, *Stilistik, Rhetorik, Poetik* (Leipzig 1900) 131ff., especially 140–141. See also S. R. Driver, *A Treatise on the Uses of the Tenses in Hebrew* (3rd ed.; Oxford, 1892) 82; M. Sekine, "Erwägungen zur hebräischen Zeitauffassung," VTSup 9 (Leiden, 1963) 81f.

24 Stilistik, 140.

25 *Treatise*, 82.

26 C. Kuhl, "Die 'Wiederaufnahme'—ein literarkritisches Prinzip?" *ZAW* 64 (1952)

have taught the Israelites the Song of 32:1–43, though he does not get around to doing so until he finishes some other business.[27] As is evident from the material already referred to, even if the present separation of v. 22 from the text of the Song be due to a later editor's insertion of the intervening verses, still—*dato non concesso!*—the separation as such would have caused him no difficulty and would not have been felt as an inconcinnity.

Against this general background prolepsis as a technique of narrative is certainly not unexpected. One excellent illustration of its use is to be found in 1 Sam 10:9a, where *wayyahăpok-lô ʾĕlōhîm lēb ʾaḥēr* is quite out of place chronologically, in this respect belonging at the end of v. 10 (cf. vv. 5–6). But the radical change in Saul effected by the spirit of God is in the author's mind the most important of the signs confirming Saul in his divine mission; this importance, as Hertzberg has correctly remarked,[28] is given expression by the inversion of the chronology.

A similar inversion is met in Exod 19:1–2a. In v. 1 Israel arrives in the desert of Sinai; v. 2, however, brings us back to the departure from Rephidim, and then, once more, the arrival in the desert of Sinai is reported. This *hysteron proteron* is almost certainly to be explained, as Noth has recognized,[29] by the importance attached by the priestly writer to the date of the arrival, with which v. 1 begins and thus introduces the entire Sinai tradition.

Alonso-Schökel has pointed out the inversions in Judg 3:18, 20 and their effectiveness; Lohfink has devoted a detailed study to the inversion in Jonah 4:5.[30] And in Joshua 2 itself Hertzberg has noted how v. 17 anticipates v. 20 and how, proleptically, v. 21b reports Rahab's tying

---

1ff.; I. L. Seeligmann, "Hebräische Erzählung und biblische Geschichtschreibung," *ThZ* 18 (1962) 314ff.

[27] O. Eissfeldt, *Das Lied Moses Deuteronomium 32,1–43 und das Lehrgedicht Asaphs Psalm 78 samt einer Analyse der Umgebung des Moses-Liedes* (Berichte der Sächsischen Akademie der Wissenschaften zu Leipzig 104/5; Berlin, 1958) 50, n. 1, proposes to translate *waylammĕdāh* by "um es . . . zu lehren." In our opinion neither GK §120f nor Job 19:18; Neh 13:9, to which he refers, justify this rendering.

[28] H. Hertzberg, *Josua*, 66f.

[29] M. Noth, *Exodus* (ATD 5; Göttingen, 1959) 124f.

[30] L. Alonso-Schökel, "Erzählkunst im Buche der Richter," *Bib* 42 (1961) 154f.; N. Lohfink, "Jona ging zur Stadt hinaus (Jon 4,5)," *BZ* NF (1961) 185ff.

the string to the window. Confronted with the difficulty of reconstructing a plausible sequence of events in vv. 12–21, he also, makes a general observation worth quoting: "Hier hilft nur die Erkenntnis, dass die hebräische Erzählungsweise nicht den gleichen logischen Gesetzen des historischen Nacheinander folgt, wie das bei uns der Fall ist. Es gibt ein Nachholen von Einzelheiten, entsprechend auch eine Vorwegnahme."[31]

In brief, prolepsis is attested as a narrative technique, and in our opinion it provides the most convincing explanation of *wayyiškĕbû šāmmâ* in Josh 2:1. It is open to none of the objections which render other explanations so improbable, and once its use is recognized as part of the Hebrew narrator's craft, it offers the obvious and natural reading of vv. 1–8. What is still puzzling is the fact that Hertzberg, so aware of its use in general and even in this chapter, failed to identify it in what seems to us a very clear example. But however we explain his failure, our task now is to analyze a little more in detail the function served by the prolepsis in the context of vv. 2–9.

"There they lay down to sleep"—the immediate effect, as the report of the spies' arrival goes to the king and he in turn dispatches his messengers to Rahab's house, is tension: the spies are in jeopardy. In v. 4a the tension increases as, with the messengers at the door calling for the spies' release, Rahab hides them with a speed that is conveyed to the reader, not by talking about it, but much more effectively by having the language itself reflect the reality: the object (the two men) is not repeated with the second verb,[32] and the two verbs *wattiṣpōn wattōʾmer*, by their juxtaposition, hardly leave time for a breath between the action and the speech.

At this point, with so many urgent questions unanswered (how could she hide them? where did she hide them? can she possibly succeed in this? and, above all, why is she doing this?), the reader must

[31] *Josua*, 20.

[32] MT reads *wattiṣpĕnô,* which cannot be right. The best solution is the generally accepted *wattiṣpōn* (MT by dittography), rather than *wattiṣpĕnēm* (so S. Holmes, *Joshua: The Hebrew and Greek Texts* [Cambridge, 1914] 18, on the basis of the LXX, but see the cautionary note of M. Margolis, *The Book of Joshua, in Greek* [Paris 1931] Part I, ad loc.), or *ʾôtām* (so Hertzberg). For the omission of explicit reference to an object already governed by a preceding verb, see König, *Stilistik,* 192ff., and cf. the double-duty pronominal suffix (M. J. Dahood, *Ugaritic-Hebrew Philology* [Rome, 1965] 9, 38ff., 74, with references to earlier literature).

listen to Rahab's detailed and, in context, painfully long reply to the royal messengers. She takes up their message point by point in vv. 4b-5:

bāʾû ʾēlay hāʾănāšîm		*hāʾănāšîm habbāʾîm ʾēlayik*	(v. 3)
wĕlōʾ yādaʿtî mēʾayin . . .	(v. 4)	Cf. *mibbĕnê Yiśrāʾēl . . .*	(v. 2)
		kî laḥpōr . . .	(v. 3)
wayhî . . . wĕhāʾănāšîm yāṣāʾû	(v. 5)	*hôṣîʾî hāʾănāšîm*	(v. 3)

But, in a partial relief of the tension, the reader smiles, too. He enjoys the opening word of the big lie: ***kēn***, "True!"[33] He appreciates the ambiguity of Rahab's last words, ***kî taśśîgûm***, "surely you can reach them," which to the messengers could mean only one thing, but for one cognizant of the situation at the moment have a deliciously ironical second sense.[34] One may also wonder if the messengers' speech in v. 3 which consists of the impv. *hôṣîʾî* plus the grounds for the order (*kî . . .*), was not intended to evoke the type of request addressed to the *paterfamilias* for the release of a guilty member of his family, that the law might take its course.[35] In this light Rahab's reply, which in its point-for-point countering is so reminiscent of a defense speech,[36] takes on a new significance, and the humor of the situation and its appeal to a popular audience are evident.

At any rate, her speech is a gem, sincere in tone, plausible in its denials, persuasive in its counsel, and absolutely untrue! How do the messengers react? The narrator leaves us with this question and in a flashback first gives us the answers to a number of the questions raised by 4a, and the woman's astuteness, already so evident in her speech, is

[33] Though this use of *kēn* is unparalleled elsewhere in the Old Testament, it is hardly suspect, and certainly the LXX does not give evidence of a different text in its Hebrew *Vorlage* (against Holmes, cf. Margolis, *Joshua,* ad loc.).

[34] Cf. the expression *taśśîg yād.*

[35] Cf. H. J. Boecker, *Redeformen des Rechtslebens im AT* (WMANT 14; Neukirchen, 1964) 21ff. The form consists of three elements: the call for release (impv.), declaration of the punishment to be imposed, grounds (*kî . . .*).

[36] Ibid., 104. The use of *kēn* belongs perhaps in a judicial setting: cf. *nākôn*, "proved, establishes" in Deut 13:15; Ugar. *knn*, "prove" (PRU II 161: 5); D. J. Wiseman, *The Alalakh Tablets* (London, 1953) text 4, where the sequence of *kinā-ēteneppušū*, "true - have been done" recalls "proved - has been done" in Deut 13:15; Akk. *kunnu*, "prove." In the same setting "I (do not) know" also fits quite well; cf. most recently N. Lohfink, *Das Hauptgebot* (AnBib 20; Rome, 1963) 128ff.

delightfully confirmed by the simplicity of the hiding-place. Then in v. 7a the complete success of her speech—could it have failed?—is realized as the messengers take off in pursuit of their quarry. As we remarked above, Weiss has called attention to the technique for achieving irony here; what is in reality only a misapprehension of the pursuers, is presented as a fact ("they pursued after them").[37] Emphasizing the irony of the situation is the line of pursuit *ʿal hammaʿbĕrôt*,[38] while the spies are really *ʿal haggāg* (v. 6). In v. 7b the scene shifts again; its strong echoes of Rahab's words in v. 5a, with the contrast in the subject of *yṣʾ* (*haššaʿar sgr, yṣʾ* of the spies in 5a, of the messengers in 7), underscore the completeness of her triumph over the king and his emissaries. And with the slow closing of the gate the first part of the drama ends—the ruse has worked!—and another begins.[39]

At this point recognition of the structure of vv. 6–8 is important both for establishing v. 7a as a "turning-point," and for appreciating the significance the author attaches to vv. 9ff. The structure is concentric:[40]

A *wĕhîʾ heʿĕlātam haggāggâ wattiṭmĕnēm . . . ʿal haggāg*
B *wĕhāʾănāšîm rādĕpû ʾaḥărêhem . . . ʿal hammaʿbĕrôt*
C *wĕhaššaʿar sāgārû ʿaḥărê. . . hārōdĕpîm ʾaḥărêhem*
B' *wĕhēmmâ ṭerem yiškābûn*
A' *wĕhîʾ ʿālĕtâ ʿălêhem ʿal haggāg.*

The formal correspondences are evident: *wĕhāʾănāšîm* (B) = *wĕhēmmā* (B');[41] in A and A' *wĕhîʾ*, *ʿly* (verb), (*haggāggā*) + *ʿal haggāg*; and, of course, position. From a purely formal viewpoint C concludes

[37] See n. 8.

[38] Though *ʿal is* frequently corrected to *ʾel* or *ʿad*, we would retain MT; it is confirmed by the LXX (cf. Margolis, *Joshua*, ad loc.), is the *lectio difficilior*, and can be explained as a pregnant construction used for the sake of contrast with *ʿal haggāg*. Cf. the rare use of *ʿālâ ʿal* (not *ʾel*) in a non-hostile sense; unquestionably its occurrence in v. 8 is determined by the desire for alliteration.

[39] For a similar coincidence of *sgr* and the closing of a scene, cf. Judg 3:23, and the remarks of Alonso-Schökel, *Bib* 42 (1961) 152. Again we would retain MT's *ʾaḥărê kaʾăšer*; it is probably grammatically defensible (cf. Noth, *Josua*, ad loc.), and if it borders on the solecistic, it can be explained by the author's straining the language to emphasize the "after" element, which is repeated no less than three times in v. 7.

[40] For this technique with references to earlier literature, see N. Lohfink, *BZ* 5 (1961) 200ff.

[41] *wĕhāʾănāšîm* in v. 7 refers to the spies, as is universally recognized.

A-B but begins B'-A'; to this formal function corresponds its contextual role: showing, as it does, the spies in the city and the pursuers locked out, the drama which began in v. 2 is effectively concluded, but at the same time the closed gate introduces another stage in the drama.

One effect of the structure is to move the attention of the reader back again, first, to the spies, and then, and principally, to Rahab, as—note the alliteration with the effective repetition of *ʿal* three times—she goes up, up, up to the roof. In the sound of the mounting steps one sense a new, important development. But the structure goes much deeper. It associates around the image of the gate the men and their retiring (B') with the men and their futile pursuit (B), and Rahab's new ascent to the roof (A') with her earlier one, when she hurried the spies up there to hide them (A). The latter association, together with the virtual identity of images, charges A' with a significance far beyond its face-value; the action of A is in a sense reassumed in A'. Similarly, B' through its structural relation to B evokes the image not only of the men before their sleep but of the pursuing messengers. Moreover, in B' with the reference to lying down to sleep we hearken back to v. 1 and the initial element of tension. Thus, the whole narrative is suddenly concentrated in v. 8, and its forward movement having been checked by the nominal sentences beginning in v. 6, it is in a sense ready to erupt. And as it breaks upon the reader that the chronology of events has been inverted, despite the initial resolution of the tension in v. 7a he is suddenly aware that a high-point has been reached.

He thus comes to vv. 9ff and to the revelation which Rahab's profession of faith brings.[42] "I know, *yādaʿtî*!" We have heard what Rahab does not know: *wĕlōʾ yādaʿtî . . . lōʾ yādaʿtî* (vv. 4b–5). Now we hear what she does know: *yādaʿtî kî nātan YHWH lākem ʾet hāʾāreṣ*! But this is not mere knowledge, it is much more. It is an acknowledgment, a recognition, which engages the whole person and commits one to action.[43] It is the knowledge which has inspired her to save the spies. And what she knows and acknowledges and professes by her action as

[42] Vv. 9b, 10b, 11b are Deuteronomic additions (Noth, *Josua*, 29f.); for the allusions in 9b (also v. 24b) to Exodus 15, see the writer's remarks, "The End of Unholy War and the Anti-Exodus," *Bib* 44 (1963) 340ff. [see above, pp. 155ff.]

[43] For this type of knowledge, see W. Zimmerli, *Erkenntnis Gottes nach dem Buche Ezechiel, Eine theologische Studie* (ATANT 27; Zürich, 1954). Cf. the declaration of faith by Jethro, another "convert," in Exod 18:11f. (see R. Knierim, "Exodus 18 und die Neuordung der mosäischen Gerichtsbarkeit," *ZAW* 73 [1961] 148, 153).

well as by her words, is nothing more nor less than the author's theology of the Conquest. She testifies to the mystery of the Sea of Reeds as a sign of and operative in the salvation of the future; it has already taken effect in Canaan, for "no sooner did we hear and our heart melted."[44] And in the crossing of the Jordan this mystery will be renewed, re-presented and extended with identical effect, when they hear of it, upon all the kings of Canaan (5:1). In other words, the popular tradition of which we hear so many echoes in vv. 1–8, is in vv. 9–11 suddenly transformed into a sacred tradition—perhaps, from the author's viewpoint, it would be more accurate to say that it is seen as such –, and it is to stress the significance of the sacred that the narrator has devoted the skills of his craft.

Of course one may still ask—a man of the western world can hardly fail to—exactly where we are to locate the repose of Rahab's guests in the sequence of events. However, the author gives us no timetable, and from the indications of the narrative itself we can do no better than fix the period generally between Rahab's speech in vv. 9ff, and her letting them out the window (v. 15). Obviously the author's interest lay elsewhere.

A more legitimate question would be why he attaches so much importance to the spies precisely as lying down to sleep. We must admit that an answer simply in terms of creating tension seems to us inadequate. Technique is not a trick or a mere device; form is not distinct from content. A writer's many drafts, a Joyce penciling in a change of phrase or a new word of dialogue in the final galleys of *Ulysses,* and a host of other possible illustrations of the struggle for adequate expression, belie any distinction of form and content. The image, therefore, of the sleeping spies in all probability goes deeper than we have suggested so far, and on further reflection one realizes that this image is most expressive of the pervasive, wondrous element of the whole story: security, even rest, in the midst of perils. And if this explains its importance for the author, one may ask if the image does not go still deeper, and functioning as a symbol of Israel suggest the deepest truth of the Conquest ahead: the people so passive, contributing so little, achieving what it does only through the intervention and protection of the God of the exodus, be it found in a spectacular crumbling of walls or in the quiet miracle of a Rahab's faith.

[44] Cf. Exod 15:14, N. Lohfink's study, *Das Siegeslied am Schilfmeer* (Frankfort-am-Main, 1965) 102ff.

CHAPTER 14

The Ancient Near Eastern Background of the Love of God in Deuteronomy

Probably no subject in the book of Deuteronomy, "le document biblique par excellence de l'*agapân*,"[1] has been so thoroughly studied as its teaching on love: Yahweh's love for Israel, and the imperative necessity of Israel's love for Yahweh in return.[2] Study of the theme has resulted in a certain consensus of opinion. It is generally agreed that the deuteronomic teaching has distinctive features, that it is not lacking in originality; it is also, though less commonly, agreed that for the conception of God and people bound by a mutual love, Deuteronomy is indebted to the prophet Hosea.[3] We propose here to broaden the basis for the discussion both of deuteronomic originality and dependence.

[1] C. Spicq, *Agapè: Prolégomènes à une étude de théologie néo-testamentaire* (Studia Hellenistica 10; Louvain—Leiden, 1955) 89.

[2] More recent studies: Spicq, *Agapè*, 71–119; V. Warnach, *Agape: Die Liebe als Grundmotiv der neutestementlichen Theologie* (Düsseldorf, 1951) 54–88; C. Wiéner, *Recherches sur l'amour pour Dieu dans l'Ancien Testament* (Paris, 1957) especially 38–46. See also W. Eichrodt, *Theologie des Alten Testaments* (4th ed.; Stuttgart - Göttingen, 1961) 200–207; G. von Rad, *Theologie des Alten Testaments* (München, 1958) 222–223.

[3] Cf. A. Alt, *Kleine Schriften zur Geschichte des Volkes Israel* (München, 1953) 2.272; H. Breit, *Die Predigt des Deuteronomium* (München, 1933) 158; Eichrodt, *Theologie*, 203; G. von Rad, *Das Gottesvolk in Deuteronomium* (BWANT 47; Stuttgart, 1929) 81; A. C. Welch, *ExpTim* 41 (1929–30) 550; cf. also H. W. Wolff, *Dodekapropheton 1: Hosea* (BKAT 14/1; Neukirchen, 1957) 76.

The point of departure for our inquiry is suggested by certain fundamental differences between Hosea's preaching on love and the doctrine of Deuteronomy. Hosea speaks of Yahweh's love (*ʾāhēb, ʾahăbâ*) for Israel, but never of Israel's "love" for Yahweh—neither as a fact (Israel's love is invariably presented as the love of other gods), nor as a present duty, nor as an ideal to be realized in the future restoration. This can hardly be explained except as a conscious, intentional avoidance of the term. In Deuteronomy, on the other hand, *ʾāhēb* is commonly predicated of Israel in relation to Yahweh; indeed, it epitomizes the book's central preoccupation, namely, observance of the Law. Secondly, in Hosea God's love for Israel is either that of a husband for his wife (3:1) or of a father for his son (11:1). In Deuteronomy we find the father-son relationship (8:5; 14:1, etc.), but never in connection with love,[4] and of the marriage-analogy there is not a trace. This absence of all allusion to marriage is the more striking in that *ʾāhēb* is the verb most apt to express conjugal love.[5]

It is evident that, if Deuteronomy does depend on Hosea, it has transformed the prophet's teaching into a notably different view of love. Can this be accounted for simply by appeal to Deuteronomy's "originality?"[6] It is doubtless better accounted for if no radical transformation need be supposed—that is, if the distinctive deuteronomic view, which nowhere draws on the image of parental or conjugal love, was guided by the analogy of another and different love-relationship.

The nature of this relationship we may hypothetically reconstruct, *mutatis mutandis*, from the distinctive features of the love Deuteronomy proposes. Love in Deuteronomy is a love that can be commanded.[7] It is also a love intimately related to fear and reverence.[8] Above all, it is a love which must be expressed in loyalty, in service, and in unqualified obedience to the demands of the Law.[9] For to love

[4] Against von Rad, *Theologie*, I. 223.

[5] On the meaning of *ʾāhēb*, see most recently Wolff, *op. cit.*, 42.

[6] Alt, *op. cit.*, 272–273, sees the necessity of allowing for others besides the prophet who prepared the ground for the deuteronomic call to the love of God. Cf. also von Rad, *Theologie*, I. 223.

[7] Wiéner, *Recherches*, 43.

[8] Eichrodt, *Theologie*, 206; Spicq, *Agapè*, 92, n.2.

[9] Eichrodt, *Theologie*, 205; Wiener, *Recherches*, 41. The Deuteronomist substitutes *ʿăbādîm* for *ʾōhăbîm* in 1 Kgs 8:23; cf. Deut 7:9.

God is, in answer to a unique claim (6:4), to be loyal to him (11:1, 22; 30:20),[10] to walk in his ways (10:12; 11:22; 19:9; 30:16), to keep his commandments (10:12; 11:1, 22; 19:9), to do them (11:22; 19:9), to heed them or his voice (11:13; 30:16), to serve him (10:12; 11:1,13). It is, in brief, a love defined by and pledged in the covenant—a covenantal love.

The problem, therefore, is: (1) is there evidence elsewhere in our sources for the existence of a comparable covenantal love; (2) if there is, is there also evidence which suggests that Deuteronomy knew of such a love and therefore may have been influenced by this knowledge?

Beginning outside the Old Testament, we may point to texts from the eighteenth to the seventh centuries B.C., in which we find the term love used to describe the loyalty and friendship joining independent kings, sovereign and vassal, king and subject.[11] In a letter to Yasmaḫ-Addu, the king of Mari, one writer declares himself the king's servant and "friend" (*rāʾimka*, literally, "the one who loves you").[12] Here, however, we must be cautious. This is an isolated example in this period, while the contents of the letter and the otherwise unknown identity of the writer do not allow us to determine the implications of this friendship. But the sequence of servant and friend, especially in the light of later texts, is noteworthy.

When we come to the Amarna period we no longer need hesitate, for then, as Korošec has briefly remarked, "love" unquestionably belongs to the terminology of international relations.[13] In the correspondence between Tušratta of Mitanni and the Egyptian court it is the principal topic, and denotes the friendship between the rulers, who are independent and equals ("brothers").[14] Like *ṭabūtu*,[15] with which

[10] We so translate *dābēq* in view of 2 Sam 20:2.

[11] For a similar semantic development cf. *amicitia* (*amo*) and *philia* (*phileō*) for the friendship between nations established by treaty.

[12] G. Dossin, *Correspondence de Iasmaḫ-Addu* (ARM 5; Paris, 1952) 76:4.

[13] V. Korošec, *Mednarodni odnošaji po klinopisnih poročilih iz el-armarnskega in hetitskega državega arhiva* [*International Relations according to Cuneiform Reports from the Tall al-Amarna and Hittite State Archives*] (Ljublijana, 1950) 340 (English summary, 393). Elsewhere in the legal language of the Akkadian sources *râmu* denotes the free choice of a person; P. Koschaker, *JCS* 5 (1951) 108, n.14.

[14] For references see the Glossary in T. A. Knudtzon, *Die El-Amarna-Tafeln* (= EA, Leipzig, 1915) 2. 1493–1494, under *raʾāmu* and *raʾamūtu*. Note especially "friendship and brotherhood," ibid., 1. 29:166.

[15] Cf. EA 8:8–12. In "A Note on the Treaty Terminology of the Sefire Stelas," *JNES* 22 (1963) 173–76, the writer attempts to show that *ṭābūtu* and related forms occur in

it is virtually synonymous, this friendship is the object of agreement and established by treaty.[16]

However, a similar love also binds sovereign and vassal. The Pharaoh is expected to love his vassal.[17] The nature of the latter's obligations is seen in the following text: "My lord, just as I love the king my lord, so (do) the king of Nuḫašše, the king of Niʾi . . .—all these kings are servants of my lord."[18] The vassal must love the Pharaoh; this is only another way of stating his basic relationship to the latter, that of servant. Rib-Adda implies the same thing when in noting the defection of still another governor (vassal), he asks: "Who will love, should I die?"[19] To love the Pharaoh is to serve him and to remain faithful to the status of vassal. And again, in describing the rebellion which closed to him the gates of his own city Byblos, the same king defines loyalty to the Pharaoh, which he assumes to be the same as loyalty to himself, in terms of "love": "Behold the city! Half of it loves the sons of 'Abd-Aširta [who fostered the rebellion], half of it (loves) my lord."[20]

Finally, subjects must love their king. Rib-Adda's loyal subjects are "those who love me," and they are opposed to the treacherous and rebellious.[21] Analogously, the Amorites "do not love 'Abd-aširta," for in general they serve the strong, and at the moment 'Abd-asirta is weak.[22]

Coming down to the first millennium, we find this terminology still in use. A vassal must still love his sovereign. The vassals convoked by Esarhaddon to insure loyalty to his successor Assurbanipal are told: "You will love as yourselves Assurbanipal."[23] In another text we find

---

Assyrian texts and in the Sefîre inscriptions (*ṭbtʾ*) with reference to the friendship established by treaties.

[16] EA 27:72–73.

[17] EA 121:61; 123:23; 158:6. Also E. F. Weidner, *Politische Dokumente aus Kleinasien* (Boghazköi-Studien 8; Leipzig, 1923) 56:59–62.

[18] EA 53:40–44.

[19] EA 114:68. For the reading and syntax of the line see the writer's remarks, "Early Canaanite *yaqtula*," *Or* 29 (1960) 14.

[20] EA 138:71–73.

[21] EA 83:51; 137:47.

[22] EA 73:15–19.

[23] D. J. Wiseman, *Iraq* 20 (1958) 49 col. iv 266–268; cf. also 43 col. iii 207. For variant readings, see R. Borger, *ZA* 54 (1961) 181–182.

a similar declaration under oath: "... the king of Assyria, our lord, we will love."[24]

In the Old Testament one passage at least clearly belongs to the same juridical vocabulary. It is 1 Kgs 5:15, where Hiram of Tyre is called David's "friend" (*ʾōhēb*). The entire section, vv. 15–26, "presents an early picture of correct historical similitude, reporting diplomatic and commercial relations between two states of Syro-Palestine—actually in its extent a fairly unique report."[25] It begins by telling of Hiram's embassy to Solomon when he heard of the latter's being anointed king, "for Hiram had always been a friend to David." It ends by informing us that Hiram and Solomon concluded a treaty. The interpretation of the designation "friend" must be guided not only by the result of the embassy, namely, a treaty, but by two other facts: 1. as follows from 2 Sam 5:11, Hiram and David were united by treaty;[26] 2. on the death of the treaty partner and the enthronement of his successor, the other party was expected to send an embassy. Thus David sends one to Hanun of Ammon,[27] and the king of Cyprus is represented in Egypt when a new Pharaoh takes the throne.[28] The importance attached to such embassies is clear from Hattusili III's letter to Rameses II, in which with some bitterness he complains that this practice had not been observed on the occasion of his own enthronement.[29] In brief, "friend" in 1 Kgs 5:15 must be understood as a reference to the treaty relationship which existed between Hiram and David, and is now renewed with David's successor.

This is the only instance in which *ʾāhēb* refers to international relations.[30] But at least two other passages are strongly reminiscent of

[24] L. Waterman, *Royal Correspondence of the Assyrian Empire* (Ann Arbor, 1930) 266, 1105:32. This document contains the oath imposed by Assurbanipal on his vassals and high officials to insure loyalty to himself in the imminent war with Šamaš-šum-ukin, his brother, in Babylon.

[25] Montgomery-Gehman, *The Books of Kings* (ICC; Edinburgh, 1951) 132.

[26] J. Bright, *A History of Israel* (London, 1960) 183.

[27] 2 Samuel 10.

[28] EA 33–34.

[29] Cf. V. Korošec, *Hethitische Staatsverträge* (Leipziger rechtswissenschaftliche Studien 60; Leipzig, 1931) 47,48. For reasons, however, to doubt that this practice fell under *parṣu ša šarrāni*, "(divine) regulation for kings," as Korošec asserts, see A. Goetze, *Kleinasien* (2d ed., Handbuch der Altertumswissenschaft, III.1.3.3.1; München, 1957) 98, n.5.

[30] It should be remarked that "friendship" was never a narrowly defined term, applicable only to one type of relationship, e.g., among equals. Cf. again *amicitia* and

some Amarna texts. In 2 Sam 19:6–7 Joab protests bitterly to David for grieving at the death of a rebellious son while showing no concern for those who had remained loyal. He charges David with "loving those who hate you and hating those who love you (*ʾōhăbêkā*)."[31] "Those who love you" have already been identified as "your servants" (v. 6). This recalls of course Rib-Adda's way of designating those loyal to him, as well as EA 53:40–44, where loving and being a servant were equated.

In view too of what we have seen one may perhaps appreciate more fully the significance of the statement in 1 Sam 18:16: "But all Israel and Judah loved (*ʾōhēb*) David, for he went out and came in before them." It is clear that the writer sees this as another important step in David's way to the throne; the north as well as the south is attached to him.[32] However, if we see in this attachment, as the Amarna and the Assyrian evidence encourages us to do, an essential requirement of the king-subject relationship, then the writer implies that the people at the point were already giving David a *de facto* recognition and allegiance, which his actual leadership and success in a sense justified.

In answer therefore to the first part of our problem, we may affirm, on the basis of biblical and extra-biblical evidence, the existence of a conception of a profane love analogous to the love of God in Deuteronomy. This profane love is also one that can be commanded, and it is a love too that may be defined in terms of loyalty, service and obedience. It is, like the love of God in Deuteronomy, a covenantal love.[33]

In a sense we have also answered the second half of our problem, namely, whether Deuteronomy knew of such a love and therefore may have been influenced by this knowledge. The biblical passages alone which we have adduced show that we may assume it did know of this profane covenantal love, and the fact that the love required of Israel is, *mutatis mutandis* (of course!), so similar, argues strongly in favor of assuming the influence of analogy.

---

the observations of D. Timpe, *Hermes* 90 (1962) 336ff., especially 338 on the wide variety of power relations covered by metaphorical terms like *amicitia* and *patrocinium*.

[31] Cf. *EA* 286:18–20: "Why do you love the ʿApiru and hate the (loyal) governors?"

[32] H. W. Hertzberg, *Die Samuelbücher* (ATD 10; Göttingen, 1960) 126.

[33] Cf. the covenant between David and Jonathan, which seals their love for each other (1 Sam 18:1.3; 20:17; cf. Spicq, *Agapè*, 76); Jonathan loves David as himself, *kĕnapšô*, which recalls the oath of the Assyrian vassals to love Assurbanipal as themselves, *kī napšātkunu*.

Other considerations support this conclusion. It should be remarked first of all that, if Deuteronomy is the biblical document par excellence of love, it is also the biblical document par excellence of the covenant. No book of the Old Testament is so penetrated in every stage of its formation by the literary form which we now know goes back as far as the vassal treaties of the second millennium.[34] If therefore there is any book of the Old Testament in which a love analogous to that required of a vassal is likely to be found, it is in the book of Deuteronomy.

We must also take into account the juridical vocabulary in which the commandment of love is embedded. The dominance of legal language in Deuteronomy is evident and needs no proof. Moreover, many of the expressions have close parallels in the treaties of the first and second millennium.[35] Once therefore we realize that love has its place in this vocabulary, it is only sound to conclude that this explains its presence in Deuteronomy.

Even if in its use of the term love Deuteronomy should represent an innovation in Israel's covenant tradition, this would not diminish the

[34] This is already clear from K. Baltzer, *Das Bundesformular* (WMANT 4; Neukirchen, 1960) 40ff. The study of N. Lohfink, *Das Hauptgebot: Eine Untersuchung literarischer Einleitungsfragen zu Dtn 5–11* (AnBib 20; Rome, 1963), offers additional arguments; see already his study on the Redaktionsgeschichte of Deut 29–32 in *BZ* 6 (1962) 32–56. A. Jepsen, *Verbannung und Heimkehr* (Festschrift Rudolph; Tübingen, 1961) 175, rejects any connection with the Hittite vassal treaties, since the Old Testament always speaks of God's covenant (Gottes *berith*) and never of Israel's covenant, and therefore God binds himself, not Israel. The strength of this argument may be judged from passages like "Keep Ḫatti's treaty of peace (*riksa u šalama ša Ḫatti uṣur*, J. Nougayrol, *Le palais royal d'Ugarit IV* [Paris, 1956] 36:19–21) and the many passages in Assyrian literature like "he sinned against my oaths (treaty)" (*ina adêya iḫṭīma),* M. Streck, *Assurbanipal und die letzten assyrischen Könige* (Vorderasiatische Bibliothek 7; Leipzig, 1916) 2. 132:93; cf. 64:85, 342, Rm II, Nr. 99:87; Waterman, *Royal Correspondence*, 1380: 5–12.

[35] Many of these have been pointed out in recent literature and need not be noted here. We would call attention only to two. First, the expression, to go after other gods. As N. Lohfink has pointed out to me, Deuteronomy never uses the pejorative *zānâ* (save once, in 31:16, and this in the latest level of the document) but prefers the juridical term, "to go after," that is, to serve; on the legal implications of the term, which is also used of vassal relationships, see P. Koschaker, *art. cit.*, 108, and cf. *EA* 136:11ff., 149:46; 280:20. Second, the expression "with all your heart," which must be considered in the light of the treaty stipulations requiring the vassal to fight with all his heart (*ina kul libbi*, Weidner, *Politische Dokumente*, 60:17–19, 61:23, 70:11ff.; 9, 132:3; *ina gammurti libbi*, Wiseman, *art. cit.*, 41 iii 169, 51 v. 310, and cf. 33 i 52–53) or to be faithful and fight with all his heart (J. Nougayrol, *Le palais royal*, 89:20–21; cf. 1 Macc 8:25).

probability of the interpretation we give the term. As we have seen, in the first millennium love still remains a duty of the vassal towards his sovereign. Influence from this direction on Deuteronomy is quite possible, for there is other evidence for very close contact with Assyrian treaty practices and expressions.

We may point first to the very long list of curses in Deuteronomy. Such length is unknown in treaties of the second millennium, but it does appear in the Esarhaddon text cited above.

More important is the presence in this same text of a curse which is substantially repeated in Deut 28:23. The Assyrian curse reads: "May they make your ground (hard) like *iron* so that none of you may flourish. Just as rain does not fall from a *brazen* heaven, so may rain and dew not come upon your fields . . . "[36] In Deut 28:23: "The sky over your heads will become like *bronze* and the earth under your feet like *iron.*" So similar are these curses that Borger writes: "Der Deuteronomist muss doch irgendwie dieses ebenso gesuchte, wie einprägsame Bild einer assyrischen Quelle entnommen haben. Kam es vielleicht auch vor in einem Vertrag zwischen den Assyrern und den Judäern?"[37]

One more example, in fact one of the most striking parallels the writer knows between cuneiform and biblical literatures in any period. In a passage of his annals which describes an Arab revolt, Assurbanipal states that the curses written in the treaties were brought down upon the rebels by the gods of Assyria. The text goes on: "The people of Arubu asked one and other again and again, 'Why has such an evil thing as this overtaken Arubu?' (and) they say, 'Because we have not kept the mighty oaths of the god Assur, we have sinned against the favor shown us by Assurbanipal, the king beloved of Enlil."[38] In Deut 29:23ff. we read: "They and all the nations will say, 'Why has the Lord dealt thus with this land? Why this fierce outburst of wrath?' And they will say, 'Because they forsook the covenant which the Lord, the God of their fathers, had made with them ... and they went and served other gods . . . "[39] Identical contexts (the curses of the treaty/covenant), iden-

[36] Wiseman, *art. cit.*, 69 col. vii 528–531.

[37] Borger, *art. cit.*, 191–192.

[38] Streck, *Assurbanipal*, 79, 68–73. The parallel to Deut 29:23ff. is pointed out by Streck, 78, n.4, with a reference to D. H. Müller's *Ezechielstudien*, 61–62.

[39] On the basis of the Assyrian parallel we have slightly modified *CCD's* translation. Since in the Assyrian text the same ones who ask the question answer it, it is to be assumed that the subjects of *wĕʾāmĕrû* in vv. 23 and 24 are identical; so also in the parallel passages 1 Kgs 9:8–9; Jer 22:8–9.

tical literary form. The biblical passage shows only insignificant differences: the question is asked and answered by future generations, not by those suffering from the curses; the biblical answer, though basically identical with the Assyrian, is considerably expanded and of course is a statement of deuteronomic theology.[40]

In view of such parallels between Assyrian treaties and Deuteronomy,[41] we may be virtually certain that deuteronomic circles were familiar with the Assyrian practice of demanding an oath of allegiance from their vassals expressed in terms of love. In line with Borger's proposal above, we may even assume that they knew of such oaths by Israelite kings.[42]

But is the term love an innovation in the Israelite covenant tradition? We think not, at least it is no innovation made by the author of Deut 6:5, which is generally considered the earliest reference to the love of God in Deuteronomy.

First, Judg 5:31:"May all your enemies perish thus, O Lord! but your friends[43] be as the sun rising in its might!" It has often been debated whether this verse, so unlike the rest of the Song of Deborah and so reminiscent of the Psalms, belongs to the original poem. The question will undoubtedly remain *sub judice*, but Weiser's cultic interpretation of the entire Song is persuasively argued, and if correct, would prove the antiquity of v. 31.[44] Certainly the conclusion has an archaic ring, and the reference to the Israelites as Yahweh's "friends" becomes perfectly intelligible in the light of our remarks on the covenant background of the term love. The Israelites are those bound to Yahweh in covenant, and therefore naturally opposed to his enemies; the war and victory described in the Song are those of the people of God. It is prob-

[40] What remains to be investigated is the *Sitz im Leben* of this form; this we leave to another occasion.

[41] The actual parallels may of course be later than the earliest texts in Deuteronomy on the love of God, but they still demonstrate the connection of the deuteronomic tradition with Assyrian treaties.

[42] For example, Manasseh may have taken the oath in Assyria to love Assurbanipal; this would be the basis for the tradition preserved in 2 Chr 33:11–13 (cf. Wiseman, *art. cit.*, 4). Since in view of the evidence of the second millennium the oath to love the sovereign hardly arose only in the early seventh century, we may safely assume that kings like Menahem also promised to love their Assyrian lord.

[43] MT, "his friends."

[44] A. Weiser, *ZAW* 71 (1959) 94–95.

able therefore that the term love goes back to a very early period in the Israelite covenant tradition.

Certainly the use of the term is earlier than its appearance in Deut 6:5. We make this assertion on the ground that Deut 6:4–18[45] is by way of commentary a series of citations and allusions to the beginning of the Decalogue. "And thou shalt love the Lord, thy God, . . ." in 6:5 presupposes therefore "those who love me" in 5:10 (= Exod 20:6).

The citations and allusions to the Decalogue in 6:10–15 are clear.[46] 6:12 ("the Lord, who brought you out of the land of Egypt, that place of slavery") cites the beginning of the Decalogue. 6:14 ("You shall not follow other gods") is a restatement of the first commandment in typically deuteronomic terminology. 6:15 ("for the Lord, your God, who is in your midst, is a jealous God") repeats the motive clause, with the addition of "in your midst," of 5:9 (= Exod 20:5).

Framing, so to speak, the concrete application of the Decalogue to the period of the settlement in Palestine are the allusions to the Decalogue in 6:5 and 6:17, which refer to 5:10 (= Exod 20:6) : *wĕʾāhabtā* = *lĕʾōhăbay, šāmôr tišmĕrûn ʾet miṣwōt YHWH ʾĕlōhêkem* = *ûlĕšōmĕrê miṣwōtāy*.[47] This seems evident from a number of considerations:

(1) In the context of 6:10–15, which is one of allusion to and citation of the Decalogue, the injunction to love Yahweh and keep his commandments is most likely also an allusion to the Decalogue.

(2) The sequence of *miṣwōt-ʿēdōt-ḥuqqîm* (6:17), though found elsewhere (1 Chr 29:19; 2 Chr 34:31; cf. 2 Kgs 23:3), never occurs in Deuteron-

[45] Deut 6:19 seems to have been added; cf. 9:4.

[46] I proposed this view of Deut 6:10–15 in my lecture notes *Adnotationes in librum Deuteronomii*, 100ff., in 1960, and compared von Rad's study of later levitical preaching ("Die levitische Predigt in den Büchern der Chronik," *Gesammelte Studien zum Alten Testament* [München, 1958] 248–261). Subsequently and quite independently, as N. Lohfink informs me, H. G. Reventlow proposed a very similar view at the 15th *Orientalistentag*. I should like to express my debt to Lohfink on two accounts: first, following his criticisms, I have here not proposed "him shall you serve and in his name shall you swear" as allusions to 5:9 (*toʿobdēm*) and 5:11, so that the order of the Decalogue is now perfectly preserved in 6:12–15 (5:6, 7, 10); second, it was the study of his dissertation (cf. n. 34 above) with its invaluable tables on the usage of the terms for law and its observance, as well as his own study of the structure of Deuteronomy 6, that allowed me to see the significance of the references to love and keeping the commandments in 6:5,17. For whatever may be correct therefore in the remarks that follow, a large share of the credit is due to Lohfink.

[47] MT, *miṣwōtāy*, Ketib, *miṣwātô;* cf. app. crit. in Kittel, *BH*[3].

omy. This points to a special reason guiding the author's choice among the many expressions for law, commandments, etc. An adequate explanation would be the desire to allude to the Decalogue.

(3) The superscription of 4:45 has the sequence *ʿēdōt-ḥuqqîm-mišpāṭîm*, which is repeated in 6:20. Since 6:17 is the only other passage in Deuteronomy where *ʿēdōt* is used, one would expect the sequence of 4:45 and 6:20. The initial position of *miṣwōt* and its replacing *mišpāṭîm* may again be explained by the influence of the Decalogue.[48]

(4) The phrase *ʾăšer ṣiwwāk* looks back to Horeb, not to the present time in Moab. In the relevant passages,[49] the general rule is that, where Yahweh is said to have commanded, and the speaker is Moses at the time of the promulgation of the deuteronomic laws,[50] then the perfect *ṣiwwâ* refers either to laws given the people at Horeb,[51] or to the command given Moses at Horeb to remain with Yahweh and learn the laws he was to communicate in Moab.[52] For this reason one never finds ". . . which Yahweh has commanded TODAY," or "just as Yahweh has commanded TODAY." The TODAY of Deuteronomy is confined to the participle *mĕṣawweh*.

Thus in 4:13 Moses speaks of the Decalogue as *ʾăšer ṣiwwâ ʾetkem*, and continues in 4:14, "but me he commanded (*ṣiwwâ*) at that time. . . ." Similarly in 5:32–6:2: in vv. 32–33 (*ṣiwwâ* twice) we have a brief parenesis on the observance of the Decalogue, recalled in 5:6–21; in 6:1 *ṣiwwâ* refers to the personal revelation to Moses at Horeb; in 6:2, however, we shift to the participle, *mĕṣawwĕkā*, because the laws revealed to Moses at Horeb are now being promulgated.

Most of the exceptions to this rule are apparent rather than real. In 13:6[53] and 17:3 the subject is the worship of other gods, and therefore based on the first commandment of the Decalogue. 20:17 is concerned with the destruction of the Canaanites, which was also commanded at

[48] Another factor in the omission of *mišpāṭîm* may have been that the Decalogue does not contain *m.*, if *m.* are customary laws (casuistic).

[49] We do not consider therefore 1:19; 1:41; 2:37; 10:5; 18:18,20; 31:23; 34:9.

[50] Therefore the following passages drop out: 6:20,24,25; 26:13,14.

[51] 4:13,23; 5:32,33; 6:17; 9:12,16; 13:6; 17:3; 20:17. The passages of the Decalogue 5:12,15,16 constitute a special problem, because the Decalogue is presented as a direct quotation. Whatever their explanation may be, they are not a difficulty for our view on the other passages with the perfect. It may also be noted that the Decalogue in Exodus does not contain these references to the past.

[52] 1:3; 4:5,14; 6:1; 28:69.

[53] Note the reference in the same verse to the historical prologue of the Decalogue.

Horeb.[54] 24:8 speaks of commands given the priests and Levites; it is difficult to say what commands are referred to, but they are not to be found in Deuteronomy.[55] 12:21 does refer to a law in Deuteronomy, namely 12:15, and 28:45 speaks of the entire law in Deuteronomy as having been commanded by Yahweh, which is quite without parallel (cf. 28:1,13,14,15). It should be observed, however, that 12:21 and 28:45 regard laws already announced to the people.

If, however, 6:5 and 6:17 allude to the Decalogue, then it is clear that *lĕʾōhăbay ulĕšōmĕrê miṣwōtay* was in the Decalogue at the time of the composition of 6:4ff.[56] No one would suggest that it was added by the author of 6:4ff. so that it could be subsequently alluded to. For this author the Decalogue in its present form represented the old normative tradition, the basis of Israelite existence, elements of which he singled out, commented upon, and applied to the Israel of his own time.

To sum up: our ancient Near Eastern sources suggest a quite new approach to the problem of the origins of the deuteronomic doctrine on the love of God. In their light it seems highly questionable whether Hosea's preaching is at all relevant, except perhaps in the sense that Hosea's highly personal vision was grounded in the older covenant tradition we find in Deuteronomy. It is of course possible that the emphasis placed on love in the deuteronomic tradition is to be partially explained by the prophet's influence. But the deuteronomic love of service is older, probably as old or almost as old as the covenant itself. If so, and if the old sovereign-vassal terminology of love is as relevant as we think it is, then what a history lies behind the Christian test of true *agape*—"If you love me, keep my commandments"!

[54] The immediate reference is to 7:2, but this is a deuteronomic reformulation of an older text (cf. S. R. Driver, *A Critical and Exegetical Commentary on Deuteronomy* [ICC; Edinburgh, 1902] 239–240, who correctly refers to Exod 23:31–33). On the relation of Exod 23:20–33; 34:10–16, and Deut 7:1–5, I again refer to Lohfink, *Hauptgebot.*

[55] C. Steuernagel, *Deuteronomium und Josua* (HKAT I/3; Göttingen, 1900) 89, thinks of laws like Lev 13f. and is probably correct in interpreting such a reference as a sign of a late addition.

[56] We agree with H. G. Reventlow, *Gebot und Predigt im Dekalog* (Gütersloh, 1962) 40, that the assumption of a "deuteronomic" redaction of the Decalogue should be buried once and for all. The Decalogue was transmitted and acquired its additions in the cult. It should be remarked that Deuteronomy itself never uses the participal—7:9 cites the Decalogue—but the participle is well attested in the Psalms (5:12; 69:37; 97:10; 145:20; cf. also 31:24).

CHAPTER 15

The Babylonian Job*

My topic is one on which I hope that as an Assyriologist I can speak with some competence, but also one, I trust, which is not without interest to biblical scholars. I shall not be comparing the book of Job. Rather, I shall be offering you what I would call Mesopotamian prolegomena to that great masterpiece of Old Testament literature.

My Job is one of the better-known works of Babylonian literature, and it has been around, in part at least, since 1875. What was published at that time was the second tablet of this composition. There one reads of a man recounting his sufferings, protesting his perfect fidelity to the gods, and therefore feeling baffled by his present state, concluding finally that man cannot know what the gods demand of him. Inevitably—this was also the time of the Babylonian Flood Story with the Babylonian Noah and of the emerging *Babel und Bibel Streit*—inevitably, the work became known as the *Poem of the Righteous Sufferer*, the *Babylonian Job*.

Over the years knowledge of the poem gradually increased. By 1960, when *Ludlul bēl nēmeqi*, "I will praise the lord of wisdom," as it came to be known from its incipit, was re-edited by Wilfred Lambert,[1] it was fairly certain that the poem originally consisted of four tablets, each of 120 lines. Of the four, we had by this time most of the first tablet, the

* Lecture delivered to the Catholic Biblical Association, 1992.

[1] W. G. Lambert, *Babylonian Wisdom Literature* (Oxford, 1960) 21–62.

second tablet virtually complete, 105 but often badly broken lines of the third tablet, and 65, also often badly broken lines, of the fourth tablet.

This fuller text showed that the sufferer's woes began with his abandonment by his personal god and goddess, and this brought with it an inevitable series of disasters. He was plotted against, rejected by the king, turned upon by almost everyone, even by his family. So the first tablet. Then after the passage we referred to above that made him appear to be a Babylonian Job, we learn how he was set upon by demonic forces that shatter his health and finally bring him to the edge of the grave. So the second tablet. Then, at his darkest hour, relief came. During the night, in a series of dreams, probably three, perhaps one for each watch of the night, the sufferer is prepared by a message and purifying rites for the deliverance that the god Marduk effects the following day. Exactly where the third tablet ended we are still not sure, but in any event the sufferer is cured and eventually we find him in Marduk's temple in Babylon, the Esangila, there to offer prayers and sacrifices and to show himself to the astonished world as a witness to, and as evidence of, the power of Babylon's god.

Though no manuscript was dated before the seventh century, Lambert argued that the work was a composition of the Kassite period, therefore, roughly of the late second millennium. Personal names that appear in the course of the narrative argue against an earlier date, and stylistic considerations against a later. This date is generally accepted.

Scholars also agree that the early inferences on the basis of the partial evidence of the second tablet were not mistaken, and that *Ludlul* does indeed address the problem of the righteous sufferer. It is, therefore, often studied and discussed together with another composition known as the *Babylonian Theodicy*, a work of probably somewhat later date. According to Wolfram von Soden, these are the two works of Mesopotamian literature in which the Job problem is faced "mit aller Leidenschaft."[2] René Labat declared that, as in the *Theodicy*, the subject of *Ludlul* is the problem of evil and the justice of the gods.[3] Thorkild Jacobsen has written that the problem of the righteous sufferer "forces itself upon religious consciousness in Mesopotamia about

[2] W. von Soden, "Das Fragen nach der Gerechtigkeit Gottes im Alten Orient," *MDOG* 96 (1965) 49.

[3] R. Labat, et al., *Les religions du Proche-Orient asiatique* (Paris, 1970) 328.

the middle of the second millennium and is dealt with in two remarkable works, *Ludlul bēl nēmeqi* . . . and the Babylonian Theodicy."[4]

To the problem of the righteous sufferer, interpreters find, broadly speaking, two solutions in *Ludlul.* They are usually seen, not as opposed, but rather as complementary, to each other. Thus, in *The Intellectual Adventure of Ancient Man*, Jacobsen saw *Ludlul* as "a counterpart of, though much inferior to, the Book of Job," in which two solutions are offered to the problem of the righteous sufferer: one for the mind, the other for the heart. In the first solution, which we find in the second tablet, "man is too small, too limited in outlook, to pass judgment on things that are divine . . . . Human judgment cannot be true judgment," and man should not "presume to set it up against that of a god." The other solution, the one for the heart, Jacobsen found in the personal history of the sufferer who eventually was cured and restored to society.[5] In other words, the gods do not abandon man, and so he must put his trust in their mercy and goodness.

In his later writings on the subject, it might be noted, Jacobsen makes no mention of the solution for the heart. This does not imply, however, as he has kindly informed me, that he has retracted his earlier position. He was simply commenting more briefly and emphasizing what he thought of greater religious significance. It might also be noted that he has restated the solution for the mind somewhat differently: "all human values are finite and yet man is held to absolutes beyond him." This he considers one of the "finest insights" of Mesopotamian religious thought, and he leaves it to the religious genius of Israel to advance further, in the Book of Job.

Occasionally a scholar has stressed the first solution to the exclusion of the second. Thus, for example, René Labat, who wrote that the sufferer "finally understands that the designs of the gods are impenetrable to mortals, and that this unfathomable mystery can alone explain the apparent injustice of the human condition."[6] But there is something misleading about that "finally understands," for this final understanding is arrived at when only a little over one-fourth of the composition is finished, and there are still 312 lines left. The account of Marduk's

[4] T. Jacobsen, *The Treasures of Darkness: A History of Mesopotamian Religion* (New Haven, 1976) 162.

[5] Jacobsen, "Mesopotamia," in *The Intellectual Adventure of Ancient Man* (Chicago, 1946) 213–16.

[6] Labat, *Religions*, 329.

intervention and the visit to his temple, the subject of tablets III and IV, constitute 50% of the entire work. Generally, then, the solution for the heart is also taken into account, some using the same general terms Jacobsen used—the gods will intervene—others being more specific and restrictive—Marduk will intervene.

This latter distinction is associated with the emphasis some scholars (for example, Jean Bottéro, Lambert, von Soden) have come to place on what they call the henotheistic atmosphere of the work. *Ludlul* is, as Bottéro put it, "résolument 'monolâtrique.'"[7] And it has been often assumed that from the beginning of his sufferings to the end the man is aware that Marduk is responsible for everything he undergoes. Indeed, it is in confronting not just any god but the ruler of the world that the problem of suffering and the assignment of responsibility takes on a new urgency and becomes immeasurably more acute.

Such, in brief summary, has been the scholarship on *Ludlul*. And I must confess it has always left me with a certain malaise, a feeling that something was wrong, that the picture was somehow out of focus, though I wasn't sure what the picture was or should be. Not the least of my problems has concerned the famous passage, the Job passage, at the beginning of Tablet II, the passage that looms so large in everyone's interpretation of the entire work. I could find no really satisfactory explanation why, if this passage is so important, so crucial to the treatment of the problem at hand, it is found so early in the work and is never again, so far as we knew, even alluded to. If this contains the message, as it were, of *Ludlul*, the very heart, as has been said, of the author's thought, I would have expected the author to save the great revelation till the end of his work or at least to come back to it in some way. In my expectations of such a grand finale I do not think I have been unduly influenced by the Book of Job. What indeed is the evidence that the author attached any kind of lasting, absolute validity to the reflections of the sufferer at this point in the narrative?

And there have been other questions. *Résolument monolâtrique?* From beginning to end? Only if Marduk is the sufferer's personal god. But is he? Does the author really avoid facing Marduk's responsibility, as has been claimed? Is in fact *Ludlul* intended to be a serious treatment of the Job problem? Compare it with the Babylonian Theodicy. There we find 27 strophes, 13 lines per strophe, a dialogue between a

[7] J. Bottéro, "Antiquités Assyro-Babyloniennes," *Annuaire de l'École pratique des hautes etudes: IVe Section* (Paris, 1965–66) 106.

sufferer and his pious friend, and they argue back and forth, strophe after strophe, about the justice of the gods. This is certainly a facing of the Job problem and a serious effort to confront it in all its complexity. But *Ludlul*? There are exactly 47 lines, the famous lines at the beginning of Tablet II, that can be said to address the problem by more than possible implication. Or so I once thought.

Then in 1980 D. J. Wiseman published his copy and edition of a fragmentary tablet found at Nimrud, ancient Kalkhu in Assyria.[8] It belongs to the first tablet of *Ludlul*, and in any reading its contribution is important. It provides, almost in their entirety, the hitherto missing lines 13–38; it indicates the restoration and probable readings of lines 39–42, and it also gives us the more or less complete restoration of the last ten lines of the tablet, lines 111–120, which previously had been known only by a few words and unintelligible signs. This means, above all, that we now have, virtually complete, the hymn with which the poem begins.[9]

When I first read the new text, the old questions about *Ludlul* came back with new force, some answered, some refocused, and another reading of the poem began to take shape. But before going public with my own fresh thoughts, I thought I would wait and see what others made of the new evidence. But alas! I have waited in vain. There have been a number of studies of specific problems of reading and translation, but nothing has appeared, so far as I am aware, that looks at the new text in the larger perspective of the entire poem.

Well, for obvious reasons, I had better not wait much longer. Besides, as Tacitus taught me long ago, one privilege of old age is to think what one wants and to say what one thinks. So here is what I think about *Ludlul*.

Let me begin with a brief description of my new reading of the text. I think that in the narrative, *after the hymn*, the author portrays someone who, when his sufferings begin, is a man of conventional personal religion. In his piety and his beliefs he is Mesopotamian Everyman. As his suffering continues, however, with no relief in sight, he is forced to see this conventional religion as problematic, a source of bewilderment, and to fall back on a conventional solution, the inscrutability of

[8] D. J. Wiseman, "A New Text of the Babylonian Poem of the Righteous Sufferer," *Anatolian Studies* 30 (1980) 101–7.

[9] W. L. Moran, "Notes on the Hymn to Marduk in *Ludlul Bēl Nēmeqi*," *JAOS* 103 (1983) 255–60.

the gods. This remains his situation until, in his hour of deepest desperation, he is made aware of another and, to him, new reality, the reality of Marduk, and there is revealed to him a new personal religion, the religion of Marduk, a religion that transforms and transcends the religion and problems of the past. To proclaim this god and this new religion is, I propose, what *Ludlul* is all about.

One of the most important things that we learn from the Nimrud text is that Marduk is not the sufferer's personal god. Lines 41–44, though still somewhat problematic, distinguish very clearly between Marduk, who is angry, and the personal god and goddess, who depart. This does not mean, of course, that the sufferer made this distinction when his tribulations began. These lines reflect his total experience, his deliverance as well as his suffering. In fact, from this point on, through the end of the second tablet, Marduk is not mentioned at all. He is finally referred to at the beginning of Tablet III, but not by name, which will appear only when Marduk is identified as the sender of the message of deliverance. The explanation for this reticence, never very plausible, though frequently cited, that the author wished to avoid associating Marduk with the suffering of his faithful servant, is now demonstrably wrong, for the opening hymn, as we shall see, not only does not avoid Marduk's responsibility, it glories in it.

The explanation for the absence of Marduk is that the narrative reflects the sufferer's perception of his problem *at the time of his suffering*, and this perception was a very conventional one, one not involving Marduk at all, but reflecting the complex of beliefs and practices associated with the cult of the personal god. It is, we may assume, the same complex that we find expressed or implied in two earlier works that anticipate in some sense the later *Ludlul*: a Sumerian composition published by Samuel Kramer and called by him "A Man and His God,"[10] and an Old Babylonian work published by Jean Nougayrol.[11]

Here suffering is a crisis of personal religion and involves one's personal god. Or to be more specific, it is the suffering of one in the prime of life that provokes the crisis. The ills of old age and the death that eventually follows do not seem to have been problematic, but were

[10] S. N. Kramer, "Man and his God: A Sumerian Variation on the 'Job' Motif," in *Wisdom in the Bible and in the Ancient Near East* (ed. M. Noth; VTSup 3; Leiden, 1955) 170–82.

[11] J. Nougayrol, "Une version ancienne du 'Juste Souffrant,'" *RB* 59 (1952) 239–50.

considered as simply belonging to the natural course of life. The personal god is the one who forms in the womb, brings one into this world, guides, protects, intercedes, and gives the additional protection of beneficent spirits. This god is not remote; he is close by. Nor is this god, in so far as a personal god, an inscrutable cosmic force. He is father, master, "my god," "my lord." He is even a man's friend. The Old Babylonian text just referred to begins, "A young man weeps to his god as to a friend." And when the time of forgiveness arrives, the personal god addresses this man: "I am your god, your creator, your refuge. My guards are awake for you, are strong for you. I will open for you a hiding place. Long life will I give you." And through this healing the god reaches out to those suffering in the community. The text continues: "Anoint the parched, feed the hungry, give water to the thirsty to drink." Integration into the community brings social obligations. In brief, sin and consequent abandonment by the personal god are inevitable—no one is perfect—but so are mercy and forgiveness inevitable—no father abandons his child forever. It is this religion of the personal god with which, so to speak, the *Ludlul* narrative begins. It is the crisis of this religion that will follow.

But before the crisis begins, at the very end of the first tablet, we find the sufferer, despite his sighs and tears at his cruel separation from society, expressing to himself his confidence that things are going to get better, and immediately. He says (I think)

> There is a festival tomorrow, good fortune will come my way.
> The new moon will be sighted; the Sun will shine on me.

We do not know what festival he refers to. From the next line, the beginning of Tablet II, "This year, and the next, the term (that is, the feast) passed by," perhaps we should think of the New Year's festival. In any case, we are certainly meant to see the thoughts of someone with a simple, naïve faith, sharing some popular belief, Everyman's religion, of a piece with a simple, unreflecting faith in a personal god, with no idea of what still lies ahead of him.

This now changes. We come to Tablet II 1–48. This passage consists of the single transitional line just quoted, and there follow four strophes. The sense of deep, personal crisis is marked structurally by introducing the first three strophes with first person verbs in initial position: "I turned around," "I looked," "I examined myself." The fourth strophe begins with a question, "Who can learn the plan of the gods in heaven's depth" (Babylonian *qerbu*) and ends "I reflected on these things," and then echoing the first line and exploiting the ambiguity of Babylonian *qerbu*, "their meaning (*qerbu*) I did not learn."

This is a very carefully composed passage. A new and important development in the sufferer's personal drama is followed and elaborated, solemn step by solemn step.

> I turned around, and there was evil, only evil.
> Wickedness to me ever increasing, I finding no redress.

The social evils of Tablet II continue. He calls out to his god and his goddess, and he calls in vain. Again, as at the beginning of his abandonment, he turns to the conventional channels of revelation and relief, diviner, magician, dream-interpreter, and he turns in vain. And now a sense of estrangement sets in:

> What strange doings everywhere.

Then,

> I looked behind—trackings, troubles.

The unremitting hostility of the world continues. He looks at himself and he finds himself treated

> Like one who did not prepare the sacrifice for his god,
> And at his meals was not mindful of his goddess.

He looks to the obligations in the cult of the personal gods—the prayers, the offerings, sharing his meals with them. He briefly mentions the public cult and the duty of the authority figure, paterfamilias and ruler of the community, to instruct his people in the service of the gods.

He reviews then his actual performance, and he finds himself without fault. Not only has he performed his duties to the gods, but he has with joy prayed for the king and instructed the people in their duties to both god and king. Then bitter and bewildered,

> Would that I knew that these things were pleasing to the god,
> What is good to oneself is an offence to the god.
> What one thinks vile is good to one's god.

"The god," "his god"—established ways of referring to the personal god. His bitterness and bewilderment concern only his personal god.

And then the famous fourth strophe:

Who can learn the plan of the gods in heaven's depth,
Who can fathom the thoughts of those deep waters,
Where has man ever learned what the god will do?

The gods are not only personal and close by; they dwell too and think their thoughts far removed from man.

He turns his thoughts to man and looks at him in a curiously detached way. The sinful man of tradition—the man who cannot help sinning—is seen, in implied contrast with the divine, first, as living vigorously and then dying miserably, next, as unstable, a creature of many and swiftly changing thoughts and moods. And finally the quiet despair of

I reflected on these things, and their meaning I did not learn.

This is, unquestionably, a remarkable passage. Most striking are the lines that stress the inscrutability of the gods. Recognition of this inscrutability was ancient and common in Mesopotamian religious thought. But here it is given a radically new twist. Not only are the gods inscrutable, but they hold man to norms of behavior that they would not reveal and he could not discover. Indeed, it even appeared that good was evil and evil good. Here is an *Umwertung aller Werte* if there ever was one, but it is the logical conclusion of two convictions: one, the possibility of innocence according to known norms; two, suffering is a consequence of personal sin.

There is here, as we have already remarked, deep bitterness and deep bewilderment. Joined with a contempt for man, the ephemeral manic-depressive, it becomes a kind of despair. It reminds one very much of the *amechania*, the sense of helplessness, that became a theme of archaic Greek poetry, and the stress the poets laid on the power to endure existence as the essential human virtue. And staying closer to home, it reminds one too of the Flood story in the Gilgamesh epic. This long account, which it is generally conceded was not part of the original epic and which made its way into the text about the same time as the composition of *Ludlul*, begins with Utnapishtim, the Babylonian Noah, telling Gilgamesh:

Shurippak—a city you yourself know,
Lying on Euphrates bank—

This city was old, the gods within it,
And their heart moved the gods to send a flood.

Why? In this version, we shall never know. In this version, the decision to destroy mankind has no prior history, no background; it simply happens. It may not be an act of sheer caprice, but we shall never know why. The waters wash over man, and he disappears, swallowed up in mystery.

The prologue to the epic portrays Gilgamesh as a wise man, and it points very emphatically to the Flood story as an important part of the knowledge that makes him wise. It is, you will agree, a chilling, frightening wisdom, and it provides a context for the chilling, frightening wisdom of *Ludlul*.

Now there is no denying that this wisdom confronts the suffering of the individual and divine governance as problems. But it is also clear that the problems center almost exclusively on the religion of the personal god. Nothing suggests in any way that without mentioning him the sufferer is struggling with the unspoken thought of the justice of Marduk, the lord of the universe.

And to state the obvious, it is also clear that this pessimistic view of the human situation is found at a certain point in the narrative. It expresses the thoughts of the sufferer while suffering and believing his personal god responsible for his plight. But these were not his last thoughts. His last thoughts are those of the opening hymn, to which we now turn.

First, a few words of introduction. In the many prayers we have in which a suffering penitent bewails his situation, confesses his sins, known and unknown, and begs for a god or goddess to heal him, a very common conclusion is the promise that, if healed, the penitent will sing to the world the praises of the healing god or goddess. Our text should be seen as the fulfillment of such a promise.

The hymn has three parts, each articulated by a verb in the first person and in initial position: "I will praise . . ." (line 1) introduces the long, objective statement of lines 1–36 that praise Marduk without reference to the speaker; "I will glorify . . ." (line 37) introduces a couplet recording the speaker's own experience; "I will have the people learn . . ." (line 39) introduces a couplet on the social and religious implications of this experience. The narrative follows.

And, to appreciate the contribution of the Nimrud text, keep in mind that lines 13–38 are completely new, and lines 39–42, despite a lingering difficulty or two, are now understood for the first time.

The opening quatrain is, *in nuce*, the entire composition.

I will praise the lord of wisdom, judicious god,
Enraged in the night, in the daylight calming.
Marduk, the lord of wisdom, judicious god,
Enraged in the night, in the daylight calming.

It declares itself an act of praise, and it declares itself boldly, with an assertion of faith. It will hymn "the lord of wisdom," or, less literally, "the all-wise lord." This wisdom, Babylonian *nēmequ*, it must be understood, is not concerned with the abstract. It is a quality of mind in the experiential and practical order that is a guide to action in all its manifold forms. It conceives of goals and determines the means to achieve these goals. The *Chicago Assyrian Dictionary* sees in it "the body of experiences, knowledge, skills, and traditions which are the basis of a craft or occupation, or form the basis of civilization as a whole" (*CAD* N/2, 160). It is, therefore, essential to that most exalted and important of occupations, that of the ruler. Indeed, anticipating by centuries the conception of the ideal ruler of the classical world and Hellenistic historiography, the Babylonians saw such practical wisdom as an essential and complementary virtue of physical strength and courage. And our hymn sings of both, both the power of Marduk and his wisdom. But it forefronts the latter, because the latter confronts the basic problem. It declares that, despite what we may call the evidence, the world makes sense. Behind suffering is a plan. We may not understand the plan. No one can. Not even the other gods. But there is a plan, there is meaning, behind what can only seem not just mysterious but even willful and capricious.

"Lord of wisdom, judicious god." "Judicious god" reaffirms this core belief. It asserts that Marduk has the mind and will to heal. A ruler must be judicious, and to be judicious is often placed in opposition to anger. Thus, in *Enuma elish* (VI 137), Marduk is "angry but judicious, raging but forgiving." Judiciousness checks anger, does not allow it to be utterly destructive, even to the disadvantage of the ruler himself. It is a quality of the mind that, like mercy, eventually saves.

The statement of faith of the opening line is followed by a statement of the problem: Marduk is angry, and suddenly, as day follows night in

Iraq, he is calm. He belongs to the darkness; he belongs to the light. He is a god of swift and startling contrasts. He is a god of wrath; he is a god of a sudden and matching mercy.

What follows repeats these qualities over and over. Thus, for example, in lines 5–6, whose underlying imagery, the darkness of the storm and the light at dawn, picks up the contrast of lines 2 and 4:

> Whose fury, like a storm blast, makes a wasteland,
> Whose breath is, like the dawn wind, pleasing.

The howling, rushing storm—the gentle breeze at the break of day: Marduk is both. Or double clause is matched by double clause, as in the following lines:

> In his rage he's irresistible, a very deluge is his wrath,
> His is a pardoning mind, his a forgiving heart.

As is evident, the hymn is concerned only with Marduk as he affects the individual. It says almost nothing, except by implication, of his rank among the gods, nothing about lineage, birthplace, cult centers, etc., the common topics of hymns to gods. It considers Marduk only as he enters the life of a man, directly, as a matter of experience. It celebrates the wrath and the mercy of Marduk.

This wrath—perhaps simply the power in lines 9–12—and mercy are hymned as matching, interfacing attributes. The semantic matching is reinforced by parallelism, clause matching clause. The dominant rhythm is established in line 5 and goes through line 16. A single clause in line 5, a single matching clause in line 6; two clauses in line 7, two matching clauses in line 8. And so on. The matching breaks off in line 17; two clauses answer the single clause of line 16. Then the text lingers on the image of Marduk tender as a mother, with an additional couplet in lines 19–20. The rhythm returns briefly in lines 21–22, then yields to less regular patterns, until the proclamation of lines 33–34, where the perfect correspondence of mercy to wrath is given final, formal expression:

> As heavy as is his hand, so merciful is his heart.
> As savage as are his weapons, so healing is his spirit.

In the collocation, as it were, of *tremendum* and *fascinans* on the same line, something that does not occur in lines 5–32, we return to the opening stanza and the Marduk who is

Enraged in the night, in the daylight calming.

A minor but important theme is, as we have already briefly noted, the suddenness with which the mercy of Marduk erupts, as it were, on the object of his wrath. Implied in the contrast of night and day in the opening quatrain, this suddenness is made explicit in lines 18–20.

He is moved to mercy, and suddenly the god is like a mother,
Hastening to treat his loved one tenderly,
And behind, like a cow with her calf, back and forth, round about he goes.

Here the cruelty of the previous line suddenly becomes the tenderness of a mother, and this sudden mercy reappears as if an essential feature in the speaker's own personal history: He took pity on me, and suddenly how he gave me life. It is in the image, too, of the rescue *in extremis*, an old topos also attested in Sumerian literature, which we find in lines 12 and 14, the body given up for dead or even being lowered into the grave and then the saving hand reaches out and raises from the dead. When Marduk will show his mercy, no one knows, but when he does, this manifestation will not be the conclusion of a process. It will simply be there, a powerful presence, an epiphany.

But if his mercy is unpredictable, it is also certain. In this hymn we clearly find the old, naïve belief in the certainty of mercy and forgiveness, but now it is shifted from the personal god to Marduk himself, the cosmic ruler. For it is precisely the cosmic ruler who is responsible. It is Bel, the Lord, who for the sufferer changes day into night, and Marduk the warrior who turns against him. If there could be any doubts about the significance of these terms at this point, they have already been anticipated and dispelled by lines 29–32 and their glorification of the Marduk whose thoughts are beyond all comprehension, even by the gods.

A warrior, but this warrior is also one who forgives, shows mercy, heals, rescues. He is a warrior, too, of great tenderness, and this tenderness transforms the object of his cruelty into his loved one (line 19). He is like a mother (line 18), like a cow with her calf to whom she is ever turning back. This image is a fairly common one in Mesopotamian art, the calves at the udders, the cow with head turned and looking back to her young. Note, too, how the language of the image, the stem *sḫr*, resonates with its earlier occurrences in lines 8 and

16 and their meaning there of forgiveness and reconciliation. And, finally, this warrior has soft palms. Soft palms are what characterize the goddess Gula, the goddess par excellence of healing, the *asugallatu*, the great physician. They are the hands of one who touches and heals, the hands of one who applies cool and healing bandages. In brief, the mercy of this cosmic ruler is not something cold, remote, archly sovereign. It is warm, gentle, touchingly tender. There is in all this the unmistakable atmosphere of the religion of the personal god.

The atmosphere, but not the reality, for this Marduk religion in effect puts an end to the old religion of the personal god. This, I think, are the clear implications of lines 15–16 and 41–46.

> 15 He frowns, and Life-force and Lady Fortune go far away.
> He looks with favor, and to the one he had rejected his god comes back again.
>
> . . . .
>
> 41 From the time the Lord turned day into night,
> And warrior Marduk turned against me,
> My god cast me away, disappeared,
> My goddess left, went *hiding* far away.
> He cut off Life-force at my side,
> Lady Fortune frightened off to look for someone else.

The first passage presents a general truth: beneficent spirits and personal gods come and go according to Marduk's moods. The second applies the truth to the individual's experience: Marduk turned against him with the apparently inevitable abandonment by the personal god. Now, this is not altogether without parallel. Frequently in prayers one of the high gods or goddesses is asked that he or she intervene and command the alienated personal god to return to his client. This is the role Marduk may play in lines 25 and 28 where he restores the personal god or is an agent of reconciliation. But in the other passages something more seems to be claimed for Marduk. The personal gods and goddesses are here simply functions or extensions of Marduk's anger or favor. As far as one's personal gods are concerned, all depends on one's relationship with Marduk; the personal gods themselves have no autonomy.

This undoubtedly should be seen as an aspect of the sovereignty of Marduk. Another aspect of this sovereignty and Marduk's power over the individual would seem to be the extraordinary and startling statement of lines 23–25 that make Marduk responsible for the individual's sin.

He *commands* and makes one give offense.
On his day of redress, absolved are guilt and sin.
It is he who ever saves, provides that *a case* be heard.

"He commands" is not quite certain, though it hard to see what other reading of the text is possible. But, in any case, whatever the correct reading may be, it can hardly palliate the following assertion, literally, "he causes sin/guilt to be acquired." To my knowledge, making a god responsible for sin in this way, in such a general statement, is without parallel. The gods may treat communities without distinction between the good and the evil ones. A hostile deity may occasionally be held responsible for one's sin. A god may deceive the individual; even the personal god may do so, though only as a punishment. But these scattered instances hardly mitigate the force of this bald, unqualified statement.

This exercise of sovereignty, it should be noted, is immediately complemented by another: just as sovereignly and paradoxically, "on his day of reckoning," guilt and sin are not punished; they are absolved. He is a god of sovereign freedom.

What is perhaps the single, most striking feature of this hymn is the mood that pervades it. A good illustration is lines 29–34.

The *exalted* lord sees into the heart of the gods,
Never does *a god* know his way.
Exalted Marduk sees into the heart of the gods,
No god, whoever he be, can learn his plan.
As heavy as is his hand, so merciful is his heart.
As savage as are his weapons, so healing is his spirit.

Lines 29–32, as we have already noted, bring us back to the opening quatrain and to the mind of Marduk. This mind, we are told, is an impenetrable mystery. The thoughts and ways of Marduk are beyond all understanding, even of the gods. And we are told this just before the final, formal statement on the relationship between the wrath and mercy of Marduk. Over the luminous certainty of these lines hangs the dark mystery of lines 29–32, but note, and note well, this is a mystery that is celebrated, not regretted.

Let us recall now the reflections of the sufferer at the beginning of Tablet II and compare what we saw there with what we have just seen in this hymn. You will, I think, agree that the differences are evident and profound. In Tablet II the dominant concern was the personal gods and the sufferer's relationship with them; in the hymn, the personal gods fade into insignificance, and all depends on one's relationship with Marduk. In Tablet II, the problem of sin and guilt was urgent and unresolved; in the hymn, the problem is not resolved but dismissed, and responsibility for sin and guilt are declared to pertain to the sovereignty of Marduk as much as mercy and forgiveness. In Tablet II, it was the plan (*ṭēmu*) and conduct (*alaktu*) of the personal gods that were found to be beyond the understanding of men; in the hymn, it is the plan and conduct of Marduk that are beyond the understanding, not only of men, but of the gods as well. The mystery is located in Marduk alone. In Tablet II, it was the gods above and man below; in the hymn, it is Marduk above and all else below.

These differences are such, it seems to me, that we must conclude that the views expressed in Tablet II are to be understood as those current at the time and the conventional answer to the problem of evil, an answer which by implication the hymn rejects. There is, I must admit, no other evidence for the currency of this view in the late second millennium, and I can only note that the remoteness and inscrutability of the gods, as Lambert has already remarked, were old theologoumena, though, it should be observed, they were applied to the gods in their governance of the universe or the nation rather than of the individual. Certainly, however, by the time of the Babylonian Theodicy, these theologoumena belong to the arguments of conventional piety and are often appealed to by the sufferer's pious friend. There is no reason to assume dependence here on *Ludlul*, nor, as far as I can see, the originality of *Ludlul*.

The discovery of Marduk's sovereignty is the subject of Tablets III and IV, and an essential part of this discovery is the visit to Marduk's temple. There is some evidence that a visit to the shrine or temple of the personal god was a necessary part of reconciliation with one's personal god. This visit is replaced by a visit to the Esangila. Note that a great part, probably all, of Tablet IV has this temple as its setting. It is here that *Ludlul* ends, and it is here that the sufferer's complete recovery takes place, as he moves from temple-gate to temple-gate. Lady

Fortune returns, life is his, his omens are clear once more, he is purified and absolved, and in the last two gates he comes to the statues of Marduk and his consort and bows in prayer before them. Then begin his offerings and sacrifices. He has learned where he must worship. *Ludlul* finally becomes a glorification of Marduk's cult as well as of Marduk himself.

Such glorification is not without parallel, and it probably should be seen, as Bottéro has already suggested, as part of the movement in the late second millennium B.C. to exalt Marduk to a unique position in the Mesopotamian pantheon. In this movement Marduk becomes absolutely supreme and, in some sense, the only god, for he alone, apart from the remote figure of the sky-god, enjoys autonomy.

This is the Marduk of *Enuma Elish*, the so-called Creation Epic, but more properly dubbed the Exaltation of Marduk. It begins with a plenitude of absence and negation, the gods inexistent, unnamed, unplaced in role and rank. "When no gods were to be seen, not one, / Were with names unnamed, with lots unlotted." It ends with an explosion of names, the fifty names of Marduk, the last of which, by making him so to speak the new Enlil and the new Ea, write finis to well over a millennium of religious history and replace the old trinity of Anu (sky-god) - Enlil (lord of the earth) - Ea (lord of the waters below) with Anu and Marduk, the latter in effect the only ruler. The Marduk of *Enuma Elish* is an absolute monarch.

The Marduk of *Ludlul* is also the Marduk that we find in compositions of the time of Nebuchadnezzar I (1125–1104 B.C.), in the late twelfth century, where Marduk's control of history, and control by his word alone, is so insisted on. If his statue was taken away by the Hittites or the Assyrians or the Elamites, it was because he ordered it. If he turns against his land and the gods all depart, it is because he told them to depart. And he knows what lies ahead. He can predict the rise of the king, the unnamed Nebuchadnezzar, who will return his statue from Elam to Babylon and restore to a new and unrivalled brilliance his temple Esangila.

Ludlul seems to be to be almost the logical extension of Marduk's lordship over creation and history into the domain of individual lives. If he rules the world and all that happens in it, he should rule the individual as well. A sovereignty less pervasive would not be absolute.

This, then, is my reading of *Ludlul*. Not a completely original reading, of course, but one, I think, with a somewhat new focus. In this reading, the solution for the mind and the one for the heart are not mutually complementary but opposed. Or more exactly, in locating the mystery of evil in Marduk, what had been a problem for the mind—I reflected on these things and did not learn their meaning—becomes a problem of the heart, and it is solved with reasons of the heart. Instead of wisdom, belief. Instead of reflection and argument, a hymn. *Credo quia absurdum.*

Ludlul bēl nēmeqi I 1–40

I will praise the lord of wisdom, judicious god,
Enraged in the night, in the daylight calming,
Marduk, the lord of wisdom, judicious god,
Enraged in the night, in the daylight calming,

Whose fury, like a storm blast, makes a wasteland,
Whose breath is, like the dawn wind, pleasing.

In his rage he's irresistible, a very deluge is his wrath,
His is a pardoning mind, his a forgiving heart.

The *full weight* of whose hands the heavens cannot support,
Whose soft palm saves a man about to die,
Marduk, the *full weight* of whose hands the heavens cannot support,
Whose soft palm saves a man about to die.

When he is angry, many are the graves to be opened,
When he pities, from the tomb he raises the fallen.

He frowns, and Life-force and Lady Fortune go far away.
He looks with favor, and to the one he had rejected his god comes back again.

Terrible is his . . . punishment to the one *still not* absolved.
He is moved to mercy, and suddenly *the god is like* a mother,
Hastening to treat his loved one tenderly,
And behind, like a cow with her calf, back and forth, round about he goes.

Sharp are the barbs of his whip, the body pierce and pierce.
His bandages are cool, giving life to death itself.

He *commands* and makes one give offense.
On his day of redress, absolved are guilt and sin.
It is he who ever saves, provides that *a case* be heard.

Through his holy spell are shivers and chills released –
Healer of *Adad's* thrusts, of Erra's wound,
Reconciler of god and goddess enraged.

The *exalted* lord sees into the heart of the gods,
Never does *a god* know his way.
Exalted Marduk sees into the heart of the gods,
No god, whoever he be, can learn his plan.

As heavy as is his hand, so merciful is his heart.
As savage as are his weapons, so healing is his spirit.

Against his will, who could cool his wound?
Would he not, which one relieve his *thrusts*?

I will glorify his fury, which like . . .
He took pity on me, and suddenly how he gave me life.

I will have the people learn adoration . . .
His good invocation *I will teach the land.*

Index of Passages

Index of Subjects

The Catholic Biblical Quarterly Monograph Series (CBQMS)

1. Patrick W. Skehan, *Studies in Israelite Poetry and Wisdom* (CBQMS 1) $9.00 ($7.20 for CBA members) ISBN 0-915170-00-0 (LC 77-153511)
2. Aloysius M. Ambrozic, *The Hidden Kingdom: A Redactional-Critical Study of the References to the Kingdom of God in Mark's Gospel* (CBQMS 2) $9.00 ($7.20 for CBA members) ISBN 0-915170-01-9 (LC 72-89100)
3. Joseph Jensen, O.S.B., *The Use of tôrâ by Isaiah: His Debate with the Wisdom Tradition* (CBQMS 3) $3.00 ($2.40 for CBA members) ISBN 0-915170-02-7 (LC 73-83134)
4. George W. Coats, *From Canaan to Egypt: Structural and Theological Context for the Joseph Story* (CBQMS 4) $4.00 ($3.20 for CBA members) ISBN 0-915170-03-5 (LC 75-11382)
5. O. Lamar Cope, *Matthew: A Scribe Trained for the Kingdom of Heaven* (CBQMS 5) $4.50 ($3.60 for CBA members) ISBN 0-915170-04-3 (LC 75-36778)
6. Madeleine Boucher, *The Mysterious Parable: A Literary Study* (CBQMS 6) $2.50 ($2.00 for CBA members) ISBN 0-915170-05-1 (LC 76-51260)
7. Jay Braverman, Jerome's Commentary on Daniel: A Study of Comparative Jewish and Christian Interpretations of the Hebrew Bible (CBQMS 7) $4.00 ($3.20 for CBA members) ISBN 0-915170-06-X (LC 78-55726)
8. Maurya P. Horgan, *Pesharim: Qumran Interpretations of Biblical Books* (CBQMS 8) $6.00 ($4.80 for CBA members) ISBN 0-915170-07-8 (LC 78-12910)
9. Harold W. Attridge and Robert A. Oden, Jr., *Philo of Byblos,* The Phoenician History (CBQMS 9) $3.50 ($2.80 for CBA members) ISBN 0-915170-08-6 (LC 80-25781)
10. Paul J. Kobelski, *Melchizedek and Melchireša'* (CBQMS 10) $4.50 ($3.60 for CBA members) ISBN 0-915170-09-4 (LC 80-28379)
11. Homer Heater, *A Septuagint Translation Technique in the Book of Job* (CBQMS 11) $4.00 ($3.20 for CBA members) ISBN 0-915170-10-8 (LC 81-10085)
12. Robert Doran, *Temple Propaganda: The Purpose and Character of 2 Maccabees* (CBQMS 12) $4.50 ($3.60 for CBA members) ISBN 0-915170-11-6 (LC 81-10084)
13. James Thompson, *The Beginnings of Christian Philosophy: The Epistle to the Hebrews* (CBQMS 13) $5.50 ($4.50 for CBA members) ISBN 0-915170-12-4 (LC 81-12295)
14. Thomas H. Tobin, S.J., *The Creation of Man: Philo and the History of Interpretation* (CBQMS 14) $6.00 ($4.80 for CBA members) ISBN 0-915170-13-2 (LC 82-19891)
15. Carolyn Osiek, *Rich and Poor in the Shepherd of Hermes* (CBQMS 15) $6.00 ($4.80 for CBA members) ISBN 0-915170--14-0 (LC 83-7385)
16. James C. VanderKam, *Enoch and the Growth of an Apocalyptic Tradition* (CBQMS 16) $6.50 ($5.20 for CBA members) ISBN 0-915170-15-9 (LC 83-10134)
17. Antony F. Campbell, S.J., *Of Prophets and Kings: A Late Ninth-Century Document (1 Samuel 1-2 Kings 10)* (CBQMS 17) $7.50 ($6.00 for CBA members) ISBN 0-915170-16-7 (LC 85-12791)
18. John C. Endres, S.J., *Biblical Interpretation in the Book of Jubilees* (CBQMS 18) $8.50 ($6.80 for CBA members) ISBN 0-915170-17-5 (LC 86-6845)

19. Sharon Pace Jeansonne, *The Old Greek Translation of Daniel* 7-12 (CBQMS 19) $5.00 ($4.00 for CBA members) ISBN 0-915170-18-3 (LC 87-15865)
20. Lloyd M. Barré, *The Rhetoric of Political Persuasion: The Narrative Artistry and Political Intentions of 2 Kings* 9 -11 (CBQMS 20) $5.00 ($4.00 for CBA members) ISBN 0-915170-19-1 (LC 87-15878)
21. John J. Clabeaux, *A Lost Edition of the Letters of Paul: A Reassessment of the Text of the Pauline Corpus Attested by Marcion* (CBQMS 21) $8.50 ($6.80 for CBA members) ISBN 0-915170-20-5 (LC 88-28511)
22. Craig Koester, *The Dwelling of God: The Tabernacle in the Old Testament, Intertestamental Jewish Literature, and the New Testament* (CBQMS 22) $9.00 ($7.20 for CBA members) ISBN 0-915170-21-3 (LC 89-9853)
23. William Michael Soll, *Psalm* 119*: Matrix, Form, and Setting* (CBQMS 23) $9.00 ($7.20 for CBA members) ISBN 0-915170-22-1 (LC 90-27610)
24. Richard J. Clifford and John J. Collins (eds.), *Creation in the Biblical Traditions* (CBQMS 24) $7.00 ($5.60 for CBA members) ISBN 0-915170-23-X (LC 92-20268)
25. John E. Course, *Speech and Response: A Rhetorical Analysis of the Introductions to the Speeches of the Book of Job, Chaps.* 4 - 24 (CBQMS 25) $8.50 ($6.80 for CBA members) ISBN 0-915170-24-8 (LC 94-26566)
26. Richard J. Clifford, *Creation Accounts in the Ancient Near East and in the Bible* (CBQMS 26) $9.00 ($7.20 for CBA members) ISBN 0-915170-25-6 (LC 94-26565)
27. John Paul Heil, *Blood and Water: The Death and Resurrection of Jesus in John* 18 – 21 (CBQMS 27) $9.00 ($7.20 for CBA members) ISBN 0-915170-26-4 (LC 95-10479)
28. John Kaltner, *The Use of Arabic in Biblical Hebrew Lexicography* (CBQMS 28) $7.50 ($6.00 for CBA members) ISBN 0-915170-27-2 (LC 95-45182)
29. Michael L. Barré, S.S., *Wisdom, You Are My Sister: Studies in Honor of Roland E. Murphy, O.Carm., on the Occasion of His Eightieth Birthday* (CBQMS 29) $13.00 ($10.40 for CBA members) ISBN 0-915170-28-0 (LC 97-16060)
30. Warren Carter and John Paul Heil, *Matthew's Parables: Audience-Oriented Perspectives* (CBQMS 30) $10.00 ($8.00 for CBA members) ISBN 0-915170-29-9 (LC 97-44677)
31. David S. Williams, *The Structure of 1 Maccabees* (CBQMS 31) $7.00 ($5.60 for CBA members) ISBN 0-915170-30-2
32. Lawrence Boadt and Mark S. Smith (eds.), *Imagery and Imagination in Biblical Literature: Essays in Honor of Aloysius Fitzgerald, F.S.C.* (CBQMS 32) $9.00 ($7.20 for CBA members) ISBN 0-915170-31-0 (LC 2001003305)
33. Stephan K. Davis, *The Antithesis of the Ages: Paul's Reconfiguration of Torah* (CBQMS 33) $11.00 ($8.80 for CBA members) ISBN 0-915170-32-9 (LC 2001007936)
34. Aloysius Fitzgerald, F.S.C., *The Lord of the East Wind* (CBQMS 34) $12.00 ($9.60 for CBA members) ISBN 0-915170-33-7 (LC 2002007068)
35. William L. Moran, *The Most Magic Word: Essays on Babylonian and Biblical Literature* (CBQMS 35) ISBN 0-915170-34-5 (LC 2002010486)

Order from: